BIG BIG BOOK OF Sudoku

 Mud Puddle Books
NEW YORK

Big Big Book of Sudoku

© 2006 Mud Puddle Books, Inc.

Mud Puddle Books, Inc.
54 W. 21st Street
Suite 601
New York, NY 10010

info@mudpuddlebooks.com

ISBN: 1-59412-142-7

Printed in the United States of America

Contents

The History of Sudoku

THE ORIGINS OF SUDOKU puzzles are likely rooted in the invention of Latin Squares by Swiss mathematician Leonhard Euler in 1783. Latin Squares are composed of square grids of some fixed dimension n x n. While a modern Sudoku is always a 9 x 9 grid, a Latin Square may be of any size (e.g., 6 x 6 or 8 x 8). A set of symbols, with a number of members equal to the dimensions of the grid, is used to fill the squares with no symbol being repeated in any row or column. In place of the numbers now commonly used, Euler filled his squares with Greek letters and so these grids are often referred to as Greco-Latin Squares.

Puzzles closely resembling modern Sudoku were devised by freelance puzzle constructor Howard Garnes in 1979. Garnes built on Euler's Latin Squares design using a consistently 9 x 9 grid and adding the nine 3 x 3 boxes, each of which must also contain all the numbers from 1 to 9. Soon thereafter these puzzles were published under the name Number Place, in Dell Magazines' *Math Puzzles and Logic Problems*.

In 1984, Nikoli, a leading puzzle publisher in Japan, brought Dell's Number Place puzzles to their Japanese fans. They originally named the puzzles *Suuji Wa Dokushin Ni Kagiru*, meaning "the numbers must be single (unmarried)" but later abbreviated this to Sudoku. In Japanese, *su* means number and *doku* means single.

The puzzles were not that popular in Japan at first, but in 1986 Nikoli made some important improvements to the way in which their Sudoku puzzles were created. From then on the number of clues given was limited to no more than thirty and they were always arranged in a rotationally symmetrical distribution. If you're unsure what this means, take a look at the placement of the clues in diagonally opposite squares of the puzzles in this book. After these improvements the puzzles became an enormous hit.

In 1989, a computerized version of these puzzles called DigitHunt was introduced by Loadstar/Softdisk Publishing for the Commodore 64. This seems to be the first home computer version of Sudoku.

Wayne Gould, a retired Hong Kong judge, puzzle fan, and computer programmer, came to enjoy Sudoku and on a 2004 visit to London he convinced *The Times* (of London) to publish them. He had written a computer program to generate Sudoku of varying difficulty levels and offered the puzzles to *The Times* for free. On November 12, 2004, they published their first Sudoku puzzle, which began the phenomenal growth in the popularity of these puzzles throughout Europe, Australia, and New Zealand.

In April 2005, Sudoku returned to the U.S. appearing as a regular feature in the *New York Post*, and in July, Sudoku spread nationwide as puzzles were added to *The Daily News* and *USA Today*. This explosive growth continues throughout the world with publication of Sudoku in more and more newspapers each month and the formation of Sudoku clubs, websites, chat rooms, competitions, books, and magazines.

How to Play Sudoku

Sudoku puzzles are solved by logic and require no math to complete. Sudoku is played on a 9 x 9 grid of squares. The grid is further divided into 9 boxes—each a 3 x 3 square grid.

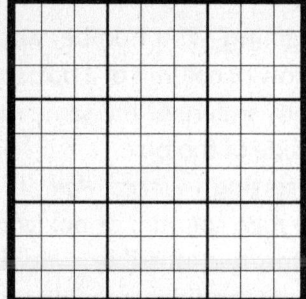

At the start, the puzzle will have some of the squares filled in with numbers. These are your clues for solving the Sudoku.

The goal is to fill in the empty squares in such a way that no number is repeated in any row, column, or 3 x 3 box. That is, each row, column, and box must contain all nine numbers in some sequence with no repetitions.

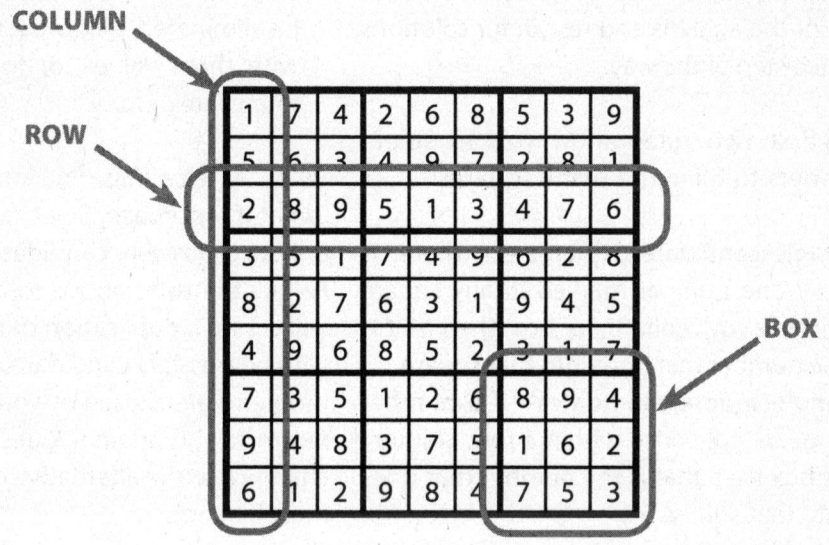

Seems simple enough, doesn't it?

Sudoku Solving Techniques

CROSS-HATCHING, the most basic solving technique, works by using the fact that boxes (the 3 x 3 square subdivisions of the grid) must contain all the numbers from 1 to 9. The first step is to determine which numbers are missing from the box. Then check the values already known in the other filled-in squares of the full row and column of each blank square in order to determine which numbers the square could contain by eliminating those that have already been used. It will often be possible to find blanks that can only contain one value. You can then fill those in and treat them just as if they were clues printed with the puzzle.

Once cross-hatching fails to isolate any more numbers it may prove useful to mark up the Sudoku. First, write small numbers (candidate lists) in each blank square indicating all the possible answers that it could contain.

You can then analyze the areas (boxes, rows, and columns) of the marked-up puzzle using a few simple rules. Remember to adjust all of your candidate lists based on each step of the analysis and rescan for solutions at each step of the way.

The first two rules allow you to select numbers to fill in the blank squares:

1) **Single-candidate squares**—If there is only one number marked in any square within a row, column, or box, then that is the number that goes into that square.
2) **Single-square candidates**—If a number appears only once within a row, column, or box then that is the number that goes into that square.

The remainder are candidate-elimination rules that potentially create single-candidate squares and/or single-square candidates:

3) **Number claiming**—If a number appears in only one row or column of a box, then it can't go in any square of the same row or column outside of the box.
4) **Naked subsetting**—*Naked Pair:* If two squares in a row, column, or box contain only the same two possible candidates, then those two candidates can be excluded from all the other squares in the same row, column, or box. *Naked Triple/Quad:* The same applies if there are three squares that only contain some combination of three candidates, or four squares with four values. Note that the squares making up a triple or quad do not need to have all of the candidates in each of them.
5) **Hidden subsetting**—If two squares in a row, column, or box are the only two to have two particular candidates, then the other candidates in those two boxes may be eliminated—likewise, for three squares with three values, or four squares with four values, etc.

When all else fails, you may resort to the "what-if" approach: Select a square that has only two possible candidates and pick one. Follow the rules above to determine if this will create a duplication or leave any square with no possible candidate. If either of these problems are caused by your selection, then return to the original "guessed" square and change it to the alternative candidate, which must be correct.

PUZZLE 1

9	5	7	6	8	4	2	1	3
7	9	2	3	5	9	6	4	1
5	3	1	2	9	7	4	8	6
4	8	9	2	3	6	7	2	8
8	2	3	7	4	5	1	6	9
1	6	4	9	2	8	5	3	7
9	1	8	4	6	3	9	5	2
2	4	5	8	7	1	3	6	4
3	7	6	4	1	2	8	9	5

PUZZLE 2

2				4		3	1	5
					8			7
		9		3	7			
5		6	8	1		7		
	1		9	6	5		4	
		8			3	5		6
			5	9		8		
7			3	2				
9	8	1		7				

Solutions on page 302

	8			9		5		
			4	3			9	
		7		2				6
	5	4		1			8	
3	6						2	7
	1			7		6	4	
9				5		7		
	7			6	9			
		2		4			5	

3		6		9		2		1
		8				9	4	
					4			5
	5		4					
9		3	8			2	1	4
						1		9
7			1					
	2	9				8		
1			4		2		6	7

Solutions on page 302

7	8				5		3	4
						5	7	
		3				9	2	
5	1	9		7				
6								9
		4				1	5	2
	5	2		1				
	4	6						
1	7		9				6	5

4	2	5	3	9	1	8	9	6
6	9	8	5	2	7		1	
1	7	3	4	6	8			
2			9	5			4	1
				4				
5	3			8	6			2
			7			1	8	
	1					4		
9			8		2		3	7

Solutions on page 303

Puzzle 7:

9					4	5		
				1	6	9		
	4		9	2			8	
		9		3				2
7		6				1		8
5				6		3		
	7			5	1		2	
	2		4	7				
	1		2					3

Puzzle 8:

	4					5		3
	6	1		5	4		7	9
					2			
7			2	9			8	
		9				4		
	2			1	3			7
			1					
4	9		5	6		8	3	
1		7					9	

Solutions on page 303

						5	3	9
9		3						1
5		1	3			4	8	
	8	7	6					
		4		9		1		
					3	7	5	
	9	8			7	3		6
1						2		5
7	2	5						

9					2			
8				4	6	2		
	7	1				5	4	
		3		5	7		4	
	5							1
	9		3	8		6		
		6	9			3	8	
		9	2	6				1
			5					4

Solutions on page 304

				6				
	1				9	3		
		9	3		2		5	8
9						2		6
	7	3	5	1	6	8	9	
8		1						7
3	9		8		5	7		
		7	6				8	
				2				

8			3		1	5	9	
		5	9	4				
4				8		6		
6		9		2	8			
			5	3		4		2
		3		6				7
				9	2	1		
		4	1	8		3		6

Solutions on page 304

				7		9		
	8		9		1	4		
5	1		2			8	7	
	3	1				2	9	
				6				
	9	5				3	6	
	6	7			2		1	9
		2	7		5		3	
		8		9				

	2		5	3	7	1	4	
			1	2	6	4	5	8
5	3	1	9	4	8	2	7	6
2		9	6	1	4	5	3	
			3	9	5	7	6	
		6	7	8	2	3	9	1
	1		8	7	3	6	8	4
9	7	4	2	6	1	8	2	
			4	5	8	9	1	

Solutions on page 305

5	6				1		4	
				5		7		
4		1				6		3
				9			8	6
1		3				2		5
8	9			4				
6		8				5		7
		7		8				
	3		5				6	9

1					2			8
		2		9		6	1	
4		7				9		
			8		9	3		1
	9						4	
7		8	1		3			
		6				4		3
	8	4		2		5		
2			5					9

Solutions on page 305

			9			1	4	
8		3				6		5
	4				2		3	
7			2	1		5		
	4						7	
		5		6	7			3
	5		1			9		
3		9				4		2
	7	2			4			

				1		6		
	8		3		2		5	7
4		6						
	7	9		4			1	8
1								2
6	3			5		7	9	
						1		3
2	6		8		1		4	
		5		3				

Solutions on page 306

Puzzle 19

4					8			
			1	5			8	
	2	9		4			7	
5					6		1	7
6		7		2		9		4
1	9		5					2
	5			6		1	9	
	7			1	9			
			4					8

Puzzle 20

	4			2			6	
	6				9	7	5	4
	8	7				9		
	3		8					
1			7	4	5			2
					2		9	
		5				6	4	
6	7	4	9				1	
	2			6			8	

Solutions on page 306

Puzzle 25:

8		3		6	1			
7	4	5						1
	1		5			2		
				7		8	3	
	6			8		5		
	8	7		3				
	2			4		6		
3						9	1	5
			6	1		3		2

Puzzle 26:

5		2		7			4	8
	8	9				7		
		1		2				3
	2	5			3			
			7		8			
			2			3	7	
6				3		5		
		7				1	3	
2	3			1		8		9

Solutions on page 308

Puzzle 27

	5	1					3	
9			1	3	8		4	
	6				7		1	
							9	7
	3		4		5	2		
2	8							
	9		5			4		
	4		2	1	3			8
	6					1	7	

Puzzle 28

		8	9			6	7	5
7					1	4		
		3			2			9
5				2				4
		1		3		8		
6				9				1
8			4			7		
		5	2					8
1	7	9			5	2		

Solutions on page 308

5		7	8			4		3
			1	9	5			
				4				
9	3					8	5	
	7	5				3	6	
	1	8					9	7
			5					
			3	7	8			
4		3			2	9		5

	1	5			3	8		
		3	5				4	
6					2			7
	4			6		7		
2		8		4		5		3
		6		3			9	
9			3					2
	8				9	6		
		1	6			4	7	

Solutions on page 309

	2		8			9		7		
					2	9		4
		9	6					
7			3	1		2		6
3								1
1		6		4	8			9
					6	5		
2		4	5					
	6		7		1		2	

	6		1	3	5			
5	9			6		2		
		7						
		6			4	1		7
9	4			8			2	5
7		2	3			6		
						8		
		3		5			6	2
			9	4	6		3	

Solutions on page 309

Puzzle 33

				4	3			
3	6				2	1		
9			1			3	6	
					1	8	9	
1			8		6			4
	8	9	5					
	4	7			5			9
		8	2				3	7
			7	1				

Puzzle 34

3					2			
8	6				3	5		7
		4	9		8	5	1	
		9			7			2
5			3				9	
		7	9	2		3	4	
1			2	5			7	6
			6					1

Solutions on page 310

Puzzle 35:

6						8		2
		7	1	3	9			4
						7	1	
7	6	5		2				
		3				9		
				6		5	3	7
	8	6						
4			7	9	8	3		
5		9						1

Puzzle 36:

			5	3				
	7		1		6	9		2
6		5	2				4	
						7		3
2	3						8	9
4		7						
	9				7	8		6
8		6	4		2		3	
				8	1			

Solutions on page 310

	3	9	7					
4				1				8
7		6		9	5			
	1		8	5				
	5		6		1		2	
				2	4		8	
			1	7		5		6
5				4				1
				9	7	3		

	2	4	7	5	3	6		
					4		5	
	9				2			
	3				7			4
8	1						6	5
7			6				2	
			1					9
	6		4					
		1	2	3	8	4	7	

Solutions on page 311

```
. . . | 3 6 . | . 2 8
8 . . | . 2 . | 3 4 .
5 . . | . . . | 6 . .
------+-------+------
. . . | 4 8 . | 5 . .
2 . 8 | . . . | 1 . 6
. . 5 | . 1 3 | . . .
------+-------+------
. . 6 | . . . | . . 7
. 8 2 | . 3 . | . . 4
1 9 . | . 5 2 | . . .
```

```
5 . . | . . 7 | . . .
. 2 7 | . . 5 | . . 9
8 3 9 | . . . | . . .
------+-------+------
2 . 1 | 5 . . | . 9 .
. 4 . | 6 . 3 | . 5 .
. 9 . | . 4 . | 7 . 6
------+-------+------
. . . | . . . | 3 1 5
4 . . | 5 . . | 9 7 .
. . . | 2 . . | . . 4
```

Solutions on page 311

Puzzle 41

9	3	8	6			1		
	5		2					8
1	2						7	
		9		3				
3	8			5			4	6
				4		2		
	1						6	2
7					1		5	
		4			5	7	9	1

Puzzle 42

2		3			9	5		8
		9	7					6
1		6			5			
		8			4			
	1		5		7		3	
			6			7		
			2			1		5
4					6	2		
6		5	3			8		9

Solutions on page 312

Level One: Easy Puzzles • 27

			7	5		6		
			9		4	2		1
5		6			2			
	9			2		8		4
	1						6	
7		5		8		9		
			1			5		2
2		7	4		5			
		1		3	8			

			7		4	1	8	
	7			9	1	6		
4			2			7		
	4					5	1	
			6		8			
	9	3					2	
		4		5				1
		9	1	6			4	
	8	6	9		3			

Solutions on page 312

Solutions on page 313

PUZZLE 45

2	3							
			8		1	2		
7		6				1		
4	5		3		2			7
		7	4	5	6	3		
6			9		8		5	1
		4				9		6
		8	7		9			
							3	4

PUZZLE 46

	9					4		
		2	1				8	6
			7	3				9
		4	2	6	7	8	5	
	1	8	4	5	3	2		
7				4	9			
1	5				8	6		
		3					7	

Puzzle 47:

6		7	5				1	
	9		7					
	1						8	5
	7				9	8	2	3
3				5				4
4	2	6	8				7	
5	8						9	
				8		3		
	4				7	6		8

Puzzle 48:

3				8				7
7	5	4	6		9	1		
	9					4		
			9	4			1	
9								2
	6			3	7			
		7					6	
		6	4		8	2	7	3
4				7				1

Solutions on page 313

1	6	4	9					
	2	8		7				
		9	4	1			6	
5						8	3	
6				2				1
	4	1						6
	3			7	6	9		
			5			6	4	
					1	7	2	5

			4	6				8
1					3			
6		5		2		1		
4		6		9	2		3	
		9		7		8		
	3		5	4		6		1
		1		3		5		2
			6					7
3				8	7			

Solutions on page 314

Puzzle 51

		8				4		
5	9		7	6				3
	3		4					
	8				4	1	9	
9		1				3		5
	5	2	3				4	
				3			5	
4			5	1			6	2
	5					7		

Puzzle 52

2		5				7		
					9		3	
1				7	2		6	
9	2			5				7
	6		7		4		8	
7				3			1	5
	9		3	2				6
	5		8					
		7					3	8

Solutions on page 314

Puzzle 53:

```
. . . | . 7 3 | . 6 1
4 . 3 | . . 5 | . . 8
. 6 . | . . . | 4 . 2
------+-------+------
2 . . | . . . | . . 3
. . 9 | 8 3 6 | 2 . .
6 . . | . . . | . . 9
------+-------+------
3 . 6 | . . . | . 2 .
8 . . | 3 . . | 7 . 5
5 2 . | 1 9 . | . . .
```

Puzzle 54:

```
2 . . | . . 7 | . . 3
. . . | 6 9 4 | . . .
9 7 . | 8 . . | 5 . .
------+-------+------
5 1 . | 7 . . | . 9 4
. . . | 4 . . | . . .
4 8 . | 2 . . | . 3 7
------+-------+------
. . 8 | 9 . . | . 4 2
. . 2 | 5 3 . | . . .
3 . . | 4 . . | . . 5
```

Solutions on page 315

Puzzle 55:

```
4 2 . | . . . | . 6 9
. . . | . 1 . | . 4 .
1 . . | . 8 . | 5 . 7
------+-------+------
. 1 . | 3 . . | 8 . .
. 5 8 | . . 9 | 3 . .
. . 2 | . . 4 | . 9 .
------+-------+------
2 . 7 | . 9 . | . . 1
. 9 . | . 4 . | . . .
8 4 . | . . . | . 2 3
```

Puzzle 56:

```
4 . 2 | 5 . . | . . .
. 5 . | . 6 . | . 7 .
. 7 . | . . . | 3 . 2
------+-------+------
. 1 4 | 3 . 7 | 8 . .
. 3 . | . 8 . | . 6 .
. . 9 | 4 . 6 | 7 1 .
------+-------+------
5 . 1 | . . . | . 4 .
. 4 . | . 2 . | . 8 .
. . . | . . 1 | 5 . 6
```

Solutions on page 315

Puzzle 57:

			7		3			9
	7	8		6		2		
		6	8	1				
6				2				4
	1		3	4	9		6	
7				8				3
				7	6	5		
		7		9			1	3
9			2		8			

Puzzle 58:

	3	8		7			2	
			2		9			8
1	2		5		3			
		9			6		8	
3				5				6
	7		9			2		
			4		7		6	2
7			8		1			
	6			2		7	9	

Solutions on page 316

	4	7					3	6
	2	6	7	1				
5			6		4	2		
			8			4		
8				4				3
	3			2				
	8	2		7				4
				8	6	9	7	
6	7					5	2	

8			6				5	
		9			3			
3		7	1	4		2		
				3			2	8
	5		8		6		1	
4	8			9				
		8	5	2		7		3
			9			5		
	9				7			1

Solutions on page 316

Puzzle 61

		5	2					
8		3						6
9		6	7	3	8	2		
		1	6					3
	6					4		
7			9			6		
	3	8	6	1		4		9
5						1		7
			5			3		

Puzzle 62

	6		1					
7	8	4		5				
				7	6	2	8	
		3	7					1
9			3	8	5			4
	7				4	9		
	4	8	5	3				
				6		4	7	1
					1		3	

Solutions on page 317

			8					4
		2					5	7
9			7	5	2			1
		8			7			6
3	6			8			9	5
1			6			2		
4			9	2	1			3
2	1					8		
6				8				

	6			9			4	7
	8	4			3	6		
1		5			2			3
				3	1			8
7			5	8				
8			6			7		1
		7	3			2	6	
3	2			1			5	

Solutions on page 317

				3	4	7		
3					9			
4			5		7	3		
1		4		8			5	
	6	3				2	9	
	7			6		8		3
		9	1		5			8
		2						5
		6	3	9				

			2			3		7
	7						6	
		6	1					8
1	9		6		4		7	
		7	3		9	6		
	2		7		8		9	1
3					1	8		
	4							1
7		1			6			

Solutions on page 318

Puzzle 67

	2		5		7			
7				1			4	
		9		8	2			
		4	3	6		8	7	
		5				3		
	8	2		7	4	6		
			6	9		4		
	9			4				6
			7		1		2	

Puzzle 68

4	5				3		8	2
		1		8	4			
		6					7	3
			4			3		5
1								6
9		3			8			
	3	9				5		
			1	3		9		
2	1		5				7	3

Solutions on page 318

	2	4			3			
				6			5	
	9	6		1	2	3		7
6			5				1	
	1			4			6	
	4				1			3
4		3	1	7		5	9	
	6			9				
			2			4	7	

3	4					6		
6			3	1				7
	8					5	1	
		5		7				1
	3		2		1		7	
1				9		8		
	2	7					8	
8				5	7			4
		3					5	9

Solutions on page 319

	2	6				5		
	5				9			7
			6	8			1	
5				4	6	8		
6			3		1			4
		7	2	5				6
	8			6	7			
9			5				3	
		5				6	4	

2	1					9		
3	7		1	2	6			
6			9	8				
		7	3		2			5
9			7		4	3		
			4	1				2
			6	9	3		4	8
		5					6	9

Solutions on page 319

Puzzle 77

	1			6		3		7
2		4			3			
				4		9	2	
1	9	8		2				
		7		1		6		
				5		4	9	1
	6	2		7				
			8			7		6
7		1		9			3	

Puzzle 78

8				3		9		
4					8		5	
2	7		1					8
		7	5	9				
5			3	2	7			6
				8	4	1		
1					3		4	7
	4			2				1
		2			1			9

Solutions on page 321

Puzzle 79:

	3	2			9			
6	1			5		9		
9								6
5	7			8	4			
	2	6		7		1	4	
		3	6				5	9
2								3
		3		1			9	5
			2			8	1	

Puzzle 80:

		7	1	5	6		8	9
4			3				6	
								1
	8			4			7	
9		5		6		3		4
	6			9			1	
5								
	4				2			3
6	3		4	7	9	2		

Solutions on page 321

Puzzle 81:

				7	9	3		1
			8					2
			5	2			4	9
	3					7	1	8
	1						2	
9	2	4				5		
5	3		4	2				
2				8				
4		6	7	1				

Puzzle 82:

7				4		9	2	
		6					5	
9	5			1	2			
	7	9						2
3		4				8		9
8						1	6	
			7	5			4	8
	9					2		
	6	8		3				5

Solutions on page 322

							9	8
		7		8				5
2				5		6		1
1			3	2			8	
9	3			1			2	4
	8			7	9			3
8		1	7					9
7				9		1		
6	5							

	8		9			3	1	
		2	5	6				8
	7	6	4					
7	1	9						
	2			9			7	
						2	6	9
					9	6	5	
8				4	5	9		
	5	4			1		3	

Solutions on page 322

		8		4				5
	9						3	
4			6		2		8	
5	8			6			9	
	1		5		4	8		
	3		7				2	1
	6		4		9			3
	4						1	
1				8		2		

				7	2		1	
	9	2			3	7		8
		6						
	1	9			6			3
6			8		4			5
5			1			2	6	
						6		
8		7	3			9	2	
	5		6	2				

Solutions on page 323

```
4 6 .  . . .  2 . .
. . .  7 . 9  . 6 .
. 7 .  . 2 8  . . 3
. 1 7  9 . .  . . 4
. 3 .  . 5 .  7 . .
9 . .  . . 6  1 8 .
7 . .  8 3 .  . 4 .
. 8 .  4 . 1  . . .
. . 6  . . .  . 3 5
```

```
. . 8  . 4 1  . . .
. 1 .  7 . .  5 . 8
. . 3  . 8 5  9 . .
1 . 5  . . .  . . .
. 9 .  2 . 7  . 3 .
. . .  . . .  4 . 6
. . 7  8 1 .  6 . .
8 . 6  . . 4  . 2 .
. . .  3 2 .  7 . .
```

Solutions on page 323

8				6		3		
		4			3	1		5
	3			4		9	2	
	9				4		7	
		7		1		6		
	2		7				9	
	6	2		7			5	
9		5	8			7		
		1		9				4

			5		8			1
	1		2	3		9	4	6
						3		
			4	6	9	7		
	7						6	
		2	3	7	1			
		5						
6	2	9		4	5		1	
1			9		3			

Solutions on page 324

				8				
			3	1	6			9
	6	4		2		3	1	
	2		9					6
	7	3		6		9	2	
8				3			7	
	8	9		7		4	5	
7				8	3	1		
				9				

				4			5	
2		4				6	3	
		1	8		7		2	
			5	7	8			9
	9						4	
8			4	2	9			
	5		1		4	2		
	4	8				3		7
	2			6				

Solutions on page 324

						5		7
			9	2	6	1		
		6	7					3
6				5	1		2	9
	3						4	
2	8		6	3				1
7					9	8		
		2	3	1	8			
1		8						

3				2	4			6
					9		4	
		7				2	8	9
	5			9		1		
	9	1				4	3	
		2		7			9	
5	7	6				3		
	4		3					
9			2	4				8

Solutions on page 325

Solutions on page 325

54 • Level One: Easy Puzzles

```
Puzzle 97
┌───────┬───────┬───────┐
│ 5 8   │   7 4 │       │
│   1   │     9 │   8   │
│ 9     │ 2 8   │ 4     │
├───────┼───────┼───────┤
│ 4   7 │       │ 6     │
│ 3     │   2   │     7 │
│   2   │       │ 5   4 │
├───────┼───────┼───────┤
│     8 │   1 6 │     5 │
│   3   │ 7     │   9   │
│       │ 9 5   │   7 6 │
└───────┴───────┴───────┘
```

```
Puzzle 98
┌───────┬───────┬───────┐
│ 3 1   │ 4     │       │
│ 2 5   │ 3     │       │
│   6   │       │ 3 1 8 │
├───────┼───────┼───────┤
│       │   5 7 │ 8 3   │
│     3 │       │ 9     │
│   9 6 │ 2 4   │       │
├───────┼───────┼───────┤
│ 1 8 9 │       │   5   │
│       │     1 │   9 2 │
│       │     4 │   8 7 │
└───────┴───────┴───────┘
```

Solutions on page 326

4					2		1	
1			5					8
		6	4					
7	1			5	6	4	8	
6				9				5
	4	8	1	3			6	9
				9	6			
8				5				1
	5		6					7

		7	2			4	9	
						8	1	5
9	1		3			6		
2	9			3				
		1				7		
				4			5	2
		3			5		6	8
5	4	9						
	7	8				1	5	

Solutions on page 326

Puzzle 101:

2	6	5						7
			5	3				
	9	1		6	2			
			7		9		1	6
	1						2	
8	7		6		4			
		8	5			6	9	
			8	6				
6						5	3	8

Puzzle 102:

1			6		3		9	
6						1	3	
	5	4		1		7		8
				8	1			
			2		6			
			4	9				
7		5		2		6	8	
	9	1						7
	3		1		5			4

Solutions on page 327

Level One: Easy Puzzles • 57

	2		3			4	1	
		9	6				2	3
			5		7			
		6		7	4			5
		7				2		
3			8	1		7		
			1			2		
2	5					3	1	
	1	3			8		4	

		9	8	5	2			
		1		6		7		
				3			6	9
	9		5					6
1		4				9		2
8					4		1	
4	2			1				
		6		4		3		
			7	9	6	2		

Solutions on page 327

				6		4		8
	8		5			3		
4		6						7
2		1	8		6			
7			9	4	1			3
			7		2	9		6
6						5		1
		4			7	8		
9		2		8				

5						2	8	
	1			5		3		4
	8				1			5
			1	4			7	
	9	7		8		4	2	
	2			9	7			
4			8				5	
8		5		2			3	
	7	9						6

Solutions on page 328

		1				8	9	
2	7				9		5	
	4			8	2			
	6		9	2		1	4	
				5				
	9	8		6	1		3	
			2	1		4		
	1			7		3	6	
	7	9				2		

8	5		4			2	6	3
	4	9			8			5
							9	
3	1		9				5	
				7				
	8				2		3	9
	3							
6			3			9	8	
5	7	1			6		4	2

Solutions on page 328

			5		8	6	7	1
				4		9		2
	5							8
		8				7		3
2		1				4		9
4		7		3				
1						8		
8		6		9				
7	2	3	6		1			

		3		4	2			
	7	4				6		
		1	8			9	2	
	3		5	7				9
			3		6			
8				2	9		7	
	5	7			4	2		
		8				3	1	
			7	6		4		

Solutions on page 329

Solutions on page 329

PUZZLE 111

		5				7	6	
	1		8			2		
			5				9	
5		1	6	9				2
7	8			3			1	6
4				7	1	3		8
	4			3				
	7			6		2		
	9	8				6		

PUZZLE 112

		2			1		3	
9	3		7			1	8	6
	8				9			
			8			4	1	
		6				9		
	7	4			2			
			2				6	
7	6	1			5		2	4
	5		6			3		

	8	4	7	1				
1			6		8			3
	6			3				
		2	4	8	5			
		6		9		3		
			3	2	6	4		
				5			8	
4			9		1			6
			6	4	2	7		

3			7				6	5
		5				7		
2			5		9			
	3	2	8			6	1	7
			9					
7	5	1	2			4	9	
			2		3			4
		8				5		
5	1			4				9

Solutions on page 330

PUZZLE
115

Puzzle 115

		1		8			9	
	5			9				8
6		8	7		4			
					2	3		6
		3	1		5	7		
1		2	8					
		7			1	9		4
5			4				7	
	3			7		8		

PUZZLE
116

Puzzle 116

6	5				4		2	
	8					5		
	9		5	1		3		
1		4		8				
		3	7			1	2	
				6			8	3
		9		7	5		6	
		8					3	
	4		3				7	2

Solutions on page 330

			7			5		
2			3	6	4		7	
				9		8	4	
4				5		1	2	
		5		2		3		
	2	1		3				6
	8	2		7				
	7		5	4	2			8
		9			8			

1	7	5					3	
	2			4				
		6		7	3	8		
4							9	
3	6		1		2		4	5
	5							8
		8	6	1		4		
				3			6	
	1					3	8	2

Solutions on page 331

Puzzle 119:

5		2	1	6		4		
7				9				2
		3		2	1			
9		4						6
	7		1			9		
8						5		7
		6	8		5			
4			6					5
		5		2	7	6		3

Puzzle 120:

5			7			2		
7					8	3	9	4
9					1			
	5			4	2	6		9
6		4	3	9			1	
			8					2
8	6	5	9					7
		9			3			6

Solutions on page 331

			9					7
	9			2				5
6	7	8				4		
9					4	5		
	5	7	1		9	3	6	
		6	3					8
		5				8	4	6
7				1			9	
8				6				

		5	9			4		6
2	8		6					1
7	6						9	
	9	6	3				4	
				7				
	1				8	9	5	
	5						1	7
9					6		8	4
6		1			5	2		

Solutions on page 332

				8	3		9	1
	7			9	5			
1			5	7				
9	2		1		8			
5								3
			2		6		1	5
				2	7			6
		2	8				7	
6	1		9	4				

2		5	1			3		7
				5	3		6	
	9	1					8	
			2	9	8	1		
	7	2	6	1				
	4					6	9	
	3		8	6				
6		7			1	5		8

Solutions on page 332

Puzzle 125:

				7	5		3	
	3			2	4	8	6	
			3			1		2
3		9						1
		7		8		6		
1						9		8
8		3			2			
	9	6	7	3			1	
	2		6	4				

Puzzle 126:

							2	
	1				9		4	
7		2		6		1		
	8	4	9			1	3	
		1	3			2	4	
		3	8			6	7	5
		5		8			9	3
	4			6				1
	9							

Solutions on page 333

					4	1		
					9	6	3	8
1	2			8				9
2							8	7
		1	7	5	2	9		
6	7							3
5				9			6	2
7	9	2	8					
		4	3					

6					1		3	
		5	7					
1			3		9	2	4	
5	2			7		4		
		6				9		
		4		9			5	8
	9	3	2		8			7
						5	8	
	5		6					1

Solutions on page 333

Puzzle 129

1					6			3
			7					6
	4	2	5			7	1	
2			4	7		1		
		3		8		9		
		9		2	5			4
	9	6			3	5	7	
5					7			
3			8					1

Puzzle 130

5							3	
2					1		4	5
6		3	4	2				
		9	3	4			6	
		2		1		7		
	6			5	9	2		
			7	3	4			9
4	1		2					8
	3							6

Solutions on page 334

Puzzle 131:

	6		8					7
			1	7	3		2	
		5	4	6				
		2			1		7	
5		8				3		6
	3		5			4		
				2	4	7		
	1		3	5	8			
3					9		5	

Puzzle 132:

1			4				7	6
					3			
9				1		2	8	5
		1		2		5		8
			7		5			
6			5		3		9	
2	8	6		7				3
			3					
3	4				8			2

Solutions on page 334

Puzzle 133:

	8					2		
	9			5	6	1	8	
1		7						5
			2			5		
3	1		5	9	8		4	6
		6			3			
7						6		1
	5	9	4	7			3	
		1					7	

Puzzle 134:

3			8	1			9	
	9	8	4		5			
4					2			6
		4				3		
	5		2		3		4	
		1				2		
6			3					5
		5		4	6	7		
	2		7	8				1

Solutions on page 335

Puzzle 135

			6				5	3
6			2					
		7	4		5			
	3	4	1	8		5	6	
	1			5		9		
	6	8		9	3	2	1	
			3		8	4		
					7			2
4	7			1				

Puzzle 136

9		6						8
7		5		2				9
4	8			3	5			
	6					2	1	4
				9				
5	4	7					8	
			3	4			7	1
2				1		4		6
1						8		2

Solutions on page 335

			6			2	1	
		4		5	2			9
	3		1		7		8	
5	4			1				
		3				9		
				3			2	4
	1		4		9		5	
2			8	7		3		
	7	6			3			

1	6	4	9					
	2	8			7			
		9	4	1			6	
5						8	3	
6				2				1
	4	1						6
	3			7	6	9		
			5			6	4	
					1	7	2	5

Solutions on page 336

8				3	9			
				2	7	1		
	7		1			2	8	6
	9						6	5
	8						1	
7	5						9	
2	3	9			1		5	
		7	9	6				
			5	7				3

	7			9		2		
	4	2	6					
	3				4	6		
4			9	1		3		
8			2		6			7
		1		4	3			9
		5	4				6	
					1	7	8	
		6		7			9	

Solutions on page 336

```
. 7 8 | . . . | 2 . 1
. . 2 | 6 8 . | . 3 .
5 . . | . 2 . | 6 . 8
------+-------+------
. . . | 9 . . | . . 6
. . 3 | . 5 . | 4 . .
2 . . | . 3 . | . . .
------+-------+------
7 . 5 | . 3 . | . . 2
. 2 . | . 6 1 | 7 . .
3 . 6 | . . . | 5 9 .
```

```
1 9 8 | . 4 . | . . .
5 . 7 | . 2 . | 8 . 3
. . . | . . 7 | . . .
------+-------+------
. 3 6 | . . . | . . .
4 . 1 | 6 . 9 | 3 . 5
. . . | . . . | 1 7 .
------+-------+------
. . . | 3 . . | . . .
9 . 4 | . 7 . | 5 . 8
. . . | . 6 . | 2 4 7
```

Solutions on page 337

		2	7		6		9	
		9			2			
	6			1		8		
6	5	4					8	
8		7		2		3		1
	3					6	5	7
		6		4			2	
			1			9		
	1		2		8	5		

1		8				5	3	6
							2	7
6						4	1	
5				7			2	
9			5	4	6			1
	6		1					9
		9	2					7
	7	6						
	4	5	8			6		3

Solutions on page 337

Puzzle 145

7			8				9	
8	6				1			
1			5			6		3
	8		6		4			
		9	1		8	2		
			9		2		6	
2		6		5				1
			2				3	7
	7				9			6

Puzzle 146

4					6		3	
2				7				
	5			8		1		2
8					3		6	1
	6	7				4	5	
5	9		6					3
6		4	5			9		
			3					4
	7		2					5

Solutions on page 338

9		2						1
		3	6					8
			9	8	1			2
	7	8		4	9			
		9				2		
			2	1		8	5	
3			7	5	8			
8					2	7		
5						3		6

PUZZLE
148

	1							7
	4	2		1		9		6
7						5		
		8	9	2	7			
2	7						3	9
			6	3	8	4		
		5						4
8		7		6		1	2	
3							6	

Solutions on page 338

Level Two: Harder (as your skills increase)

Solutions on page 339

PUZZLE 149

	2		9				4	
	9		7			6		5
1				8			3	9
7	3	6				5		
				5				
		5				2	1	3
4	5			2				7
3		9			5		8	
	7				4		5	

PUZZLE 150

				8		9		7
		6		7				5
			6	5			4	8
		2			8	6	3	
8								2
	7	9	2			8		
2	9			6	1			
3				9		4		
6		8		2				

PUZZLE 151

PUZZLE 152

Solutions on page 339

Puzzle 153:

			5		3	2	7	8
8		3				5	6	
						9		
			5	8		2		
5			1	2	4			7
	4		6	9				
		7						
	8	5				1		9
9	3	6	8		5			

Puzzle 154:

				5		3	1	
1		3				4	2	8
	2	8						
8		4	3		5	2		
		9	2		1	8		3
						5	8	
4	7	5				6		9
	8	1		3				

Solutions on page 340

Puzzle 155:

7				4					
5	4	2	8		1	7		
	1		5			8	2	
				1	2			
	2						6	
			6	9				
	7	4		5			1	
		1	3		4	6	7	2
				7				9

Puzzle 156:

				4				
9	7				5		1	
1	8	5		3	6			
7				6		5		8
8								9
5		9		7				4
			3	2		7	9	1
	3		1				5	6
			5					

Solutions on page 340

2	6							7
9				7		6	2	
			4		2			3
			9				7	8
	9	8				3	1	
7	3				6			
8			6		4			
	1	7		5				9
3							5	4

	3	4			7			2
					5	8		3
		6		3	2	1		
	7		1			9		4
			8					
3		1			9		6	
	5	3	7			2		
7		8	5					
4			9			5	1	

Solutions on page 341

		5					1	
			6	1			3	5
		2		5		6		4
5			8		9	7		3
				2				
8			3	4		1		9
1		8		3		4		
2	9			8	5			
	5					8		

		2			1			5
		4	2	8		6	1	
	8			3				
	1					5		8
		6	5		2	3		
5		9					6	
				2			9	
	3	7		9	8	4		
4			6			8		

Solutions on page 341

Puzzle 161

					9		7	4
2	9		7				8	
		7	5		1		3	
		9		7				2
		3		4		8		
5				9		3		
	1		4		3	9		
	5				7		6	3
6	3		9					

Puzzle 162

			2					5
	5	6			1		4	
		8		9	4			6
			4		9		5	
		5	6		3	2		
	9		7		8			
7			8	3		4		
	6		9				1	2
8					2			

Solutions on page 342

Puzzle 163:

```
9 . . | 5 . . | 7 . .
. 6 3 | 1 . . | . 5 4
5 8 . | 6 . . | . . .
------+-------+------
. . . | . . 6 | . . 5
1 9 . | . 4 . | . 3 2
7 . . | 3 . . | . . .
------+-------+------
. . . | . 3 . | . 4 9
6 7 . | . 8 . | 2 1 .
. . . | 4 . 1 | . . 7
```

Puzzle 164:

```
4 . 7 | . 1 . | 9 8 .
. . . | 8 9 . | . . .
. . . | . . . | 4 . 1
------+-------+------
. 7 5 | . . 2 | 8 . .
. 1 . | 9 . 7 | . 5 .
. . 9 | 5 . . | 3 2 .
------+-------+------
7 . 1 | . . . | . . .
. . . | 6 9 . | . . .
. 2 6 | . 7 . | 5 . 3
```

Solutions on page 342

```
Puzzle 165
5 . 6 | 2 . . | 8 1 3
7 . . | . . . | . 4 .
. . 1 | . . 6 | . . 9
------+-------+------
. 4 3 | . 1 . | . . .
. . . | 3 9 7 | . . .
. . . | . 5 . | 9 3 .
------+-------+------
3 . . | 9 . . | 7 . .
. 7 . | . . . | . . 6
2 6 9 | . . 1 | 3 . 8
```

```
Puzzle 166
. 9 3 | 8 1 . | . . .
8 6 . | . . . | . . 1
1 . 5 | . 6 . | 4 3 .
------+-------+------
. . 6 | 3 . . | . . .
. . . | 2 8 6 | . . .
. . . | . 5 3 | . . .
------+-------+------
. 3 1 | . 4 . | 2 . 7
9 . . | . . . | . 1 3
. . . | 3 2 9 | 6 . .
```

```
 8 .  2 | 4 . . | . . .
 7 .  . | . . 3 | . . 8
 . 5  . | . 9 . | . . 7
---------+-------+-------
 . 1  . | 9 . 2 | . 4 .
 . 9  . | 8 1 6 | . 3 .
 . 2  . | 7 . 5 | . 8 .
---------+-------+-------
 1 .  . | . 8 . | . 5 .
 9 .  . | 2 . . | . . 4
 . .  . | . . 4 | 8 . 1
```

```
 2 . 3 | . . . | . 4 7
 9 8 . | 1 7 . | . 2 .
 1 . . | . . 2 | . . .
-------+-------+-------
 6 . . | . . . | 5 7 .
 . . 8 | . . . | 3 . .
 . 3 1 | . . . | . . 2
-------+-------+-------
 . . . | 6 . . | . . 1
 . 1 . | 5 8 . | 6 9 .
 3 2 . | . . . | 8 . 4
```

Solutions on page 343

6	3		7					
	8	7		1				
9		2						4
5				6		7	4	
		9	5		3	1		
	6	3		7				9
1						4		2
			8			3	6	
					7		9	1

6							3	
9			1				6	
	7		3	9			5	2
3			4		7	5		
	5						4	
		4	2		3			8
8	4			1	2		9	
	9				8			4
	2							5

Solutions on page 344

8				6	1			9
	4			9				1
6			5		8		7	3
		1				8	3	
	8	7				1		
1	9		3		4			8
3				2			1	
5			6	1				2

		7	6		3			
	2			4			3	5
				1			6	
9			5				4	6
		8	2	3	6	5		
5	6			7				3
	4			2				
2	9			6			5	
			1		5	9		

Solutions on page 344

9			6	4				
		1	9		8	5		4
3				7	2		8	
	1						9	
2								6
	3						4	
	7		3	5				2
5		9	7		6	3		
				1	9			7

2	3				6	4		
		9	4			1		
							7	8
4		2		5		3		7
7								6
6		3		1		5		4
9	2							
		7			4	8		
		8	7				5	2

Solutions on page 345

```
. . . | . . 2 | . . .
. 8 . | 1 . . | . . 4
6 5 4 | . 8 9 | . . .
------+-------+------
. . 6 | . 3 5 | 8 . 1
. . . | 4 . 8 | . . .
2 . 3 | 7 1 . | 4 . .
------+-------+------
. . . | 5 9 . | 1 4 6
9 . . | . . 4 | 7 . .
. . . | 8 . . | . . .
```

```
. . . | . 6 . | 1 . .
. 9 1 | . . . | . 8 .
. 7 . | 5 . 1 | . . 9
------+-------+------
. . 3 | 6 7 4 | . 1 .
. 5 . | . 8 . | . . 6
. 1 . | 3 5 2 | 9 . .
------+-------+------
1 . . | 7 . 3 | . 4 .
. 6 . | . . . | . 2 9
. . . | 9 . 4 | . . .
```

Solutions on page 345

Puzzle 177:

			9	3		5	8	
				5	7		9	4
			4	1				
5	7							9
6		3				4		1
8							5	6
				7	6			
2	1		5	8				
	8	6		4	1			

Puzzle 178:

	3	8						
1	4	2					3	8
		5		8	4			
	2		8			3		
4			1		9			5
		7			3		2	
			2	9		7		
8	6					2	4	9
							5	8

Solutions on page 346

Puzzle 179:

		3	4		2			6
				6			3	
4		9	3		7			
6						1	2	
		1	6	2	8	7		
	2	8						9
			9		5	4		2
	8		3					
7			8		6	5		

Puzzle 180:

		7			6	9	8	2
1		2	8	9				
		3	7					
				4			1	
	1		9		7		5	
	4			8				
					3	2		
				6	9	1		8
9	2	6	1			5		

Solutions on page 346

Puzzle 181

2					1	5		
	5		2	7			4	1
8				3		2		
			1	8				
7	2			5			3	8
			9	3				
	9			2				6
3	8		4	7		9		
	7		9					5

Puzzle 182

			6		8	2		
		2				5		8
					2		3	6
2			9	8	5		6	
		8		2		1		
	6		1	7	3			5
1	5		8					
4			3			7		
			9	3		1		

Solutions on page 347

Solutions on page 347

	2		9		6	1	4	
8					1		2	
		4				7		
7			2	1				
2	4						7	6
				6	7			3
		8				9		
	1		6					2
	7	2	8		4		5	

3	8	4				9		
		5	6		8			3
2				3		8		
				8	5			
8		6				3		2
			3	2				
		9		5				4
4			9		1	5		
		3				2	7	9

Solutions on page 348

	7	4				9		
2	5			9		4	3	
9				6			2	
		8		5	2			
	8					5		
	7	2		9				
8			2				7	
5	2		1			6	8	
	3					1	9	

1			5					9
7	2	3			1	6		
			6					
		2		4	3	7	5	
5				1				4
	4	6	2	7		3		
					4			
		4	7			1	6	2
6					8			3

Solutions on page 348

Puzzle 189:

3		5	1	6	2			
			4			5		7
2		9						
		3		7			1	
7		6				8		5
	2		3			7		
						3		8
1		2		4				
			6	7	8	2		1

Puzzle 190:

		3				4		
7	4			9		6	8	
6			5				7	3
		1		6			3	
4								7
	8		4			1		
1	9				4			8
	6	4	2				1	5
		8				3		

Solutions on page 349

Puzzle 191:

	5				1			
7	6	9						
2				7		5	6	9
		3	7					1
		4	2		8	6		
8				3		7		
9	8	2	5					3
						4	5	2
			7				9	

Puzzle 192:

			3	6			4	8
8		3		4				
1	6						3	
		6	2			5	9	4
9	8	5			7	2		
	5						6	7
				7		4		2
6	7		8	9				

Solutions on page 349

	3				2		6	7
		1	6	5	9	3		
4			7		8			9
		3	9	4	5	1		
1			2		6			4
		7	4	6	1	5		
6	4		5				9	

				6			2	8
		7	1					5
5		3	8	7			9	
9			4					
	4	8				1	3	
					3			9
	5			4	8	2		7
7						1	9	.
1	9			5				

Solutions on page 350

Puzzle 195:

		8	9	7				
3	6	1			4			9
	7		6			1		
					5			6
5			7	8	6			2
8			4					
		3		9			2	
4			5			8	3	1
				2	8	6		

Puzzle 196:

	3			2	8			5
		2	1			4		
4				6		2		7
	2		8					
3		9				8		4
					3		1	
5		3		7				1
		6			1	5		
1			3	5			6	

Solutions on page 350

104 ● Level Two: Harder Puzzles

Puzzle 197:

			3					
2	9	3		5		1	8	
1		7	8					
					7			3
3	1	2				7	4	6
5			1					
				2		6		1
	5	9		7		8	3	2
				5				

Puzzle 198:

		2	3		8		6	
	4	9			1	7		
	3			6		2		
							1	5
		5	9		2	4		
	1	6						
		4		3				2
		1	5				8	3
	2			1		6	5	

Solutions on page 351

Solutions on page 351

Puzzle 201:

4					1	6		
	7	1	2		4		9	
						1		8
	3	8	6	1				
		7				3		
				9	7	8	1	
3		2						
	1		7		8	2	6	
		9	1					5

Puzzle 202:

	7	3						
4	6		3					9
8		9			1	2		
7		6		3				
3			2	8	6			1
			1			3		4
		4	6			9		7
6					2		5	3
						6	8	

Solutions on page 352

```
6 3 . | . . 4 | . . .
8 . 7 | . . 9 | . . .
. 5 4 | 6 . 2 | 7 . .
------+-------+------
. . . | . . 3 | 1 . .
1 . . | 8 5 7 | . . 6
. 8 4 | . . . | . . .
------+-------+------
. . 6 | 2 . 5 | 4 7 .
. . . | 7 . . | 3 . 5
. . . | 3 . . | . 8 1
```

```
5 4 . | . . . | 1 . .
3 . . | . 2 7 | . . .
6 7 . | . 3 . | . . 9
------+-------+------
. . . | 6 . . | 5 . .
2 5 . | 1 . 9 | . 6 4
. . 6 | . . 2 | . . .
------+-------+------
1 . . | . 9 . | . 4 6
. . . | 8 1 . | . . 3
. . 9 | . . . | . 5 1
```

Solutions on page 352

Puzzle 205 grid:

				7			8	
9			3		1	7		
	7		5		4	3	1	6
6				2			5	
				1				
	9			5				4
7	2	1	8		5		6	
		3	9		7			8
	4			6				

Puzzle 206 grid:

						3	6	8
	7		9			4		1
5						2	4	7
	3					7		
		2	3			9	7	
			6				2	
4	8		1					2
2			4			5		3
	5	1	2					

Solutions on page 353

6							2	3
4	5		9			6		
					7	4		8
2		6	7		9			4
				4				
5			6		3	2		1
7		3	1					
		2			8		4	5
1	8							2

						8	4	9
8	7		4					3
9	4	3			8			5
				5	1	3		
				7				
		7	8	6				
3			7			9	2	4
7					3		5	6
1	6	2						

Solutions on page 353

Puzzle 209

		4			1			2
		3	6			9		1
7		6		9				
		7			6		2	9
		5				3		
8	2		4			7		
				7		4		5
1		3		4	2			
5			6			2		

Puzzle 210

	2		8			1		
	9						4	1
		8	4	6			9	2
1					8	5		
7								1
		2	3					4
4	8			7	6	1		
	6	3					7	
			5		3		4	

Solutions on page 354

5	2	4		3			8	
		7		5				
		1	6	2	9			4
				8	4			
	4		7				2	
	3	5						
4		6	8	5		3		
			6			8		
	8			1		6	9	7

	6				7			3
8		5		6			7	
9				4	5			
	1		8	7				
	2		9		1		5	
			2	5			3	
		8	7					2
	4			3		7		9
3			4				6	

Solutions on page 354

```
. . . | . . . | . . 8
1 . . | . . . | 4 . 2
. 8 7 | . 2 9 | . 3 .
------+-------+------
. 3 . | . 8 4 | . . 7
. 7 . | 1 . 6 | . 5 .
6 . . | 5 7 . | . 4 .
------+-------+------
. 5 . | 6 3 . | 9 8 .
3 . 8 | . . . | . . 4
7 . . | . . . | . . .
```

```
. 8 . | 7 . . | . . 1
3 . . | . . 4 | 2 . 9
5 7 . | . . . | . . .
------+-------+------
. 3 8 | . . 5 | . 9 .
4 . . | 9 . 8 | . . 7
. 9 . | 6 . . | 3 8 .
------+-------+------
. . . | . . . | . 5 8
7 . . | 1 3 . | . . 2
8 . . | . . 7 | . 1 .
```

Solutions on page 355

3	1		7	8		2		
8	6						5	
								3
		8		9	1			7
	2		8		6		9	
7			4	2		6		
4								
	9						8	1
		6		5	7		3	4

	6			7	1	5		
		5	9			2		8
			2	8			3	
	3	9		2				
2								9
				3		4	6	
	2			6	4			
5		6			2	1		
		1	8	5			2	

Solutions on page 355

3			4				5	
						4		9
		8	9			1	3	
	3	5			9			2
		6	2		8	9		
7			3			5	4	
	8	2			7	3		
6		3						
	1				3			5

		6	7	3	4	5		
				2			6	
7	4			8		3		
5			9			8	7	
	3	7			8			6
		1		6			2	5
	6			1				
		5	8	9	3	6		

Solutions on page 356

9		8			2		1	
				4		9		
		4	9			8		7
		1					7	
7	8		2		4		5	1
	3					2		
4		6		9	5			
		3		6				
	9		7			1		4

3		1			6	2		
					5			9
		8	9					
	3	5			9	6	1	
		6	2		8	9		
	2	9	3			5	4	
					7	3		
6			5					
		4	8			7		5

Solutions on page 356

Puzzle 221:

		7			6	9	8	2
			8				3	5
8	9	3						
			6			8		9
	8			3		6		
6		9			1			
						2	9	6
5	3				9			
9	2	6	1			5		

Puzzle 222:

6					1			9
9		5				1		
		7		9			4	5
		9	8					3
	1		4		3		7	
3				2	6			
4	9		2			5		
		1				8		4
2			6					1

Solutions on page 357

Puzzle 223:

			5		3	2		
8		3	9				6	4
7		4	2	8				
1	7					4		
		2					5	1
			3	9	6			5
4	8				2	1		9
		6	8		5			

Puzzle 224:

3			7		5			
	5			1		2		
				4		5		
	6	5	8	7				1
		8	2			1	4	
1				9	3	8	6	
		7		3				
		6		5			2	
			6		2			9

Solutions on page 357

2					5	4		
	8			6		7	1	
4	9	6	7		1			
			8			9		
			5		7			
		1			3			
			1		8	3	9	4
	5	3		7			2	
		8	9					7

						6	9	
1		2					3	
			7		5		6	1
		5	6	4	2			9
2								4
6			5	8	1	3		
7	8		4		3			
	3					1		8
		6	1					

Solutions on page 358

1	8			3		4		
		9		8			1	6
								2
	5		3	7		2		9
		7				3		
2		1		9	4		5	
5								
4	2			5		9		
		3		6			7	4

			9		6	1		
8						6	2	5
1							3	
7	3		2	1				4
		1				8		
9				6	7		1	3
	5							7
3	1	9						2
		2	8		4			

Solutions on page 358

Puzzle 229

1			6					
3		8			7	9		
	5				9			7
	4			3	5	8		1
			4		8			
2		3	7	1			5	
8			5				4	
		1	2			7		5
					1			2

Puzzle 230

1			7	5				
3				6		2		
	9		8	1			4	
6	3			2			1	
8								5
	4			8			2	3
	8			7	6		9	
		7		9				8
				3	8			6

Solutions on page 359

PUZZLE
231

8	7	2				3	1	
1	3							
				3	7	4		
	9		8				3	1
		7		6		2		
4	2				3		9	
		3	5	9				
							2	9
		8	1			6	5	3

PUZZLE
232

			7			5	3	
3		6				2	7	
	7				3		6	
		8	2				9	6
		5				1		
2	9				1	3		
	2		4				5	
	5	1				9		2
	4	9			7			

Solutions on page 359

PUZZLE 233

		8		5				6
			2				5	4
	4	9		7		1		
1			3			4	9	
			8		9			
	6	2			4			1
	9		5		1	7		
7	2			9				
4			2			1		

PUZZLE 234

			9			4		
5					7	8	1	
2		3		8			5	
1			6	7		5		
		8				6		
		7		3	5			8
	3			6		7		5
	8	5	9					4
		4		5				

Solutions on page 360

Puzzle 235:

			6	4			7	5
	6	5			2			
9		4		8				
7						8		3
1			8		6			4
4		9						1
			3			2		9
			2			4	3	
2	9			1	4			

Puzzle 236:

4	8				6			
		6		3				
5		3						2
		7	3		1	9		4
		5	2			9	7	
6		9	4			7	1	
7						3		9
				4		2		
			8				6	7

Solutions on page 360

PUZZLE 237

3			8			5	9	
	9	8	4	6				
					2	8		6
2						3		
7	5						4	9
		1						8
6		7	3					
				9	4	6	7	
	2	9			8			1

PUZZLE 238

	5			7		8		3
7			8	5				1
			2					
6		2	1		5		3	
	8						5	
	4		9		2	6		7
				8				
2				1	6			9
5		6		9			7	

Solutions on page 361

Puzzle 239

```
. 7 . | . . 2 | . . .
. . 1 | . 6 9 | 7 . 5
. . . | . . 7 | 8 6 9
------+-------+------
. . . | . . 1 | . . 6
. 5 . | 6 . 3 | . 7 .
8 . . | 9 . . | . . .
------+-------+------
4 2 7 | 3 . . | . . .
9 . 6 | 2 4 . | 3 . .
. . . | 7 . . | . 4 .
```

Puzzle 240

```
. . 2 | . . 1 | . 3 .
. . 3 | 5 7 . | . 2 .
. 6 . | . . 9 | . . 7
------+-------+------
. . . | . 1 5 | 9 4 .
3 . . | . 9 . | . . 8
. 1 9 | 8 4 . | . . .
------+-------+------
4 . . | 2 . . | . 1 .
. 3 . | . 8 4 | 2 . .
. 2 . | 1 . . | 8 . .
```

Solutions on page 361

	9	1			3			
8	2		9		1			
		4				9	1	3
				5	8			6
5								7
3			6	9				
2	1	7				6		
			7		2		3	9
			8			7	4	

6	4				7			1
8		1		3	6			
	9			4				
		5	3	6				
		8	5	1	2	6		
				9	8	4		
				7			2	
		1	8			9		7
5			4				3	6

Solutions on page 362

PUZZLE 243

9			8		4	7	5	
	8	3				6	9	
		6	5					
3	2					4		
1				8				5
		9					7	1
				7		5		
	9	1				3	4	
	5	8	4		3			6

PUZZLE 244

9		6		7	2		4	
4								6
			4			2	9	1
		9	6	5				
2								9
				4	9	5		
3	8	4			6			
7								8
		1	9	8		7		4

Solutions on page 362

128 • Level Two: Harder Puzzles

Puzzle 245:

	2	1		7	9			4
5		9	2			1	7	
	6							
		6			4	9		8
				2				
4		2	7			6		
							9	
	3	4			8	5		2
2			3	6		8	4	

Puzzle 246:

9		6		7	4			
	3				6	1		9
4				5		2		
3	6					2		
8								5
		7					8	3
	9		3					1
2		3	7			9		
			6	5		8		2

Solutions on page 363

Puzzle 247

1							6	
5	4	7	1	2				
				7	4			
	6	7		5	9			4
		1		8		3		
8		9	4		2	1		
		2	3					
				7	1	5	3	8
	1							7

Puzzle 248

		7		9			1	5
			1					7
1		6			5			
6	7			3			9	
		1	5		7	8		
	3			6			5	4
			8			4		6
7					9			
4	1			5		3		

Solutions on page 363

4			5			2		
				9				8
	7		6	2	8			3
		7			2			4
	2	3				7	9	
9			3			1		
7			8	3	5		4	
3			4					
		6			7			5

2					1		6	3
		1	8	5	4			
		7			2			
	1		2					6
	3	9				4	1	
8					3		5	
			1				2	
			5	6	7	8		
1	5		3					4

Solutions on page 364

Puzzle 251:

	1			6	7	3		
	6		9					5
2			4					
1	7	5						
	3	6	5		8	7	2	
						5	1	3
				3				9
7						6		5
		9	1	4			3	

Puzzle 252:

		5			8		4	
				3	4			8
	4	7			2			6
2		1			5			3
	3						7	
9			1			8		5
1			8			3	9	
4			2	6				
	2		3			6		

Solutions on page 364

				1		5	2	3
		8	9	3	2		1	
							9	
		6	7			3		4
			2		1			
5		4			3	2		
	4							
	6		3	7	8	1		
1	8	5		9				

8				4	3			
	6				2			
9			1	5		3	6	
	5	6						
1	3	2		9		7	5	4
						6	2	
	4	7		8	5			9
			2				3	
			7	1				6

Solutions on page 365

Puzzle 255:

				1	5	4		2
				2		9	6	
		6					1	7
7	9						5	3
		6				8		
8	3						4	9
4	1			9				
6	7		3					
3		9	2	8				

Puzzle 256:

7								4
		4	5		1			7
		3	8	4				
	5				9	2	4	1
		9				5		
1	2	7	3				9	
				6	8	4		
4			1		2	7		
6								8

Solutions on page 365

Puzzle 257

1					3	6	8	
	7			6		2		
				1		3	4	
6		9	5					
8			3		9			5
				1	9			3
	8	3		7				
		7		9			3	
	5	1	2					6

Puzzle 258

			7		3	6		
3	7	8	9				5	
	9			1		3		
			5		7		1	
		2				7		
	4		6			1		
		3		7			9	
	6				5	1	3	8
		1	2		8			

Solutions on page 366

				1				
			3			2		7
		5	6	7		9	3	
	4		8			6		3
		1	2		7	8		
5		6			1			9
	6	9		4	3	5		
1		2			8			
				2				

9	7	3		6				
						4		9
	4		8	2			7	
		6		9			3	5
			3		6			
2	3			4		6		
	6			3	4		8	
8		2						
				8		9	1	6

Solutions on page 366

136 • Level Two: Harder Puzzles

	8	4			3			
		2		7		3	4	
3					6		8	
		6				8		2
	9		5		8		3	
1		8				5		
	7		6					3
	1	3		2		4		
			3			6	7	

	1		8	7				
	3				4			
4			9	6			5	2
	8	9				5		1
2								3
1		4				9	7	
8	4		5	1				6
			7				1	
				4	9		8	

Solutions on page 367

			8	1		6		2
	1						4	3
			4				7	9
	2		5					4
	4	9				3	2	
3				4		7		
1	6				4			
7	9						3	
4		3		6	8			

2	1		4	5	9			6
		7						
		5	1	3				
1					3			
	6	4	5			1	9	2
			6					3
				6	8	3		
						5		
8			2	9	5		6	1

Solutions on page 367

5					7			9
	1						5	2
				2			3	7
2	8	1			6			
	6		8	7	2		9	
			5			6	2	8
7	5			9				
6	4						1	
1			7					5

		5	4			8		6
8	2							
	9		1				5	7
		9		6	5			8
2								3
1			8	3		2		
9	6				4		8	
							3	5
5			1			8	4	

Solutions on page 368

	2	9			7		6	4
				4	2			
	4		9		3			2
				1		4		
	8	1		9		7	3	
	6		7					
4			8		9		7	
			3	7				
5	3		1			6	9	

2		8		3			7	
		4			8			
	3						8	6
3			5	2		1		
9			6		7			5
		2		1	9			8
6	1						5	
			8			9		
	2			4		7		1

Solutions on page 368

5		2	3				4	
			4	5			1	
	7			2	9		5	
	2							6
1		3				2		5
8							7	
	1		9	3			2	
	5			8	2			
	3			7	8			9

8	1	9	2					
2	7					1		
			1	4	7	9		
							5	7
4			3		9			2
	2	3						
			2	4	7	1		
		5					1	6
					6	2	3	4

Solutions on page 369

Puzzle 271:

		6	5		1			2
	4		3					6
2	1		4					
	9		6					3
	5	8				6	7	
4				5		9		
				4			2	5
7				2			6	
6			7		3	1		

Puzzle 272:

			2	1			5	
	1	2			5			
5			4			8		
			1	2		6	9	
	5	8		6		4	1	
	6	1		7	4			
		7		2				4
			9			1	3	
	8		5	1				

Solutions on page 369

Puzzle 273

9		2			5		7	
			9	3				
3	5		1				8	9
4			2	6				
	9						3	
			9	7				1
1	7				4		6	2
				2	6			
	2		8			4		7

Puzzle 274

		2	6					1
	1			5	3		2	4
				2		3	8	6
		9					3	
		6		7		1		
	4					7		
2	8	1		9				
7	6			4	1		9	
4						6	8	

Solutions on page 370

Puzzle 275:

	4						3	5
8		3	1	7	6	6		9
	7				6			4
3		6						
			6		2			
						3		8
7			2				9	
1		2	8	6		5		7
4	3						1	

Puzzle 276:

1	2				3			
			9		4			
		9	8				4	7
6	3		5			1		
8			3		9			5
		4			1		2	3
4	8				6		9	
			4		5			
			2				7	6

Solutions on page 370

1		5			6	9		
8			9					6
9		6	5	7	3			
	8							
3		9				7		5
							1	
			6	1	7	4		9
5					8			7
		7	4			3		2

2		6		1		7		8
3			9	2				
					7			3
5	3					2		
7			3		1			9
		8					1	6
8			6					
			5	8				7
6			9		3		4	5

Solutions on page 371

Puzzle 279

2		7		9		6		
6	8				7			
		5						
	6			4	2			
4	9	2	6		3	8	7	5
			8	7			6	
						7		
			4				9	1
		3		8		5		2

Puzzle 280

9		7						6
	2	6		1	9	8	4	
		1	6		4			
				6	3			
8								3
			1	7				
			2			7	3	
	3	5	4	8		9	7	
6						5		8

Solutions on page 371

Puzzle 281:

	9					8		
4		7	8					
	2	5			9			3
3	7		9	1			6	
		4		6		7		
	6			7	5		3	8
6			5			2	8	
					6	5		4
		9					1	

Puzzle 282:

				6		3		
4		8			3			
			4		8	5		2
2	3	6		7				1
		5		4		6		
	7			1		2	5	3
6		2	5		9			
			1			9		6
		3		8				

Solutions on page 372

Puzzle 283

					6	1	8	5
				7				
	9		4	1				6
	8		2				5	4
4	5						9	8
2	6			8		3		
9				8	3		1	
				5				
8	3	4	1					

Puzzle 284

1		4						
	2	8	6				9	
7		9		1	8			
5						8	3	9
6								1
8	4	1						6
			2	7		9		8
	1				9	6	4	
							7	5

Solutions on page 372

```
Puzzle 285
. . . | 8 6 . | . 3 1
3 . . | . . . | 7 5 .
. 1 4 | . . . | . . 8
------+-------+------
. . . | 5 1 . | 3 . .
. . 6 | 7 . 8 | 5 . .
. . 8 | . 2 4 | . . .
------+-------+------
4 . . | . . . | 2 7 .
. 2 9 | . . . | . . 5
7 6 . | . 4 5 | . . .
```

```
Puzzle 286
. . 2 | . . 9 | . . .
. . 1 | . . . | . 9 5
. . 6 | . 8 1 | . 3 .
------+-------+------
6 . . | . . 3 | . 2 8
9 8 . | . 2 . | . 5 1
5 2 . | 4 . . | . . 6
------+-------+------
. 6 . | 8 7 . | 5 . .
3 4 . | . . . | 2 . .
. . . | 3 . . | 6 . .
```

Solutions on page 373

				5		6		
3		8						1
5	9	6	8					
		9	5	2		8	1	
			3		9			
	4	5		8	1	9		
				6		5	9	2
2						1		8
		1		3				

		3		6	1			
	9		3			4		
5			4					6
		5	2				1	7
8			1		6			3
6	2				3	8		
4					7			1
		8			5		2	
			8	4		3		

Solutions on page 373

	4				7			
2	6							
	8	7		3	4			
		2	8		6	1		5
1	9						3	2
7		8	3		2	4		
			2	7		6	4	
							1	3
			4				8	

	5		3		2			6
1				8			3	
	6	4	9		1			
			5			3		
7		9		3		6		1
		5			7			
			1		9	5	8	
	1		4					2
5			7		3		6	

Solutions on page 374

Puzzle 291:

```
. . 2 | . . 7 | 3 8 .
. 1 2 | . 6 . | . . .
. 3 . | 4 1 . | . . 2
------+-------+------
. 1 5 | . . . | . 7 .
. . . | 5 . 2 | . . .
. 2 . | . . . | 4 1 .
------+-------+------
1 . . | 6 7 . | 8 . .
. . . | 1 . 3 | 9 . .
. 8 7 | 4 . . | 1 . .
```

Puzzle 292:

```
9 . . | . 5 3 | . . .
. . . | . . . | 8 5 3
. . . | 2 . . | . 9 1
------+-------+------
. 8 . | 3 . . | 7 . .
4 7 1 | . . . | 2 3 8
. . 2 | . . 7 | . 4 .
------+-------+------
7 4 . | . . 5 | . . .
8 9 5 | . . . | . . .
. . . | 8 6 . | . . 5
```

Solutions on page 374

Puzzle 293:

	6	5	7	3			1	
4							5	
2			1					8
6		7	5	9			2	
				2				
	2			8	4	1		5
1				3				7
	4							1
	5			1	6	3	8	

Puzzle 294:

	6						7	
			7	3		5		8
7	2		6	8				4
		5	4			2	9	
				5				
	7	2			8	4		
2				1	9		4	3
8		6		7	4			
	4						8	

Solutions on page 375

							8	
	2				6	4		7
4			8				9	6
2	7			8			5	4
		5		7		9		
8	3			5			7	1
9	6				3			5
1		4	9				2	
	5							

3	1	7					6	
	5	8	3			7		
		4		2	5			
			9				3	6
		3		6		9		
8	9				3			
			6	7		4		
		5			1	6	9	
	3					1	8	7

Solutions on page 375

Solutions on page 376

PUZZLE 297

		6					5	7
						2		
	7			2		6	4	8
7		5		6	4		3	
			9		7			
	2		8	1		7		6
1	6	2		8			7	
		4						
8	3					4		

PUZZLE 298

9	1			8		7	5	
	6			9	3		1	
			1			6		
		8			1			6
		4				9		
7			2			1		
		9		5				
	8		7	1			6	
	3	1		2			7	9

Puzzle 299:

```
2 7 3 | . 6 . | 5 . .
. . . | . 1 . | . 2 .
. . 6 | . 2 . | 3 . .
------+-------+------
7 6 . | . . 4 | . . 2
9 . . | . . . | . . 4
5 . . | 6 . . | . 8 1
------+-------+------
. . 7 | . 4 . | 1 . .
. 8 . | . 5 . | . . .
. . 5 | . 7 . | 8 4 9
```

Puzzle 300:

```
2 9 . | . . . | . 8 .
. 3 . | . 6 9 | . . .
. 1 . | 3 5 . | 6 . 9
------+-------+------
. . 2 | . 8 4 | . 6 .
. . . | . . . | . . .
. 8 . | 1 9 . | 4 . .
------+-------+------
1 . 9 | . 3 5 | . 4 .
. . . | 2 7 . | . 9 .
. 6 . | . . . | . 3 2
```

Solutions on page 376

		8	6					7
						8	5	3
			7	8				1
5			3			7	1	
4			5		6			8
	3	2			7			9
7			9	3				
8	9	5						
1					4	9		

	2			5	3			
		8	9					
	9	6		1		3	4	
6		9			7			4
8								5
7			6			9		3
	8	3		7		5	9	
					5	1		
			2	3			7	

Solutions on page 377

7			5				6	2
6			1		7	4		
	2				9			
	3			1	4			
1	8			9			4	6
			7	8			9	
		5					2	
		4	2		1			5
3	6				8			9

		2	6					1
	9	5					7	2
		7			2	8		
	5				4			8
7			5		3			4
9			1				3	
		9	4			1		
2	7						4	6
4					5	2		

Solutions on page 377

158 • Level Three: Tough Puzzles

Puzzle 305:

		1			7		9	2
				6	8			
		5					6	
6			1	4				8
9		3	6	2	8	7		4
4				7	9			6
	3					2		
		4	9					
2	8		4			5		

Puzzle 306:

4		8				2		
2			7				6	8
				2				3
6	1		9	8				
		3	1	5	4	7		
				7	6		8	2
7				3				
3	8				1			7
		6					8	5

Solutions on page 378

9	1	8		5			2	
		7			9			
		4		7				1
	8		3	4	2		1	
	3		1	8	7		4	
7				3		1		
				7		3		
	2			6		9	7	5

9		8		5			2	

		7					2	
	5			1	9	4		
9			3		2	8	7	
5	6					3		
			2	9	1			
		1					4	9
	4	5	9		7			8
		3	8	6			9	
		9				2		

Solutions on page 378

5	9		1	4	7	3		2
			5			4		7
			8					6
	7	1					5	
	3					2	7	
9				3				
1		4		5				
7		3	4	2	8		6	9

	1	6	3				5	7
			7	9	6			3
								8
7		5	2	6				
			9		7			
				1	5	7		6
1								
9			6	7	3			
8	3					2	4	6

Solutions on page 379

Puzzle 311

1			7					
3	7				4	2		
5		6	8	1				
		9		7		1		
8			3		9			5
	4		6			9		
				7	6	5		2
		7	4				3	8
				8				6

Puzzle 312

			7				8	
	7		9					1
5					2	3	4	
		9	5	2			1	4
		2				7		
7	4			8	1	9		
	8	3	1					2
2					5		3	
	5			8				

Solutions on page 379

4			6			5	8	
							6		3
					9			1
3			9	1	2	7		
		9	4		3	2		
		2	5	7	8			4
9			3					
8		7						
	5	6			4			7

							9	5
	5		9		4	1		2
	2		3	7				4
1	4		2			5		
		9			6		4	1
6				3	9		1	
3		5	4		1		2	
4	1							

Solutions on page 380

6					8			
8	5				7		2	9
	7	9	3				8	
		6		4				
9			6	3	2			1
			1			3		
	6				1	8	9	
1	9		8				4	7
			7					6

6	7		3	8				
		5		9		4	3	
3			5					
9		6			5	2		
	3						4	
		7	2			8		3
					6			5
	5	2		1		6		
			5	8		9	2	

Solutions on page 380

6				4	8	9		2
					1	4		
2					6			
1	7							
3	9	8		5		1	6	4
							7	9
			6					7
		2	9					1
9			3	1	2			8

		9		2		5		
				8				
4				3	5	2	8	9
			8	9		1		
	9	1				4	3	
		2		7	1			
5	7	6	9	1				4
				5				
		3		4		6		

Solutions on page 381

PUZZLE 319

2							7	
	4			8				3
	3		9			5		
3		6	5	2			9	
	4		6		7		2	
	5		1	9		6		8
		9	7				5	
4			8			9		
	2							1

PUZZLE 320

9		6				8		
			5	9		3	7	
				6	3			1
			6	5	7			3
	5						6	
1			2	4	9			
3			7	1				
	9	5		2	4			
		2				7		4

Solutions on page 381

Puzzle 321:

4		7	9			1		2
			7				5	
8	9			1				
				7		3		5
	7	5				8	4	
9		3		5				
				4			6	1
	6				7			
2		8			6	4		3

Puzzle 322:

			5	9		2	7	
5						9	4	
2				1		3		5
			4	6				
		3	8		2	1		
				7	1			
7		5		8				9
	2	9						3
	8	4		2	3			

Solutions on page 382

```
. . 2 | 6 . 5 | . . 3
. . . | . . . | 5 2 .
. 5 . | 1 7 . | . 8 .
------+-------+------
. 1 7 | . 6 . | . . .
2 9 . | . . . | . 3 6
. . . | . 9 . | 2 4 .
------+-------+------
. 7 . | . 5 4 | . 6 .
. 4 9 | . . . | . . .
6 . . | 8 . . | 9 4 .
```

```
1 5 2 | . . . | . . .
. . . | 2 . 3 | . 1 .
9 . . | 6 . . | 2 . .
------+-------+------
4 . 1 | . . 6 | 5 3 .
. 9 . | . . . | . 2 .
. 2 5 | 8 . . | 9 . 7
------+-------+------
. . 6 | . . 4 | . . 3
. 1 . | 3 . 2 | . . .
. . . | . . . | 7 5 2
```

Solutions on page 382

Puzzle 325:

9					7		1	
			9			7		
			2		8	9	5	
	5		7	2				6
3		9				4		5
7				4	5		9	
	7	1	5		3			
		6			4			
	9		6					8

Puzzle 326:

	4	8	6				2	
				2		4		
		6	9		4	1		
			4	5	9		7	
7								5
	9		2	7	1			
		9	1			2	5	
		5		4				
		6			3	8	4	

Solutions on page 383

Puzzle 327:

9		4	8		7			2
2	1							
		6		3				9
		2				9		4
	4		7		6		2	
3		1				7		
1				7		2		
							3	6
4			9		8	5		7

Puzzle 328:

	2			8		4		
		5	7		4		3	2
					5		8	
	9		5	7			4	
	4						6	
	7			4	8		2	
	1		9					
4	5		8		7	6		
		3		1			9	

Solutions on page 383

1	3		9			7		
		5						4
	8	4		3		9		
		9	7		8			1
3				6				7
2			3		9	8		
		7		9		1	2	
9						5		
		3			6		8	9

			7		9		5	2
					2		3	7
			3	5			1	
				4		7	8	
5	9						4	3
	4	8		7				
	7			9	5			
6	8		4					
9	1		2		7			

Solutions on page 384

PUZZLE **331**

				5		8		
			7		6			3
2							5	6
	6	7	3	2				4
	4		1		7		2	
3				4	9	6	1	
7	9							5
5			2		4			
		4		9				

PUZZLE **332**

	4		5			3	6	
		3	1		9		5	
5				3			2	1
					6		7	
1								2
	5		3					
8	1			7				9
	7		9			8	2	
	2	9			1		8	

Solutions on page 384

172 • Level Three: Tough Puzzles

1				4	3			2
			2			8		
6		3	8		7			
2		6						4
4	7						2	5
8						1		6
			3		4	6		9
	4			7				
3			9	6				7

9			4				5	
				1		9		2
		5	3	7				
7		9				2		
6	2	3				8	1	5
		1				3		7
			8	5		6		
3		6	4					
	9			7				4

Solutions on page 385

Puzzle 335:

1						3			8	
	7			9	6			2		
5						2			4	
6						7				4
		2		3		9		7		
7				6						3
	8			1						2
		7			9	5			3	
	5			2						6

Puzzle 336:

4		7				6			8	2
					9				3	5
		3							6	1
3				6		2				9
6				5		1				7
7	8							2		
5	3				6					
9	2			1				5		3

Solutions on page 385

PUZZLE 337

			1	2		4	8	
		4		8			6	
				7				1
		7	8	5	9			
	9	1				8	5	
			4	3	1	7		
7				4				
	5			9		3		
	3	8	5	2				

PUZZLE 338

							5	2
1					2	9		7
	2		3	5		8		
					3		8	5
	9	7				6	4	
3	4		5					
		3		9	5		2	
6			2	4				9
9	1							

Solutions on page 386

		5			2	3	1	
1			5	6	3			8
		6			8			
7		9	2					3
5				7	2			9
			7			6		
8			3	4	5			1
	5	4	6			8		

		2	4					
		8		5	3		1	
9	3			1	7			
	7			2			3	
	9	3				6	2	
	2			3			4	
			5	7			9	3
	1		3	9		8		
						8	7	

Solutions on page 386

2			9	7		5		
	6	1			4	2	7	
								8
7				9				
5		9	7		6	4		2
				1				7
6								
	9	2	5			8	3	
		7		2	8			4

		1				6	9	
	5			1		2		7
7								3
2		5	8				3	
9		8		6		4		5
	7				3	8		2
5								6
8		6		5			2	
	1	3				7		

Solutions on page 387

	2			9				4
			6	1				
6		7	3			1		8
5			9	8			2	6
7	6			3	2			9
8		9			3	5		7
				5	1			
2				7			1	

		5				9		4
	2			4	1		7	6
9							2	
	8				5		9	3
			1		2			
7	5		3				1	
	3							9
5	9		2	3			6	
6		7				3		

Solutions on page 387

7	2					4		
		5	7					
		9	2		4		7	
			6	9			5	
3	6		1		5		2	8
	5			3	8			
	4		5		7	1		
					1	2		
		1					6	5

					4		7	3
			7		1	2		5
	5		3		2		8	
4							5	7
8								9
1	6							4
	3		2		9		4	
7		2	6		5			
6	9		8					

Solutions on page 388

Puzzle 347

7			5				6	2
6			1		7	4		
	2					9		
	3			1	4			
1	8			9			4	6
			7	8			9	
		5					2	
		4	2		1			5
3	6				8			9

Puzzle 348

		3	8	6				
	6	1	3			8		9
			4	7				
				4	3	5	2	
3				8				1
	8	2	1	5				
				3	8			
6			8			2	4	5
				9	4	6		

Solutions on page 388

Puzzle 349:

					1			9
4	1	3	9					
	9				4	6		
1	8	6	2			4		
5								2
		9			5	3	8	6
		1	4				2	
					2	7	6	1
9			5					

Puzzle 350:

			5			2		
			1	9	6			2
		7					6	8
		8		5				
5	1	4	3		7	8	9	6
					4		7	
1			6					4
3				7	9	5		
			4			3		

Solutions on page 389

Solutions on page 389

	3	4			7			
6	2						3	4
1			2			7		
	6			3	9			8
			4		5			
8			1	2			7	
		6			8			2
2	8						1	3
			6			8	4	

	7		5	2				
5				7			6	
		9		4		5		
8			6		2			4
	1		7		4		2	
7			1		3			5
		7		6		9		
	4			3				8
			1	8		3		

Solutions on page 390

Puzzle 355

					8			6
	3		5	2		8		
			4			5	7	1
	4							7
	8	7	3		1	9	5	
1						6		
2	5	4		6				
	7		2	1			4	
9			4					

Puzzle 356

		2			3		6	
	1	3			5			8
		5				4	3	
			5	4				
1	5	9				2	4	7
				1	7			
	9	6				1		
8			3			7	9	
	2		1			3		

Solutions on page 390

Puzzle 357

3					5			
6		9			8		4	
	8		9			5		
2	6		8	7		9	3	
	7	4		9	3		6	2
		7			9		8	
	9		1			3		4
			6					9

Puzzle 358

							5	
	2	8			3	4		9
6	4			2			7	
		6			2	7		
5	1						2	4
		7	5			6		
	6			3			8	2
8		2	6			3	4	
	5							

Solutions on page 391

Solutions on page 391

			5	3		4		
	2		4					5
4		5				2		1
8			9	4	3		5	
				1				
	4		2	7	5			8
2		1				8		7
3					9		6	
		9		2	8			

	6	2		1			9	
	9				5		2	3
				2	8			
	8		1	5			6	
7								9
	3			4	6		5	
		7	3					
8	1		5				7	
	2			7		4	3	

Solutions on page 392

Puzzle 363:

				7		9		5
	5		3		1			
		8				3	1	
	3			2		8	5	
4		5				2		7
	9	2		5			3	
	2	1				4		
			9		7		2	
8		9	6					

Puzzle 364:

	2	4	7		3		8	
					4	2	5	
		6	8	1		3		
6				2				
		2				7		
				8				3
		3		7	6	5		
	6	7	4					
	5		2		8	4	7	

Solutions on page 392

Puzzle 365:

	1				2		6	
		4		3		1		5
		3				9		
7		2			6		9	
3			2	1	8			4
	5		3			2		6
		9				5		
5		7		8		6		
	3		9				7	

Puzzle 366:

	1	3					4	
5			7	1	3		8	
			2		6			
		8						1
2	7		4		1		3	9
9						4		
			8		2			
		9	3	6	4			5
		2				7	6	

Solutions on page 393

Puzzle 367:

		8	4				7	
4			7				6	
7						9		
1	8		4	6		2		7
6				5				1
3		2		9	8		5	6
		7						3
	3				4			9
	4			2		7		

Puzzle 368:

		4		1		2		
	2		8					
	6	1		4				5
	7				5	9		
3	8	9				1	5	2
		5	9				8	
4				2		3	1	
					6		4	
	1		3			2		

Solutions on page 393

Puzzle 369

		5	7			6		8
							2	5
		6			8	4		
6		4	1				7	
2			4		9			1
	1				3	8		4
		8	6			7		
9	5							
7		2			4	1		

Puzzle 370

				9	6		8	
	1	6	8	7			4	
5		8						6
		7			9	6		
			7		1			
		9	5			7		
9						4		7
	7			5	4	8	2	
	3		1	2				

Solutions on page 394

	1	3			8	2	5	
		2	3			7		
			4				3	8
		4		1	6			
	7						6	
			3	4		9		
9	3				4			
		1		8			3	
	4	8	7			1	9	

1			4		9			
	6	8			3	4		
	3							
	7				6	5		8
	9	3	7	4	5	6	2	
6		5	8				4	
							9	
		7	3			8	6	
			1		8			2

Solutions on page 394

Puzzle 373:

	3			5				6
				1			2	
7	5		3				4	
	1	4				2		
6		7	5		9	8		1
		8				4	6	
	7			4			8	2
	4		9					
8				3		5		

Puzzle 374:

					9	4	7	6
	9	6	4					
				5			9	
			8				4	5
5	4		6	2	1		3	9
8	2				4			
	6			1				
						5	1	2
1	5	2	3					

Solutions on page 395

		2	8	7				
	4				6	2		3
				9				1
2	6	3		8		1		
4				1				2
		7		6		5	8	4
3			6					
6		4	7				1	
				9	5	4		

					1		3	9
4	5		3			8		
			8		2	6		4
6			5	2			9	
	8			1	7			6
5		4	2		8			
		3			5		6	1
7	9		1					

Solutions on page 395

Puzzle 377

		2		1				
6					2	1		5
		5	4		7	2		3
		4					1	8
	6						5	
5	8					9		
2		6	9		4	5		
4		3	5					6
				6		4		

Puzzle 378

	7			9	5		8	
		4	8					
					1			2
	8	9	5			1		
5	2	7		6		8	9	3
		6				9	2	5
9			7					
						8	6	
	5		6	4			3	

Solutions on page 396

PUZZLE 379

5			1			6		
2			5		9		8	3
	7						5	
	5				1	9	6	
			4	2	5			
	2	1	6				3	
	9						4	
6	3		7		2			8
		2			8			6

PUZZLE 380

3			2				8	
	5	6			1			2
2			5	9				6
	3		4					1
	8			1			9	
1					8		3	
7				3	5			9
5			9			1	2	
	4				2			3

Solutions on page 396

Puzzle 381:

		1				9	7	5
3		5		2				
9			1	5		6		
7				1		9		
			8		6			
	8		5					1
	4			8	5			9
			2			4		7
2	9	3				5		

Puzzle 382:

	2		5	1				
1		3	4					7
				3				2
			3	1	8			6
	1		4		6	7		
3		4	7	5				
4			8					
6			7			4		1
			2	4		9		

Solutions on page 397

Puzzle 383:

		8			5		4	
1	4					9		
		9	1	2	4			8
				8	3	2		
8								7
	6	1	7					
7			4	3	9	1		
		4					8	3
	1		8			5		

Puzzle 384:

			9			2		
5								6
	9	7			4			5
		1	4	6	9		3	
9			8		2			4
	6		3	7	1	5		
7			1			4	2	
6								3
		4		2				

Solutions on page 397

Puzzle 385:

8		9	2					
2			9	8		1	6	
	3				7			8
		8	6			5		
4								2
		3			8	4		
3			4				5	
	4	5		3	2			6
				6	2			4

Puzzle 386:

							2	4
1			6	8		9		
	3		1			6		8
4		7	9			3		
			2		6			
		1			3	8		9
7		5			9		6	
		4		6	1			3
		1	6					

Solutions on page 398

Puzzle 387:

	7			5			3	
3				6	9	7		5
		5	1					9
					1			6
	5	4				9	7	
8			9					
4				5	6			
9		6	2	4				7
	3			9			4	

Puzzle 388:

	4				9		8	
7	1			5				4
9				3		7	6	
	5		1	4			7	
	2			9	7		1	
	3	1		7				2
8				2			3	7
	7		5				4	

Solutions on page 398

9	4		5					
		8	1			9	5	
		5			9	3		
			8	2		7	1	
2								9
	8	7		1	3			
		4	3			8		
	5	6				2	1	
					1		9	4

	7			9				
4	6	1	3	2				
8		9	4					6
		6			3			
	4	5				7	9	
			1			3		
5					8	9		7
			1	2	4	5	3	
			5				8	

Solutions on page 399

Solutions on page 399

8		6			3		9	4
	1	2	9			3		6
			2	4		8		
6			7	1	8			9
		8		3	9			
3		9			5	4	2	
1	4		3			9		7

	2				7		6	
7	5	3				2	4	
1					2			7
	1				5			2
			8		9			
3			1				9	
2			6					1
	9	1				7	8	6
	4		7				2	

Solutions on page 400

	5		6	7				
		3					6	
8		1		4		7		
				8	5	9	3	
	9	4		7	1			
	4	5	9	3				
		7		2		3		6
	3					5		
				9	4		7	

6		3						8
		4		6		2		
2			4		7		1	
	1		2	7			8	
7								4
	4			9	5		6	
	2		7		9			1
	6		5			9		
4							8	5

Solutions on page 400

		4		3			5	8
			1					
		1		9	5	4		
			6			8	4	
6	5	8				7	1	3
	9	7			1			
		6	9	7		3		
					8			
7	8			1		9		

		7				8		
			7	1	2		6	
1		2		4	8			7
			8	9			2	
	5			2			3	
	2			3	7			
5			2	7		9		6
	1		9	5	4			
		9				1		

Solutions on page 401

9		4		2	6			
8							6	
	6		5	4		7		9
					2			1
	3	1				5	8	
2			1					
3		6		9	7		1	
	8							6
			8	6		3		4

3	2			9		4		7
	9	1				8		6
	8	4						
			7		3			
8		6		4		5		
	5		8					
				6	2			
4		6		8	1			
9		7	3		6	4		

Solutions on page 401

Puzzle 401:

	9	1					5	7
2		7				4	8	
4				7				6
				4		6		2
			2	5	8			
7		9		6				
5				1				4
	7	3				8		1
9	1					7	6	

Puzzle 402:

			8			7		
	5							1
8	1	7	4		5			9
9		4			2	5		
7								8
		8	7			2		4
1			3		8	4	7	6
3							9	
		2			6			

Solutions on page 402

Puzzle 403:

					9	3		5
	8			3				6
4		3	6				9	7
			8	4				
8			5		6			9
			1		2			
9	4				8	7		2
7			2				5	
2		8	1					

Puzzle 404:

	3		1		9			
	9	6				5		
	8	1	7	5				2
			8				4	
5		7				8		9
	2				4			
9				1	8	7	5	
		8					1	2
			3		7			6

Solutions on page 402

```
5 . 9 | . . . | . . .
. . . | . 7 4 | . 6 9
. . . | . 8 1 | 5 7 .
------+-------+------
2 . . | 8 . 6 | . 4 .
. . 5 | . . . | 2 . .
. 4 . | 7 . 2 | . . 6
------+-------+------
6 8 7 | 4 . . | . . .
3 5 . | 6 1 . | . . .
. . . | . . . | 6 . 4
```

```
1 2 4 | . . 3 | 6 8 9
. . . | . 6 . | . . .
. . 6 | . . . | . 4 7
------+-------+------
6 3 . | . 2 7 | . . .
. . . | . . . | . . .
. . . | 6 8 . | . 2 3
------+-------+------
4 8 . | . . . | 5 . .
. . . | . 9 . | . . .
9 5 1 | 2 . . | 4 7 6
```

Solutions on page 403

PUZZLE 407

						7		9
		3	7				5	
			2		4	8		
3			1	8			7	
	9	2	3		6	4	1	
	6				7	2		3
		6	5		3			
	7				8	3		
2		8						

PUZZLE 408

		3			5	1		9
	8						3	2
			9	3		5	6	
8					3		2	
	3						5	
	9		7					1
	5	9		2	7			
1	4						7	
7			6	4			8	

Solutions on page 403

Puzzle 409:

5		3		7	4	6		
	1				9			
9								
4			8		1	9		2
	6	9				8	1	
8		1	6		7			4
								5
			7				9	
		2	9	5		3		6

Puzzle 410:

		2	6					1
	9	5					7	2
		7			2	8		
	5				4			8
7			5		3			4
9			1				3	
		9	4			1		
2	7					4	6	
4				5	2			

Solutions on page 404

PUZZLE 411

4		7	5	6		8		
	9	5	7					
1				4				7
		4					2	
9		1		2		7		8
	2					4		
5				7				6
					4	2	8	
		9		8	3	1		5

PUZZLE 412

1			8					
8					1			6
9	4		5	7	3			
	8					2	9	3
3								5
7	5	2					1	
			6	1	7		5	9
5			2					7
				9				2

Solutions on page 404

4		6	9	5				
8		9	7		6			
2				8	3			
1			3				9	
			1		7			
	2				9			7
			6	3				5
			2		4	1		9
				9	5	7		2

	5	9					3	7
		3		6		1		
1		2		7	3			
				2	9			
2			3		1			5
			5	8				
			6	3		8		9
		1		5		4		
4	3					5	2	

Solutions on page 405

		1				6	9	
	5			1		2		7
7								3
2		5	8				3	
9		8		6		4		5
	7				3	8		2
5								6
8		6		5			2	
	1	3				7		

					9			7
		2		1			8	
7		9	2	4	6		1	
4		8						1
	7						3	
9						4		2
	6		8	7	2	3		4
	9			6		1		
3			1					

Solutions on page 405

Puzzle 417:

			7					
	3			2			5	
8		5	6					3
	7			1	2	4		5
9	5						2	1
2		1	4	7			3	
6					4	2		7
	8			3			9	
					7			

Puzzle 418:

6			4	2				5
			1			4	8	
		8		6	9			7
7		1					5	
	6						7	
	4					6		2
5			6	7		9		
	7	6			1			
1				5	2			8

Solutions on page 406

		8						
	5	6		2		8		
6			8	9	3			
	4	7	3		9			2
	3						7	
7		6		4	1	5		
	3	8	9				1	
	2		4		3	6		
						8		

1					8	5		
	6	3	4				8	
				1	3			6
		1				6		8
	2		6		1		4	
4		6				3		
7			1	2				
	4				5	1	6	
		2	9					3

Solutions on page 406

```
8 4 . | . . . | . 3 .
. 2 5 | 1 . . | 7 4 9
. 1 . | . 9 5 | . . .
------+-------+------
5 9 . | 8 . . | . . .
. . . | . . . | . . .
. . . | 3 . . | 9 7 .
------+-------+------
. . 2 | 4 . . | 5 . .
1 5 3 | . . 2 | 9 6 .
. 8 . | . . . | . 7 3
```

```
1 . 8 | . . . | . 3 .
. . 2 | 1 . 3 | . . .
5 3 . | 2 . 4 | . 7 .
------+-------+------
. 6 . | 7 . 5 | . . 3
. . . | . . . | . . .
7 . . | 3 . 6 | . 1 .
------+-------+------
. 5 . | 4 . 9 | . 8 2
. . . | 6 . 2 | 4 . .
. 2 . | . . . | 6 . 1
```

Solutions on page 407

Puzzle 423:

8				3		5		
4	6	5						
	7		5	4			8	6
			4	8				5
		6				4		
7			2	1				
2	3		4	8			5	
						8	2	1
		8	7					3

Puzzle 424:

1	4				3			8
	5	3	4				1	
	8		1	2		5		
		5					9	
7								5
	2					6		
		4		9	2		7	
	1				7	8	6	
8			6				5	2

Solutions on page 407

				4				
7	6		9					4
3	5		1		2			
		7	2	6		8	9	
	9						3	
	3	6		9	7	2		
			3		4		6	2
5					6		1	8
				1				

	9					6		
8			5	2	3		9	
	2	5		6				
4	8				1			2
		7				1		
2			4				8	6
				4		2	5	
	4		6	5	7			3
		8					6	

Solutions on page 408

		7	2				5	
9		5			4	2		
				8	7			9
2	6			9				
4			6		1			7
			3				6	4
8		6	1					
		1	9			3		8
	7				2	6		

			2	5		4		6
							1	2
		2	6	3		9		
	7	5		1				4
		8				2		
1				4		8	7	
		4		2	5	7		
7	9							
5			3		9	6		

Solutions on page 408

		8			9			
		5	3			8	2	
6	9		8			3		7
		7	1				6	
			4	3	7			
	2				8	5		
7		9			3		8	4
	5	6			4	9		
			9			7		

	5				4	3		
		7			8		4	6
		6						2
5					2		9	
6		3	4		5	2		1
	8		7					4
1						4		
7	4		2			9		
	6		8				7	

Solutions on page 409

PUZZLE **431**

5			2					
	6		9		1		4	5
		8		3			7	1
1							8	
	3	6				7	2	
	8							3
8	2			5		4		
7	4		8		6		5	
					2			7

PUZZLE **432**

2						7	9	6
4				9		5		
	5		3				4	
	1			6	3			
		7	5	4	9	8		
			1	7			6	
	7				4		8	
		3		8				7
8	6	1				9		

Solutions on page 409

222 ● **Level Three: Tough Puzzles**

					2	4	3	
3				9			5	
	1		3		7	9		8
				1		3		4
	4						9	
5		8		2				
4		1	6		9		7	
	2			7				5
	6	3	2					

9				6				
8			4		7		2	
	6			5	1		8	7
		2		8				6
6								1
7				1		2		
3	9		5	2			4	
	7		1		3			2
				7				5

Solutions on page 410

	3	8	9		2			
	4				6			
7			3			1		
	2	6	8			3		
4			1		9			5
		7			3	8	2	
		4			8			6
			7				4	
			4		1	5	8	

				4		5		
		1		9			2	7
	7	9		5	2	6	1	
6					3			
		5		8		7		
			4					6
	1	4	2	6		9	7	
8	2			7		4		
		6		3				

Solutions on page 410

437

	2	4		5	3			9
			9		4	2		
			8					7
6	3	9		2				4
7				8		9	2	3
4					6			
		7	4		5			
9			2	3		4	7	

438

	7		4			5		
9				7		6	2	
				2	9			7
2				1		9		
	5		7		2		6	
		9		4				2
4			2	5				
	3	6		8				5
		5			6		9	

Solutions on page 411

		5	8		6	9		
	2				1			
9		6						
	8		7	6				3
	6	9	1		2	7	4	
7				9	4		1	
						4		9
			2				6	
		7	4		9	3		

	9			4	3	2		
		3	9				6	
				8	6		1	3
			3	5				6
	6						9	
3				9	7			
2	1		4	3				
	8				2	1		
		6	8	1			4	

Solutions on page 411

5			3	7				
3		8	1		4		9	6
		6				3		
	8	5			7	1		
			3					
		3	8			9	4	
		7				5		
4	5		7		8	6		2
				2	5			4

			5		8	2		
5	1			3				
		7			4		8	
8		1				7	3	
9	7						6	4
	6	2				5		8
	3		1			4		
				4			1	3
		4	9		3			

Solutions on page 412

Level Four: Tougher (we really mean it!)

Solutions on page 412

8			6					5
				5		9		7
		9	1			4	8	
			8	2				
3		7	9		5	2		8
				1	3			
	6	3			1	8		
7		5		8				
9					2			3

		4				6		
3			9	6				
5	9		8			3	4	
		9			7	8	1	
			3	4	9			
	4	5	6			9		
	8	3			6		9	2
			9	5				8
		1				4		

Solutions on page 413

Puzzle 447:

	8			1	9		6	
2	9			5				4
		7	8			3		
9							1	3
		2			7			
5	7							8
		4			2	6		
6				7			3	2
	2		6	3			7	

Puzzle 448:

		2	7	8			1	
		9				8		
4	8			2				7
	1	7	6		3			
	9						3	
			5		8	1	2	
9				6			8	3
		3				2		
	2			3	4	6		

Solutions on page 413

3				8			6	
		8		6				9
9			7			3	1	8
	2	1						6
5								4
8						5	7	
1	8	9			2			3
7			8			6		
	3			9				7

	2		7		3			
			9					
5				1	2		4	7
6		9	5	2		8		
8								5
		5		8	1	9		3
4	8		1	7				2
				5				
			2		8		7	

Solutions on page 414

Puzzle 451:

		7						3
	1	5				6	2	
2		3			1		8	
			7					6
6		4	3		2	8		1
7				5				
	9		5			7		8
	7	8				9	6	
4						3		

Puzzle 452:

4		7			6			1
	5	2		1				3
			3			8		
5			4				1	2
			2		1			
2	8				3			9
		5			7			
7				6		1	9	
6			1			2		7

Solutions on page 414

2			7	9		4		
1	7		3			8		
				1				7
		7		2			6	3
		1		3		2		
4	2			9		5		
7				5				
		6			4		1	2
	4		9	6				5

		5				6		8
	7		9		6		2	5
3			5			4		
					5		7	
2		7				5		1
	1		2					
		8			2			3
9	5		8		7		4	
7		2				1		

Solutions on page 415

	5		8		4		2	
3		7		2				
			5		7			6
1	2					6		
	6	3				2	9	
		5					1	3
2			1		5			
				4		9		5
	4		3		8		7	

PUZZLE

456

	6		1		9			3
5	1		7	6				9
3								
1	3			5		8		6
				9				
2		5		3			4	1
								7
9				7	4		5	8
7			9		6		3	

Solutions on page 415

Puzzle 457

	1					2		
6		2	3					
			4	1	6	3		
3			5		6			7
	7	5				4	6	
8			3		7			5
	3	7	1		4			
				8		3		4
		8					9	

Puzzle 458

9							2	3
					9	4	6	
	6				3			
	7	2		8	5		3	4
			4		7			
1	4		9	3		6	8	
			5				1	
	3	8	7					
5	1							8

Solutions on page 416

Puzzle 459:

	2							9
				6			5	1
5	9		8		2	3		
	3		5	2				4
8								5
7				8	1		2	
	3	1		6			9	2
2	6			9				
9						7		

Puzzle 460:

5					7	9		
			9	3			4	
	9	3				8		
7			3	4	2		6	
			6		8			
	6		7	5	9			3
		6				4	5	
	1			9	6			
		7	5					6

Solutions on page 416

Puzzle 461:

2					9			
4	3	7		2				9
		1	3			2		4
						6	4	
3			5		1			7
	5	9						
5		1		6	8			
9				1		5	7	8
			2					1

Puzzle 462:

		4		5			8	
3	7				4	2		1
					2		4	7
6	3				7	8		
				4				
		5	6				2	3
4	8		1					
2			7	4			3	8
		5		3		4		

Solutions on page 417

				3		8		
8	7		4					3
9				2	8	6		
	2	8	9				6	
6								2
	3				2	4	9	
		5	7	1				4
7					3		5	6
		2		4				

1				3	2	4		9
			4		1	6		
		9			7	2		
8							5	
	3		8		6		2	
	4							8
		1	3				9	
		4	7		9			
6		9	1	2				3

Solutions on page 417

6	9	8		4				
3			9					
	4	1			6		9	
8	1				7	4		6
9		6	8				1	7
	6		2			8	4	
				8				3
			5			2	6	1

	6				2	4	7	5
								9
	4		8	6	7			
	8		9	7		1		
			2		8			
		7		3	5		2	
			5	8	1		4	
7								
8	1	4	7				9	

Solutions on page 418

Level Four: Tougher Puzzles •

PUZZLE 467

PUZZLE 468

Solutions on page 418

4	8	1				5		
			5	3		8		
5			1					
	2			6	1	9		
		5	2		9	7		
		9	4	5			2	
					2			9
		8		4	3			
		2				4	6	7

9					6		5	
8		5	7					
	6	3					2	9
	5			2	9			
6	3			7			8	2
		8	1				4	
3	4					8	1	
					1	2		6
	1		8					4

Solutions on page 419

Puzzle 471:

6				8		2	4	9
		3		2		5		
				5	4		1	
	8	6		3	9			
				7				
			1	4		3	8	
	7		4	6				
		5		9		7		
9	6	2		1				4

Puzzle 472:

							3	4
3					9	7		
		4		1			6	9
		3		2				
1	5	4	6		3	9	7	2
				7		5		
4	2				5		9	
		6	2					7
5	3							

Solutions on page 419

Puzzle 473

	2	4			1	6		7
6				3				
			4			3	9	
		6	7	2		5		
	3			5			8	
		2		1	9	7		
	8	5			6			
				4				5
2		1	5			9	4	

Puzzle 474

6	7		2					
2		4		3	6		7	
		5	4					
	8						4	6
		7	1		4	8		
4	1						5	
					3	4		
	4		9	1		6		5
					2		3	9

Solutions on page 420

Puzzle 475:

```
. . . | . . 5 | . 9 8
. 5 . | 3 . . | . . .
7 . 2 | . 4 . | 5 . 3
------+-------+------
2 . 5 | . 4 . | . . .
9 3 . | . 6 . | . 7 5
. . . | 5 . . | 8 . 2
------+-------+------
5 . 7 | . 3 . | 1 . 6
. . . | . 7 . | 2 . .
4 1 . | 6 . . | . . .
```

Puzzle 476:

```
. 5 . | 4 8 9 | . 7 6
. . . | 2 . . | 4 . 9
. . . | . 1 . | . 8 .
------+-------+------
4 7 . | . . 6 | . . .
. . 3 | . . . | 6 . .
. . . | 8 . . | . 4 7
------+-------+------
. 8 . | . 7 . | . . .
5 . 7 | . . 2 | . . .
3 4 . | 1 6 8 | . 5 .
```

Solutions on page 420

Puzzle 477:

3			7			5		
	5		3	6		9	7	
	1	6						
	3	7			6			9
	6			2			8	
8			4			7	5	
						4	1	
	7	3		4	2		9	
		9			8			7

Puzzle 478:

	2		3					
9		3		6		2		
6			5	1	2	8		
5				8				
	8	2				9	1	
			2					8
		6	7	2	3			9
		7		8		1		4
					4		3	

Solutions on page 421

PUZZLE
479

Puzzle 479:

1				5	8			
		6	7					3
7		9		2		1	4	
	1	4			3		7	
	9		1			4	6	
	7	5		1		3		2
2					5	6		
			2	3				4

PUZZLE
480

Puzzle 480:

8				7	6	2		9
		2				5		
		4		9			1	
	2				1		8	7
1				4				5
7	4		5				6	
	9			8		6		
		7				8		
2		8	6	5				1

Solutions on page 421

Puzzle 481:

	4	8	6		5	7	2	
								6
2	7					1	5	
			4					1
		4	3		8	2		
5				1				
	3	9					6	7
8								
	6	7	5		3	8	4	

Puzzle 482:

	9		6					
		8		5	7		6	
		4	3				1	
7							2	1
	1	9	4	2	8	6	7	
2	8							9
	7				3	1		
	3		2	6		7		
					1		9	

Solutions on page 422

Puzzle 483

```
. . . | 8 . . | 1 . 6
. . . | . 1 . | . 9 7
. 7 . | 9 . . | 5 . 2
------+-------+------
. . 7 | . 9 . | 6 . 3
. . 4 | . 6 . | 2 . .
6 . 1 | 3 . . | 7 . .
------+-------+------
2 . 9 | . 7 . | . 6 .
8 4 . | 5 . . | . . .
7 . 5 | . 3 . | . . .
```

Puzzle 484

```
. 6 . | 7 . . | . . .
. . 4 | 2 8 . | . . .
. . . | . 3 6 | . 4 7
------+-------+------
. 1 3 | . . 9 | 5 . 8
. . 6 | . . . | 3 . .
5 . 9 | 8 . . | 1 6 .
------+-------+------
6 5 . | 3 2 . | . . .
. . . | 9 8 . | 4 . .
. . . | 7 . . | 3 . .
```

Solutions on page 422

		4			3			
3	7			6				
5	9	6	8	1				
6	3		5					
8	1						6	5
					1		2	3
			7	6		5	9	2
			9				3	8
			2			4		

		4		5	3		8	9
			9			2		
	9	6	8		2			
6								4
8			3		9			5
7								3
			1		6	5	9	
		7			5			
9	5		2	3		4		

Solutions on page 423

	7				2		5	
	2	5	1					
		1		6	4	7		
	4		8		5			7
2								9
5			2		9		6	
		9	4	2		3		
					3	6	8	
	6		7				9	

		3	7		5			
		7	4		2			6
5							1	
		1						3
2	4	6	9		3	8	7	1
8						2		
	1							8
6			3		1	9		
			2		7	1		

Solutions on page 423

Puzzle 489:

							6	
6				8	7		1	4
				1	9			2
	5			2		6		1
	1		4		5		9	
2		6		1			4	
8		7	5					
9	6		8	4				3
	2							

Puzzle 490:

			7		3			
3				6		2		
	9	6		1				7
		9		7			1	4
8			3		9			5
7	4		6			9		
4				7		5	9	
		7		9				8
			2		8			

Solutions on page 424

Puzzle 491:

```
. . 2 | 6 . . | . 5 .
3 9 . | . . 1 | 6 7 .
. 6 . | . 2 . | . . .
------+-------+------
. 3 . | 9 . . | . 1 8
. . 5 | . 3 . | . . .
9 2 . | . 8 . | 5 . .
------+-------+------
. . 4 | . . . | 8 . .
. 7 1 | 9 . . | . 6 5
. 8 . | . . 5 | 2 . .
```

Puzzle 492:

```
5 2 . | 9 3 1 | . . 6
. . . | . 8 5 | . . .
. . 1 | . . . | . 5 .
------+-------+------
. 5 . | 1 . . | . 7 .
1 . 8 | . . . | 5 . 9
. 7 . | . . 9 | . 6 .
------+-------+------
. 9 . | . . . | 3 . .
. . . | 6 9 . | . . .
3 . . | 2 1 4 | . 9 7
```

Solutions on page 424

9		4				3	5	
	6				1	4		9
				5		8		
	7		9	5		8	4	
	9	6		8	2		3	
	4		5					
1		7	6				9	
	3	5				1		4

	2		7			4	5	
					3			
6			5			2	7	3
		1	9		6	8		
4				8				7
		7	4		5	1		
1	9	2			4			8
			8					
	7	8			9		4	

Solutions on page 425

5			2	7			6	
2		1	3	6		8		
		8	1			2		
	6	7		3				
			7					
			2			7	4	
		4			2	6		
		3	6	5		4		8
	1		7	4				3

1	2						8	
		8						1
			8	1	2	3		7
	3				7			4
	1		3	4	9		6	
7			6				2	
4		3	1	7	6			
2						1		
	5						7	6

Solutions on page 425

	8						9	4
		4		5		3		
			7	4			8	1
9	2		6					
		6	5		4	9		
				9			6	7
4	5			3	7			
		9		6		8		
8	6						5	

6	7		8		3		2	1
		3	7			8		
			6		9			
				1			7	2
9								3
5	1			3				
			4		6			
		8			5	2		
1	6		3		2		9	4

Solutions on page 426

Puzzle 499

9							2	3
					9	4	6	
	6			3				
	7	2		8	5		3	4
			4		7			
1	4		9	3		6	8	
			5				1	
	3	8	7					
5	1							8

Puzzle 500

9			7	6			3	
					4	2		9
		2			3	8	6	
	3				5		9	
		5		3		1		
	9		6				8	
	2	3	4			7		
7		1	3					
	4			2	7			3

Solutions on page 426

3			7			5		
	5		3	6		9	7	
	1	6						
	3	7			6			9
	6			2			8	
8			4			7	5	
						4	1	
	7	3		4	2		9	
		9			8			7

4			8	3				5
				5	2			
		8		7	4		1	
7	9						4	
	4	2		6		8	5	
	5						3	9
	1		4	2			9	
			5	9				
9				8	1			3

Solutions on page 427

	8				3	6	9	
	5		2		9			8
		6		1				
		4					2	5
		5	1		2	9		
8	2					7		
				3		2		
3			6		5		8	
	9	8	7				3	

2			6					1
4	3			7		8		
		6			8	3		
	2		1				8	4
		7				1		
6	1				9		7	
		1	2			9		
		2		3			1	8
3					5			2

Solutions on page 427

Puzzle 505:

	2	4			1	6		7
6				3				
			4			3	9	
		6	7	2		5		
	3			5			8	
		2		1	9	7		
	8	5			6			
				4				5
2		1	5			9	4	

Puzzle 506:

			6				4	1
	3		5		1	8		6
1				2		3		
9		3	1					
		7				1		
					9	2		3
		1		8				5
5			2	7		6		1
3	8				5			

Solutions on page 428

Puzzle 507:

	4	1					6	
2						7		4
	8	7		3	4			
	3			9				
	9	6	7		5	8	3	
				1			9	
			2	7		6	4	
6		4						3
	2					5	8	

Puzzle 508:

	1			6	3	5		
	5		4			6	3	
3								9
4			3		7			
1		3		4		2		7
			5		1			3
6								5
	4	9			5		7	
		7	6	8			9	

Solutions on page 428

7	1			3	8	2		
4		8		9				1
3		9		1				
		3			2			
		1		5		9		
			1			4		
			3			1		5
1				8		6		7
		4	7	1			2	8

	9						4	
	5			4		9	8	
						3	1	5
			2			1	8	
	8	1	4	9	6	7	3	
		4	7			8		
	1	2	8					
	9	8		7			2	
5						6		

Solutions on page 429

Puzzle 511:

2								6
				3		5	8	1
	8		7			3	9	
	1	9	8			2		
	4						3	
		3			4	6	1	
	6	4			8		5	
3	7	8		6				
1								8

Puzzle 512:

							9	2
6			7					5
3		4		1			6	8
		3		8	1	2		
			2	3	6			
		2	4	9		8		
7	4			2		6		1
2					4			7
8	3							

Solutions on page 429

Puzzle 513:

	9	8		4				2
2				8		3		5
8	1			9	7	4		
5	7			3			2	8
		6	8	2			1	7
1		5		7				9
7				5		2	6	

Puzzle 514:

			3		1			6
		8					1	7
6		3	4	7			5	
2			7					1
		6					8	
	9				3			5
	6			5	4	7		2
1		7					5	
5			9		7			

Solutions on page 430

Puzzle 515

	5		4	8	9		7	6
			2			4		9
			1			8		
4	7				6			
	3					6		
			8				4	7
	8			7				
5		7		2				
3	4		1	6	8		5	

Puzzle 516

2					4			
		6	8	1		9		
			6				8	1
	2	3	1		6		5	
		5				1		
		6	5		8	3	2	
5	3			1				
	1		6	4		9		
			8					2

Solutions on page 430

• Level Four: Tougher Puzzles

6			9			2	4	8
				8				7
	2				4		3	
2	4	7	8			6		
				6				
		6			1	7	9	2
	6		1				2	
1				9				
	3	8	5		6			9

							3	
	7		1		3		4	8
		6	2	8		1	7	
4			7			8		3
7		5			6			4
	5	7		1	9	3		
8	1		6		2		5	
	2							

Solutions on page 431

9			7		5	4		2
		7			2			
5								7
			8	2		6		3
2			9	5	3			1
8		5		7	6			
4								8
			3			9		
3		9	2		7			4

			1	7			2	
2					9	7		
	7		2	8	3	4		
	5	7						
3		9				8		7
						5	3	
		8	3	1	6		4	
		5	7					8
	4			5	8			

Solutions on page 431

				8			7	
7			2				1	
9	3				7	2		
			9	2		5		
8	9		7		5		2	1
		5		3	1			
		6	5				9	3
	1				2			4
	4			6				

						4	1	
		7			1		2	5
5			2					7
	2	5	7					
9		4	1	2	5	7		8
					6	5	9	
3				8				1
1	5		3			6		
		8	6					

Solutions on page 432

Puzzle 523:

7		9	2			3		
								9
	6				8	5	7	2
2			9	7	5			4
				4				
9			8	1	6			3
6	4	2	5				8	
5								
		3			7	4		5

Puzzle 524:

					7		6	4
2		1	4		6			
			1				3	
4	6			1	3	9	8	
				7				
	9	5	2	6			4	1
	5				2			
		6			1	4		8
8	1		7					

Solutions on page 432

	5	7	3			9	8	
	6		8					5
	9				5			1
				4	2			
		8	9		7	6		
			5	8				
7			4				9	
5					9		7	
	2	6			8	5	4	

7	6		3			9	4	
	3		4	1			6	
				6				1
	2			4				5
			7		6			
9				2			8	
1				9				
	9			7	2		5	
	8	6			4		9	7

Solutions on page 433

				7	5	3	4	
		7			4	8		
		8					7	2
6			4			2	8	
			7		1			
	5	4			3			9
1	2					4		
		9	5			1		
	6	5	1	4				

				2			9	8
6				1	8	2		7
			9			5		
2	6		8					1
		8				4		
1					3		6	2
		7			9			
8			6	1	5			4
4	1			8				

Solutions on page 433

```
. 2 5 | . 3 1 | . 9 .
. 7 1 | 9 . . | . . .
3 . . | . . . | . . 7
------+-------+------
6 3 . | 1 . . | 9 . .
2 . . | . 6 . | . . 1
. . 9 | . . 3 | . 6 4
------+-------+------
1 . . | . . . | . . 3
. . . | . . 7 | 2 4 .
. 6 . | 3 5 . | 1 8 .
```

```
. . 3 | 9 . 2 | . 5 .
1 5 . | . . . | . . 9
. 8 9 | . 5 . | . . .
------+-------+------
. . . | . 7 . | 5 8 .
. . 5 | 1 . 8 | 2 . .
. 4 2 | . 9 . | . . .
------+-------+------
. . . | . 4 . | 6 3 .
3 . . | . . . | . 4 2
. 9 . | 6 . . | 3 8 .
```

Solutions on page 434

Puzzle 531

							3	4
3				9	7			
	4		1				6	9
	3		2					
1	5	4	6		3	9	7	2
			7		5			
4	2			5		9		
		6	2					7
5	3							

Puzzle 532

7	3			9	8	2		
9				4			7	
						3		
8			9		5	4	6	
2				3				7
		4	3	1		7		2
		7						
	6			1				4
		2	3	7			8	6

Solutions on page 434

PUZZLE 533

1		4			3		8	9
	7					2		
5						3		
6	3		5	2				
8			3		9			5
				8	1		2	3
		3						2
		7					3	
9	5		2			4		6

PUZZLE 534

6		7		2		1	9	5
	5		1					6
		8					3	
	2				6			9
3								4
8			7				1	
	8					9		
2					1		4	
1	9	4		5		7		8

Solutions on page 435

Puzzle 535:

					8			9
5	6		4				8	1
	8			1				
3		1		4		6		
	7		6	3	1	9		
	6			5		3		7
				2			9	
9	4				5		6	2
6			9					

Puzzle 536:

		4	6					7
5		3			9	1		
			3				4	
2						7		3
3	6		2		5		9	1
1		8						5
	5				2			
		6	9			3		2
7					6	9		

Solutions on page 435

		8				7		
9	5				7	4	3	
			9	3				8
6				5	9	3		
			3		8			
		3	2	7				4
4				8	2			
	2	5	7				1	3
		7				8		

					8	7	3	
9	3	1					2	
	5				3	1	6	
				5				
	7	2	4		1	3	8	
			7					
	2	5	3				1	
	4					5	9	7
	1	9	8					

Solutions on page 436

9				6			2		
1		8	7				6	
6								3
	8	6		9	2	7		5
2		7	5	4			6	9
7								2
	9				5	3		7
		4		8				6

	6				1	5	3	
				9				
		9	8	5			1	
6	4		5	2		1		
1								2
		2		1	7		5	6
	1		6	8	9			
			7					
	9	6	1				8	

Solutions on page 436

5					7			9
	1		6			4	5	2
							3	
	8	1	9	3		5		
		5		7			3	
		3		4	1	6	2	
	5							
6	4	9			8		1	
1			7					5

2	7	3			9			
			7					6
	4			2		3		
7						9	5	2
		2	5	8	7	6		
5	3	4						1
	7			4			6	
4					6			
			3			8	4	9

Solutions on page 437

Puzzle 543

4				2	9			
	1			6	3			
3			8			6		2
1					7		9	6
		7				3		
2	9		6					1
8		3			2			7
			3	7			5	
			9	8				4

Puzzle 544

 		4	6					7
5		3			9	1		
			3				4	
2						7		3
3	6		2		5		9	1
1		8						5
	5				2			
		6	9			3		2
7					6	9		

Solutions on page 437

		3	8	9	5			
	8							5
1		5			2			
6				3	1	5		
5	9						1	6
		1	5	8				2
			6			7		1
4							6	
			7	1	9	8		

5					7	9		
			9	3			4	
	9	3				8		
7			3	4	2		6	
			6		8			
	6		7	5	9			3
		6				4	5	
	1			9	6			
		7	5					6

Solutions on page 438

PUZZLE 547

1								7
	2	8	6			1		
		9			8		6	2
	7			6	4			9
6								1
8			7	9			5	
4	3		2			9		
		7			9	6	4	
9								5

PUZZLE 548

8	7	2						
			5			6		
		1		2	9	4	8	
		7		1				3
		4	7		2	1		
6				4		7		
	9	8	2	5		3		
		6			4			
						8	9	4

Solutions on page 438

	2	4			1	6		7
6				3				
			4			3	9	
		6	7	2		5		
	3			5			8	
		2		1	9	7		
	8	5			6			
				4				5
2		1	5			9	4	

5	9	6	1					2
			5		6			
4				3		5		
2	7	1						4
			2	7	1			
8						2	7	1
		2		1				5
		9		5				
7					8	1	6	9

Solutions on page 439

	2				3			
				6	4		5	
5	9		8		2	3		
		9		2				4
8			3		9			5
7				8		9		
		3	1		6		9	2
	6		4	9				
			2				7	

PUZZLE
552

4			7			6		
	7	1		4	6	3		
		6				4		
	3	4			5		7	
	8							3
	1		2			8	6	
		8				7		
	3		8	1		2	4	
		2			4			9

Solutions on page 439

Puzzle 553:

```
8 4 . | . 5 . | 6 . .
. 2 5 | . . 8 | . . 9
7 1 . | 3 . . | . 8 .
------+-------+------
. . 1 | . 8 4 | . . .
. . . | . . . | . . .
. . . | 5 3 . | 4 . .
------+-------+------
. 7 . | . . 3 | . 5 8
1 . . | 8 . . | 9 6 .
. . 4 | . 1 . | . 7 3
```

Puzzle 554:

```
. . . | . . 7 | 1 6 .
2 . 1 | . . . | 8 . 5
. . 8 | 1 . 5 | . 3 .
------+-------+------
4 6 . | . . . | 9 . .
1 . . | . . . | . . 6
. . 5 | . . . | . 4 1
------+-------+------
. 5 . | 3 . 2 | 6 . .
9 . 3 | . . . | . 4 8
. . 1 | 6 7 . | . . .
```

Solutions on page 440

PUZZLE 555

PUZZLE 556

Solutions on page 440

Puzzle 557:

1				5					
		8			4		2		
	9		8	1					7
6	3		5					1	
	1		3	4	9			6	
	4				1			2	3
4					7	6		9	
		7	4				1		
					3				6

Puzzle 558:

5	2			9	3	1			6
					8	5			
		1							5	
	5			1					7	
1		8						5		9
	7					9		6	
	9							3		
				6	9					
3				2	1	4		9	7

Solutions on page 441

```
Puzzle 559
+-------+-------+-------+
| 4 . 9 | 7 . 5 | . . 6 |
| . 1 . | . . 9 | . . . |
| 7 5 2 | . . 8 | . . . |
+-------+-------+-------+
| . . 4 | . . . | . . 2 |
| 6 . 1 | . . . | 4 . 8 |
| 9 . . | . . . | 7 . . |
+-------+-------+-------+
| . . . | 1 . . | 9 7 3 |
| . . . | 6 . . | . 1 . |
| 1 . . | 5 . 3 | 6 . 4 |
+-------+-------+-------+
```

```
Puzzle 560
+-------+-------+-------+
| 1 . . | 4 . . | 3 . 6 |
| . 6 . | . . 3 | . 1 . |
| 9 . . | . 1 . | . . 5 |
+-------+-------+-------+
| . . . | . 2 . | 5 . 8 |
| . 9 . | 7 . 5 | . 2 . |
| 6 . 5 | . 3 . | . . . |
+-------+-------+-------+
| 2 . . | . 7 . | . . 3 |
| . 1 . | 3 . . | . 6 . |
| 3 . 9 | . . 8 | . . 2 |
+-------+-------+-------+
```

Solutions on page 441

Puzzle 561:

				1	2		9	
	5	3		6				
9				5				4
	4	6	2				3	
5	8			4			6	9
	3			6	8	4		
6			5					8
				8		7	2	
	1		6	2				

Puzzle 562:

	1					9		7
	4	8	7				1	
				2	1			
	9	5	2					1
6		1		3		5		4
4					5	7	9	
			4	8				
	5					3	1	8
8		7					6	

Solutions on page 442

Puzzle 563

```
1 8 . | 2 . . | . . .
. . . | . 1 4 | 2 . .
. . 2 | . . . | 7 . 9
------+-------+------
2 . . | 4 . . | 1 . 5
4 5 . | . . . | . 2 7
7 . 9 | . 5 . | . . 4
------+-------+------
8 . 6 | . . . | 5 . .
. . 1 | 9 6 . | . . .
. . . | . . 2 | . 9 1
```

Puzzle 564

```
. 8 4 | 2 . 5 | . 1 .
2 . . | . . . | . . 7
6 . . | 3 . . | . 4 .
------+-------+------
. . . | 7 . . | . 5 1
. . 9 | 8 . 6 | 4 . .
5 3 . | . . 2 | . . .
------+-------+------
. 2 . | . . 9 | . . 4
3 . . | . . . | . . 5
. 5 . | 6 . 8 | 1 3 .
```

Solutions on page 442

Puzzle 565:

```
2 . . | 6 8 . | . . .
. 7 . | . 9 . | . . 2
. . 9 | 5 7 . | 8 . .
------+-------+------
9 . . | . . . | . 4 7
. 6 1 | . . . | 2 8 .
7 8 . | . . . | . . 5
------+-------+------
. . 8 | . 2 7 | 1 . .
3 . . | 8 . . | . 7 .
. . . | . 4 5 | . . 8
```

Puzzle 566:

```
1 . . | . 5 . | . . .
. . 8 | 9 . 4 | . 5 .
. 9 . | 8 . . | 3 . 7
------+-------+------
6 3 . | . . . | . 1 .
. 1 2 | . 4 . | 7 6 .
. 4 . | . . . | . 2 3
------+-------+------
4 . 3 | . . 6 | . 9 .
. 6 . | 4 . 5 | 1 . .
. . . | . 3 . | . . 6
```

Solutions on page 443

					8			2
8		9	2			4	3	
	4			6			8	
7	5	4						
3	8				1			4
				3	5	7		
8		6			2			
6	2			5	3			1
9		1						

	6			7		8	2	
	8		9			1		
4	1			2		9		
		1	3				4	
6			7				8	
8				4	2			
6		7				4	5	
8			6		7			
7	5		4		1			

Solutions on page 443

					7			1
		1				7	4	
7	9	3		4	1	5		
					4			8
	7	8		1		6	9	
3			7					
		9	6	7		8	2	4
	6	4				9		
5			4					

9	8			4		7		
2					1	6	3	
		1						4
4	3			8				9
		5		1		8		
8			4				7	3
3						2		
	4	8	2					7
		9		6			8	5

Solutions on page 444

	6	5		9	8			
7	8	4	2					
3					6		8	
4					9	8	1	
	7	2	6					3
	4		5					2
				2	4	7	1	
			9	4		5	3	

4			7				3	
	3			5	2	4	8	9
	2	9						1
							1	7
		7		2		9		
1	9							
2						1	9	
3	7	8	2	1			4	
	6				5			8

Solutions on page 444

PUZZLE 573

5				6	3		2	
			5				6	9
4		6	2				5	
			8					5
7		5				2		3
8				2				
	8				9	5		1
3	5			7				
	1		3	8				4

PUZZLE 574

	3		8			9	4	
		8		5				3
					4		2	8
3		9			5			1
	2						5	
6			7			8		9
7	1		5					
5				4		7		
	8	6			9		1	

Solutions on page 445

Puzzle 575:

9							5	
2			7		6		3	
	4			2	5			6
	8	9				5		2
7								8
5		1				3	4	
3			6	5			2	
	9		4		3			5
	1							3

Puzzle 576:

		6	3	4				7
		8	7				1	
	7				1			
	9	5				8		1
	8	1				5	2	
4		3				7	9	
			4				7	
	5				3	1		
8				5	2	4		

Solutions on page 445

8		2	4					3
7	4			2				
	5	1	6					
5	1	8			2			6
				1				
6			7			1	8	9
					9	6	5	
				6			7	4
2					4	8		1

6	7					3		
		4			6		7	
8		5			1			2
	8		5		7	1		
5								3
		6	3		9		5	
9			7			4		8
	4		9			6		
		8					3	9

Solutions on page 446

9	4	6	8				1	
		3		7				8
7			4	1				
	1					2		6
	3						5	
5		9					7	
				6	4			1
4			1			6		
	8				9	7	4	2

	2		8	6			9	4
8					1			
1	9		5				8	3
	8					3		
6								5
		7					6	
2	3				5		4	1
			2					7
4	7			1	9		2	

Solutions on page 446

PUZZLE 581

			2	7				5
		6	3			7		
	7	8	5		4	3		
6				2				1
	8						9	
1				5				4
		1	8		5	4	6	
		3			7	1		
8				6	2			

PUZZLE 582

8				7	6	2		9
		2				5		
		4		9			1	
	2				1		8	7
1				4				5
7	4		5				6	
	9			8		6		
		7					8	
2			8	6	5			1

Solutions on page 447

PUZZLE
583

5			1			4		9
			4		9		6	2
				7			5	
9			7		3			6
	7						9	
8			2		4			7
	9			4				
4	2		6		1			
1		5			7			3

PUZZLE
584

5				3	9	2		
8			4					
		6	7	5	2			1
		8					3	6
			2		4			
1	9					2		
4			9	2	1	7		
				6				9
	7	9	3				1	

Solutions on page 447

Puzzle 585:

	2		6	1			3	
			4					
	8	1	3	5		2		
2				9				3
	6	7				8	9	
1				6				5
		9		3	2	6	7	
					4			
	3			8	6		1	

Puzzle 586:

			3		8		5	
		8	7		6		1	
	7			2		6		
	9	5	2					1
6				3				4
4					5	7	9	
		2		8			7	
	5		6			3	1	
	3		1			2		

Solutions on page 448

Puzzle 587

3			7			5		
	5		3	6		9	7	
	1	6						
	3	7			6			9
	6			2			8	
8			4			7	5	
						4	1	
	7	3		4	2		9	
		9			8			7

Puzzle 588

6				1	2		8	
			3					7
	2				4		3	
2			8			6		
	9	1	2		7	8	5	
		6			1			2
	6		1				2	
1				8				
	3		5	2				9

Solutions on page 448

SOLUTIONS

Solution to Puzzle 1

9	5	7	6	8	4	2	1	3
1	8	4	3	5	2	6	7	9
6	3	2	1	9	7	4	8	5
5	4	9	2	1	6	8	3	7
8	2	3	7	4	5	9	6	1
7	6	1	9	3	8	5	2	4
3	1	8	4	6	9	7	5	2
2	9	5	8	7	1	3	4	6
4	7	6	5	2	3	1	9	8

Solution to Puzzle 2

8	7	2	6	4	9	3	1	5
1	3	4	2	5	8	9	6	7
6	5	9	1	3	7	4	8	2
5	9	6	8	2	4	7	3	1
3	1	7	9	6	5	2	4	8
4	2	8	7	1	3	5	9	6
2	6	3	5	9	1	8	7	4
7	4	5	3	8	6	1	2	9
9	8	1	4	7	2	6	5	3

Solution to Puzzle 3

4	8	3	1	9	6	5	7	2
5	2	6	4	3	7	8	9	1
1	9	7	8	2	5	4	3	6
7	5	4	6	1	2	3	8	9
3	6	9	5	8	4	1	2	7
2	1	8	9	7	3	6	4	5
9	4	1	2	5	8	7	6	3
8	7	5	3	6	9	2	1	4
6	3	2	7	4	1	9	5	8

Solution to Puzzle 4

3	4	6	5	9	8	2	7	1
5	1	8	2	3	7	9	4	6
2	9	7	6	1	4	3	8	5
8	5	1	4	6	9	7	3	2
9	7	3	8	5	2	1	6	4
4	6	2	3	7	1	5	9	8
7	3	5	1	8	6	4	2	9
6	2	9	7	4	5	8	1	3
1	8	4	9	2	3	6	5	7

Solution to Puzzle 5

7	8	1	2	9	5	6	3	4
2	9	3	1	4	6	5	7	8
4	6	5	3	7	8	9	2	1
5	1	9	8	2	7	3	4	6
6	2	4	5	1	3	7	8	9
8	3	7	4	6	9	1	5	2
3	5	2	6	8	1	4	9	7
9	4	6	7	5	2	8	1	3
1	7	8	9	3	4	2	6	5

Solution to Puzzle 6

4	2	9	3	7	1	8	5	6
6	5	8	4	2	9	7	1	3
1	7	3	5	6	8	2	9	4
2	8	6	9	5	7	3	4	1
7	9	1	2	4	3	5	6	8
5	3	4	1	8	6	9	7	2
3	6	2	7	9	4	1	8	5
8	1	7	6	3	5	4	2	9
9	4	5	8	1	2	6	3	7

Solution to Puzzle 7

9	6	7	3	8	4	2	5	1
2	5	8	7	1	6	9	3	4
1	4	3	9	2	5	7	8	6
4	8	9	1	3	7	5	6	2
7	3	6	5	4	2	1	9	8
5	2	1	8	6	9	3	4	7
3	7	4	6	5	1	8	2	9
8	9	2	4	7	3	6	1	5
6	1	5	2	9	8	4	7	3

Solution to Puzzle 8

2	4	8	9	7	1	5	6	3
3	6	1	8	5	4	2	7	9
9	7	5	6	3	2	1	4	8
7	1	4	2	9	5	3	8	6
5	3	9	7	8	6	4	1	2
8	2	6	4	1	3	9	5	7
6	8	3	1	4	9	7	2	5
4	9	2	5	6	7	8	3	1
1	5	7	3	2	8	6	9	4

Solution to Puzzle 9

8	7	2	4	6	1	5	3	9
9	4	3	5	7	8	6	2	1
5	6	1	3	2	9	4	8	7
2	8	7	6	1	5	9	4	3
3	5	4	7	9	2	1	6	8
6	1	9	8	4	3	7	5	2
4	9	8	2	5	7	3	1	6
1	3	6	9	8	4	2	7	5
7	2	5	1	3	6	8	9	4

Solution to Puzzle 10

9	6	4	7	3	2	1	5	8
8	3	5	1	4	6	2	9	7
2	7	1	8	9	5	4	3	6
1	2	3	6	5	7	8	4	9
6	5	8	4	2	9	7	1	3
4	9	7	3	8	1	6	2	5
5	1	6	9	7	4	3	8	2
3	4	9	2	6	8	5	7	1
7	8	2	5	1	3	9	6	4

Solution to Puzzle 11

5	3	2	1	6	8	4	7	9
7	1	8	4	5	9	3	6	2
6	4	9	3	7	2	1	5	8
9	5	4	7	8	3	2	1	6
2	7	3	5	1	6	8	9	4
8	6	1	2	9	4	5	3	7
3	9	6	8	4	5	7	2	1
4	2	7	6	3	1	9	8	5
1	8	5	9	2	7	6	4	3

Solution to Puzzle 12

8	6	2	3	7	1	5	9	4
3	1	5	9	4	6	2	7	8
4	9	7	2	8	5	6	3	1
6	3	9	4	2	8	7	1	5
2	5	4	6	1	7	3	8	9
1	7	8	5	3	9	4	6	2
9	2	3	1	6	4	8	5	7
5	8	6	7	9	2	1	4	3
7	4	1	8	5	3	9	2	6

Solution to Puzzle 13

4	2	3	8	7	6	9	5	1
7	8	6	9	5	1	4	2	3
5	1	9	2	3	4	8	7	6
6	3	1	5	4	8	2	9	7
2	7	4	3	6	9	1	8	5
8	9	5	1	2	7	3	6	4
3	6	7	4	8	2	5	1	9
9	4	2	7	1	5	6	3	8
1	5	8	6	9	3	7	4	2

Solution to Puzzle 14

7	4	8	5	3	9	1	6	2
6	9	3	1	2	7	4	5	8
5	2	1	8	4	6	9	7	3
2	3	9	6	1	4	5	8	7
1	8	7	3	9	5	2	4	6
4	5	6	7	8	2	3	9	1
8	1	5	9	7	3	6	2	4
9	7	4	2	6	1	8	3	5
3	6	2	4	5	8	7	1	9

Solution to Puzzle 15

5	6	2	3	7	1	9	4	8
3	8	9	4	5	6	7	1	2
4	7	1	8	2	9	6	5	3
7	2	5	1	9	3	4	8	6
1	4	3	7	6	8	2	9	5
8	9	6	2	4	5	3	7	1
6	1	8	9	3	4	5	2	7
9	5	7	6	8	2	1	3	4
2	3	4	5	1	7	8	6	9

Solution to Puzzle 16

1	6	9	4	3	2	7	5	8
8	3	2	7	9	5	6	1	4
4	5	7	6	1	8	9	3	2
6	2	5	8	4	9	3	7	1
3	9	1	2	7	6	8	4	5
7	4	8	1	5	3	2	9	6
5	1	6	9	8	7	4	2	3
9	8	4	3	2	1	5	6	7
2	7	3	5	6	4	1	8	9

Solution to Puzzle 17

5	2	7	9	3	6	1	4	8
8	9	3	7	4	1	6	2	5
1	6	4	5	8	2	7	3	9
7	3	6	2	1	8	5	9	4
2	4	1	3	5	9	8	7	6
9	8	5	4	6	7	2	1	3
4	5	8	1	2	3	9	6	7
3	1	9	6	7	5	4	8	2
6	7	2	8	9	4	3	5	1

Solution to Puzzle 18

3	2	7	5	1	4	6	8	9
9	8	1	3	6	2	4	5	7
4	5	6	9	8	7	2	3	1
5	7	9	2	4	6	3	1	8
1	4	8	7	9	3	5	6	2
6	3	2	1	5	8	7	9	4
8	9	4	6	2	5	1	7	3
2	6	3	8	7	1	9	4	5
7	1	5	4	3	9	8	2	6

Solution to Puzzle 19

4	1	5	7	9	8	2	3	6
7	3	6	1	5	2	4	8	9
8	2	9	6	4	3	5	7	1
5	4	2	9	8	6	3	1	7
6	8	7	3	2	1	9	5	4
1	9	3	5	7	4	8	6	2
2	5	4	8	6	7	1	9	3
3	7	8	2	1	9	6	4	5
9	6	1	4	3	5	7	2	8

Solution to Puzzle 20

9	4	1	5	2	7	3	6	8
2	6	3	1	8	9	7	5	4
5	8	7	6	3	4	9	2	1
4	3	2	8	9	6	1	7	5
1	9	6	7	4	5	8	3	2
7	5	8	3	1	2	4	9	6
8	1	5	2	7	3	6	4	9
6	7	4	9	5	8	2	1	3
3	2	9	4	6	1	5	8	7

Solution to Puzzle 21

4	2	1	8	3	9	6	7	5
6	3	7	1	5	2	9	8	4
5	8	9	6	7	4	3	1	2
7	9	8	3	1	5	2	4	6
3	4	2	9	6	7	8	5	1
1	5	6	2	4	8	7	3	9
8	1	3	4	2	6	5	9	7
2	7	4	5	9	3	1	6	8
9	6	5	7	8	1	4	2	3

Solution to Puzzle 22

6	4	1	9	2	8	7	3	5
8	5	3	4	1	7	6	2	9
2	7	9	3	5	6	1	8	4
3	1	6	5	8	4	9	7	2
9	8	7	6	3	2	4	5	1
5	2	4	1	7	9	3	6	8
7	6	5	2	4	1	8	9	3
1	9	2	8	6	3	5	4	7
4	3	8	7	9	5	2	1	6

Solution to Puzzle 23

6	7	9	8	5	2	1	3	4
3	8	1	4	6	9	7	2	5
2	4	5	1	3	7	8	6	9
7	9	3	5	2	1	4	8	6
1	5	4	6	8	3	9	7	2
8	6	2	9	7	4	5	1	3
4	2	7	3	1	5	6	9	8
9	1	6	2	4	8	3	5	7
5	3	8	7	9	6	2	4	1

Solution to Puzzle 24

4	3	6	9	5	2	8	7	1
8	5	9	7	1	6	2	4	3
2	7	1	4	8	3	9	5	6
1	6	7	3	2	8	5	9	4
9	4	5	1	6	7	3	2	8
3	2	8	5	4	9	6	1	7
7	9	2	6	3	1	4	8	5
5	8	3	2	7	4	1	6	9
6	1	4	8	9	5	7	3	2

Solution to Puzzle 25

8	2	3	7	6	1	4	5	9
7	4	5	2	9	3	6	8	1
6	1	9	5	4	8	2	7	3
2	5	1	9	7	6	8	3	4
4	3	6	1	8	2	5	9	7
9	8	7	4	3	5	1	2	6
1	9	2	3	5	4	7	6	8
3	6	4	8	2	7	9	1	5
5	7	8	6	1	9	3	4	2

Solution to Puzzle 26

5	6	2	3	7	1	9	4	8
3	8	9	4	5	6	7	1	2
4	7	1	8	2	9	6	5	3
7	2	5	1	9	3	4	8	6
1	4	3	7	6	8	2	9	5
8	9	6	2	4	5	3	7	1
6	1	8	9	3	4	5	2	7
9	5	7	6	8	2	1	3	4
2	3	4	5	1	7	8	6	9

Solution to Puzzle 27

8	5	1	6	2	4	7	3	9
9	2	7	1	3	8	5	4	6
4	3	6	9	5	7	8	1	2
5	1	4	3	8	2	6	9	7
6	7	3	4	9	5	2	8	1
2	8	9	7	6	1	3	5	4
1	9	8	5	7	6	4	2	3
7	4	5	2	1	3	9	6	8
3	6	2	8	4	9	1	7	5

Solution to Puzzle 28

2	1	8	9	4	3	6	7	5
7	9	6	8	5	1	4	3	2
4	5	3	6	7	2	1	8	9
5	8	7	1	2	6	3	9	4
9	2	1	5	3	4	8	6	7
6	3	4	7	9	8	5	2	1
8	6	2	4	1	9	7	5	3
3	4	5	2	6	7	9	1	8
1	7	9	3	8	5	2	4	6

Solution to Puzzle 29

5	9	7	8	2	6	4	1	3
3	4	2	1	9	5	7	8	6
8	6	1	7	3	4	5	2	9
9	3	4	2	6	7	8	5	1
2	7	5	9	8	1	3	6	4
6	1	8	4	5	3	2	9	7
7	2	6	5	4	9	1	3	8
1	5	9	3	7	8	6	4	2
4	8	3	6	1	2	9	7	5

Solution to Puzzle 30

7	1	5	4	9	3	8	2	6
8	2	3	5	7	6	9	4	1
6	9	4	1	8	2	3	5	7
3	4	9	2	6	5	7	1	8
2	7	8	9	4	1	5	6	3
1	5	6	8	3	7	2	9	4
9	6	7	3	5	4	1	8	2
4	8	2	7	1	9	6	3	5
5	3	1	6	2	8	4	7	9

Solution to Puzzle 31

4	2	1	8	3	9	6	7	5
6	3	7	1	5	2	9	8	4
5	8	9	6	7	4	3	1	2
7	9	8	3	1	5	2	4	6
3	4	2	9	6	7	8	5	1
1	5	6	2	4	8	7	3	9
8	1	3	4	2	6	5	9	7
2	7	4	5	9	3	1	6	8
9	6	5	7	8	1	4	2	3

Solution to Puzzle 32

2	6	8	1	3	5	4	7	9
5	9	4	7	6	8	2	1	3
1	3	7	4	9	2	5	8	6
3	8	6	5	2	4	1	9	7
9	4	1	6	8	7	3	2	5
7	5	2	3	1	9	6	4	8
6	1	9	2	7	3	8	5	4
4	7	3	8	5	1	9	6	2
8	2	5	9	4	6	7	3	1

Solution to Puzzle 33

8	2	1	6	4	3	9	7	5
3	6	5	9	7	2	1	4	8
9	7	4	1	5	8	3	6	2
7	5	6	4	2	1	8	9	3
1	3	2	8	9	6	7	5	4
4	8	9	5	3	7	6	2	1
6	4	7	3	8	5	2	1	9
5	1	8	2	6	9	4	3	7
2	9	3	7	1	4	5	8	6

Solution to Puzzle 34

3	7	5	1	6	2	4	8	9
8	6	1	4	9	3	5	2	7
2	4	9	7	8	5	1	6	3
4	9	3	8	5	7	6	1	2
7	1	6	2	4	9	8	3	5
5	2	8	3	1	6	7	9	4
6	5	7	9	2	1	3	4	8
1	8	2	5	3	4	9	7	6
9	3	4	6	7	8	2	5	1

Solution to Puzzle 35

6	3	1	5	7	4	8	9	2
8	2	7	1	3	9	6	5	4
9	5	4	6	8	2	7	1	3
7	6	5	9	2	3	1	4	8
1	4	3	8	5	7	9	2	6
2	9	8	4	6	1	5	3	7
3	8	6	2	1	5	4	7	9
4	1	2	7	9	8	3	6	5
5	7	9	3	4	6	2	8	1

Solution to Puzzle 36

9	4	2	5	3	8	6	7	1
3	7	8	1	4	6	9	5	2
6	1	5	2	7	9	3	4	8
5	6	9	8	2	4	7	1	3
2	3	1	7	6	5	4	8	9
4	8	7	9	1	3	2	6	5
1	9	4	3	5	7	8	2	6
8	5	6	4	9	2	1	3	7
7	2	3	6	8	1	5	9	4

Solution to Puzzle 37

1	3	9	7	8	2	6	5	4
4	2	5	3	1	6	9	7	8
7	8	6	4	9	5	2	1	3
2	1	4	8	5	7	3	6	9
9	5	8	6	3	1	4	2	7
6	7	3	9	2	4	1	8	5
3	9	2	1	7	8	5	4	6
5	6	7	2	4	3	8	9	1
8	4	1	5	6	9	7	3	2

Solution to Puzzle 38

1	2	4	7	5	3	6	8	9
3	7	8	9	6	4	2	5	1
5	9	6	8	1	2	3	4	7
6	3	9	5	2	7	8	1	4
8	1	2	3	4	9	7	6	5
7	4	5	6	8	1	9	2	3
4	8	3	1	7	6	5	9	2
2	6	7	4	9	5	1	3	8
9	5	1	2	3	8	4	7	6

Solution to Puzzle 39

4	1	9	3	6	5	7	2	8
8	6	7	1	2	9	3	4	5
5	2	3	8	7	4	6	9	1
9	3	1	4	8	6	5	7	2
2	4	8	5	9	7	1	3	6
6	7	5	2	1	3	4	8	9
3	5	6	9	4	8	2	1	7
7	8	2	6	3	1	9	5	4
1	9	4	7	5	2	8	6	3

Solution to Puzzle 40

5	1	4	9	2	7	6	3	8
6	2	7	3	8	5	1	4	9
8	3	9	4	1	6	5	2	7
2	6	1	7	5	8	4	9	3
7	4	8	6	9	3	2	5	1
3	9	5	1	4	2	7	8	6
9	7	2	8	6	4	3	1	5
4	8	6	5	3	1	9	7	2
1	5	3	2	7	9	8	6	4

Solution to Puzzle 41

9	3	8	6	7	4	1	2	5
4	5	7	2	1	9	6	3	8
1	2	6	5	8	3	4	7	9
2	4	9	1	3	6	5	8	7
3	8	1	7	5	2	9	4	6
6	7	5	9	4	8	2	1	3
5	1	3	4	9	7	8	6	2
7	9	2	8	6	1	3	5	4
8	6	4	3	2	5	7	9	1

Solution to Puzzle 42

2	7	3	4	6	9	5	1	8
8	5	9	7	1	3	4	2	6
1	4	6	8	2	5	3	9	7
7	6	8	1	3	4	9	5	2
9	1	2	5	8	7	6	3	4
5	3	4	6	9	2	7	8	1
3	9	7	2	4	8	1	6	5
4	8	1	9	5	6	2	7	3
6	2	5	3	7	1	8	4	9

Solution to Puzzle 43

1	2	4	7	5	3	6	8	9
3	7	8	9	6	4	2	5	1
5	9	6	8	1	2	3	4	7
6	3	9	5	2	7	8	1	4
8	1	2	3	4	9	7	6	5
7	4	5	6	8	1	9	2	3
4	8	3	1	7	6	5	9	2
2	6	7	4	9	5	1	3	8
9	5	1	2	3	8	4	7	6

Solution to Puzzle 44

9	6	5	7	3	4	1	8	2
8	7	2	5	9	1	6	3	4
4	3	1	2	8	6	7	5	9
6	4	8	3	2	9	5	1	7
2	1	7	6	5	8	4	9	3
5	9	3	4	1	7	8	2	6
3	2	4	8	7	5	9	6	1
7	5	9	1	6	2	3	4	8
1	8	6	9	4	3	2	7	5

Solution to Puzzle 45

2	3	1	5	9	7	6	4	8
9	4	5	8	6	1	2	7	3
7	8	6	2	3	4	1	9	5
4	5	9	3	1	2	8	6	7
8	1	7	4	5	6	3	2	9
6	2	3	9	7	8	4	5	1
5	7	4	1	2	3	9	8	6
3	6	8	7	4	9	5	1	2
1	9	2	6	8	5	7	3	4

Solution to Puzzle 46

5	9	7	8	2	6	4	1	3
3	4	2	1	9	5	7	8	6
8	6	1	7	3	4	5	2	9
9	3	4	2	6	7	8	5	1
2	7	5	9	8	1	3	6	4
6	1	8	4	5	3	2	9	7
7	2	6	5	4	9	1	3	8
1	5	9	3	7	8	6	4	2
4	8	3	6	1	2	9	7	5

Solution to Puzzle 47

6	3	7	5	4	8	9	1	2
8	5	9	2	7	1	4	3	6
2	1	4	3	9	6	7	8	5
1	7	5	4	6	9	8	2	3
3	9	8	7	5	2	1	6	4
4	2	6	8	1	3	5	7	9
5	8	1	6	3	4	2	9	7
7	6	2	9	8	5	3	4	1
9	4	3	1	2	7	6	5	8

Solution to Puzzle 48

3	2	1	5	8	4	6	9	7
7	5	4	6	2	9	1	3	8
6	9	8	7	1	3	4	2	5
8	7	5	9	4	2	3	1	6
9	4	3	1	6	5	7	8	2
1	6	2	8	3	7	5	4	9
2	8	7	3	5	1	9	6	4
5	1	6	4	9	8	2	7	3
4	3	9	2	7	6	8	5	1

Solution to Puzzle 49

1	6	4	9	3	2	5	8	7
3	2	8	6	5	7	1	9	4
7	5	9	4	1	8	3	6	2
5	7	2	1	6	4	8	3	9
6	9	3	8	2	5	4	7	1
8	4	1	7	9	3	2	5	6
4	3	5	2	7	6	9	1	8
2	1	7	5	8	9	6	4	3
9	8	6	3	4	1	7	2	5

Solution to Puzzle 50

9	7	3	4	6	1	2	5	8
1	2	8	7	5	3	4	6	9
6	4	5	8	2	9	1	7	3
4	8	6	1	9	2	7	3	5
5	1	9	3	7	6	8	2	4
2	3	7	5	4	8	6	9	1
7	6	1	9	3	4	5	8	2
8	9	2	6	1	5	3	4	7
3	5	4	2	8	7	9	1	6

Solution to Puzzle 51

2	6	8	1	3	5	4	7	9
5	9	4	7	6	8	2	1	3
1	3	7	4	9	2	5	8	6
3	8	6	5	2	4	1	9	7
9	4	1	6	8	7	3	2	5
7	5	2	3	1	9	6	4	8
6	1	9	2	7	3	8	5	4
4	7	3	8	5	1	9	6	2
8	2	5	9	4	6	7	3	1

Solution to Puzzle 52

2	4	5	6	8	3	7	9	1
8	7	6	4	1	9	5	3	2
1	3	9	5	7	2	8	6	4
9	2	3	1	5	8	6	4	7
5	6	1	7	9	4	2	8	3
7	8	4	2	3	6	9	1	5
4	9	8	3	2	7	1	5	6
3	5	2	8	6	1	4	7	9
6	1	7	9	4	5	3	2	8

Solution to Puzzle 53

9	8	2	4	7	3	5	6	1
4	1	3	6	2	5	9	7	8
7	6	5	9	8	1	4	3	2
2	7	8	5	4	9	6	1	3
1	5	9	8	3	6	2	4	7
6	3	4	2	1	7	8	5	9
3	9	6	7	5	8	1	2	4
8	4	1	3	6	2	7	9	5
5	2	7	1	9	4	3	8	6

Solution to Puzzle 54

2	6	4	1	5	7	9	8	3
8	3	5	2	6	9	4	7	1
9	7	1	3	8	4	5	2	6
5	1	6	8	7	3	2	9	4
7	2	3	9	4	1	6	5	8
4	8	9	6	2	5	1	3	7
1	5	8	7	9	6	3	4	2
6	4	2	5	3	8	7	1	9
3	9	7	4	1	2	8	6	5

Solution to Puzzle 55

4	2	8	5	3	7	1	6	9
7	5	3	9	1	6	2	4	8
1	6	9	4	8	2	5	3	7
9	1	4	3	6	5	8	7	2
6	7	5	8	2	9	3	1	4
3	8	2	1	7	4	6	9	5
2	3	7	6	9	8	4	5	1
5	9	1	2	4	3	7	8	6
8	4	6	7	5	1	9	2	3

Solution to Puzzle 56

4	8	2	5	7	3	6	9	1
1	5	3	2	6	9	4	7	8
9	7	6	8	1	4	3	5	2
6	1	4	3	9	7	8	2	5
7	3	5	1	8	2	9	6	4
8	2	9	4	5	6	7	1	3
5	6	1	9	3	8	2	4	7
3	4	7	6	2	5	1	8	9
2	9	8	7	4	1	5	3	6

Solution to Puzzle 57

1	2	4	7	5	3	6	8	9
3	7	8	9	6	4	2	5	1
5	9	6	8	1	2	3	4	7
6	3	9	5	2	7	8	1	4
8	1	2	3	4	9	7	6	5
7	4	5	6	8	1	9	2	3
4	8	3	1	7	6	5	9	2
2	6	7	4	9	5	1	3	8
9	5	1	2	3	8	4	7	6

Solution to Puzzle 58

9	3	8	6	7	4	1	2	5
4	5	7	2	1	9	6	3	8
1	2	6	5	8	3	4	7	9
2	4	9	1	3	6	5	8	7
3	8	1	7	5	2	9	4	6
6	7	5	9	4	8	2	1	3
5	1	3	4	9	7	8	6	2
7	9	2	8	6	1	3	5	4
8	6	4	3	2	5	7	9	1

Solution to Puzzle 59

9	4	7	5	2	8	1	3	6
3	2	6	7	1	9	8	4	5
5	8	1	6	3	4	2	9	7
7	1	9	8	6	3	4	5	2
8	6	2	9	4	5	7	1	3
4	5	3	1	7	2	6	8	9
1	9	8	2	5	7	3	6	4
2	3	5	4	8	6	9	7	1
6	7	4	3	9	1	5	2	8

Solution to Puzzle 60

8	2	1	6	7	9	3	5	4
5	4	9	2	8	3	1	7	6
3	6	7	1	4	5	2	8	9
1	7	6	5	3	4	9	2	8
9	5	3	8	2	6	4	1	7
4	8	2	7	9	1	6	3	5
6	1	8	4	5	2	7	9	3
7	3	4	9	1	8	5	6	2
2	9	5	3	6	7	8	4	1

Solution to Puzzle 61

1	7	5	8	2	6	9	3	4
8	2	3	9	4	1	5	7	6
9	4	6	5	7	3	8	2	1
4	8	1	7	6	5	2	9	3
3	6	9	1	8	2	7	4	5
7	5	2	3	9	4	6	1	8
2	3	8	6	1	7	4	5	9
5	9	4	2	3	8	1	6	7
6	1	7	4	5	9	3	8	2

Solution to Puzzle 62

2	6	5	1	9	8	3	4	7
7	8	4	2	5	3	1	6	9
3	9	1	4	7	6	2	8	5
4	5	3	7	2	9	8	1	6
9	1	6	3	8	5	7	2	4
8	7	2	6	1	4	9	5	3
1	4	8	5	3	7	6	9	2
5	3	9	8	6	2	4	7	1
6	2	7	9	4	1	5	3	8

Solution to Puzzle 63

7	5	1	8	6	3	9	2	4
8	3	2	4	1	9	6	5	7
9	4	6	7	5	2	3	8	1
5	2	8	1	9	7	4	3	6
3	6	7	2	8	4	1	9	5
1	9	4	6	3	5	2	7	8
4	8	5	9	2	1	7	6	3
2	1	3	5	7	6	8	4	9
6	7	9	3	4	8	5	1	2

Solution to Puzzle 64

2	6	3	8	9	5	1	4	7
9	8	4	1	7	3	6	2	5
1	7	5	4	6	2	9	8	3
6	4	2	9	3	1	5	7	8
5	9	8	2	4	7	3	1	6
7	3	1	5	8	6	4	9	2
8	5	9	6	2	4	7	3	1
4	1	7	3	5	8	2	6	9
3	2	6	7	1	9	8	5	4

Solution to Puzzle 65

6	5	1	8	3	4	7	2	9
3	8	7	6	2	9	5	4	1
4	9	2	5	1	7	3	8	6
1	2	4	9	8	3	6	5	7
8	6	3	7	5	1	2	9	4
9	7	5	4	6	2	8	1	3
2	3	9	1	7	5	4	6	8
7	1	8	2	4	6	9	3	5
5	4	6	3	9	8	1	7	2

Solution to Puzzle 66

8	1	9	2	6	5	3	4	7
2	7	4	9	8	3	1	6	5
5	3	6	1	4	7	9	2	8
1	9	8	6	2	4	5	7	3
4	5	7	3	1	9	6	8	2
6	2	3	7	5	8	4	9	1
3	6	2	4	7	1	8	5	9
9	4	5	8	3	2	7	1	6
7	8	1	5	9	6	2	3	4

Solution to Puzzle 67

4	2	8	5	3	7	1	6	9
7	5	3	9	1	6	2	4	8
1	6	9	4	8	2	5	3	7
9	1	4	3	6	5	8	7	2
6	7	5	8	2	9	3	1	4
3	8	2	1	7	4	6	9	5
2	3	7	6	9	8	4	5	1
5	9	1	2	4	3	7	8	6
8	4	6	7	5	1	9	2	3

Solution to Puzzle 68

4	5	7	9	6	3	1	8	2
3	2	1	7	8	4	6	5	9
8	9	6	2	1	5	7	3	4
6	8	2	4	7	1	3	9	5
1	7	5	3	2	9	8	4	6
9	4	3	6	5	8	2	1	7
7	3	9	8	4	2	5	6	1
5	6	4	1	3	7	9	2	8
2	1	8	5	9	6	4	7	3

Solution to Puzzle 69

1	2	4	7	5	3	6	8	9
3	7	8	9	6	4	2	5	1
5	9	6	8	1	2	3	4	7
6	3	9	5	2	7	8	1	4
8	1	2	3	4	9	7	6	5
7	4	5	6	8	1	9	2	3
4	8	3	1	7	6	5	9	2
2	6	7	4	9	5	1	3	8
9	5	1	2	3	8	4	7	6

Solution to Puzzle 70

3	4	1	7	2	5	6	9	8
6	5	9	3	1	8	2	4	7
7	8	2	9	4	6	5	1	3
2	6	5	8	7	4	9	3	1
9	3	8	2	6	1	4	7	5
1	7	4	5	9	3	8	6	2
5	2	7	4	3	9	1	8	6
8	9	6	1	5	7	3	2	4
4	1	3	6	8	2	7	5	9

Solution to Puzzle 71

1	2	6	7	3	4	5	8	9
8	5	3	1	2	9	4	6	7
7	4	9	6	8	5	3	1	2
5	1	2	9	4	6	8	7	3
6	9	8	3	7	1	2	5	4
4	3	7	2	5	8	1	9	6
3	8	1	4	6	7	9	2	5
9	6	4	5	1	2	7	3	8
2	7	5	8	9	3	6	4	1

Solution to Puzzle 72

2	1	8	4	3	5	9	7	6
3	7	9	1	2	6	8	5	4
6	5	4	9	8	7	2	1	3
1	8	7	3	6	2	4	9	5
5	4	3	8	1	9	6	2	7
9	6	2	7	5	4	3	8	1
8	9	6	5	4	1	7	3	2
7	2	1	6	9	3	5	4	8
4	3	5	2	7	8	1	6	9

Solution to Puzzle 73

6	1	3	5	8	9	2	4	7
5	4	2	7	1	3	9	8	6
7	8	9	2	4	6	5	1	3
4	3	8	9	2	7	6	5	1
2	7	6	4	5	1	8	3	9
9	5	1	6	3	8	4	7	2
1	6	5	8	7	2	3	9	4
8	9	7	3	6	4	1	2	5
3	2	4	1	9	5	7	6	8

Solution to Puzzle 74

9	1	8	3	5	4	7	2	6
3	4	5	6	7	2	1	8	9
2	6	7	1	8	9	3	4	5
1	8	4	7	3	5	9	6	2
5	3	2	9	6	8	4	7	1
7	9	6	2	4	1	5	3	8
6	5	3	8	9	7	2	1	4
8	2	9	4	1	3	6	5	7
4	7	1	5	2	6	8	9	3

Solution to Puzzle 75

5	3	4	1	8	2	9	6	7
9	8	6	3	7	4	2	1	5
7	2	1	6	5	9	3	4	8
4	5	2	7	1	8	6	3	9
8	6	3	9	4	5	1	7	2
1	7	9	2	3	6	8	5	4
2	9	7	4	6	1	5	8	3
3	1	5	8	9	7	4	2	6
6	4	8	5	2	3	7	9	1

Solution to Puzzle 76

6	2	5	3	8	9	4	1	7
8	7	9	6	4	1	5	2	3
4	3	1	5	2	7	8	9	6
1	8	6	2	7	4	9	3	5
5	4	7	9	3	6	2	8	1
3	9	2	8	1	5	7	6	4
7	6	4	1	9	2	3	5	8
2	5	8	4	6	3	1	7	9
9	1	3	7	5	8	6	4	2

Solution to Puzzle 77

8	1	9	2	6	5	3	4	7
2	7	4	9	8	3	1	6	5
5	3	6	1	4	7	9	2	8
1	9	8	6	2	4	5	7	3
4	5	7	3	1	9	6	8	2
6	2	3	7	5	8	4	9	1
3	6	2	4	7	1	8	5	9
9	4	5	8	3	2	7	1	6
7	8	1	5	9	6	2	3	4

Solution to Puzzle 78

8	6	5	7	3	2	9	1	4
4	3	1	9	6	8	7	5	2
2	7	9	1	4	5	6	3	8
6	8	7	5	9	1	4	2	3
5	1	4	3	2	7	8	9	6
9	2	3	6	8	4	1	7	5
1	9	6	8	5	3	2	4	7
3	4	8	2	7	9	5	6	1
7	5	2	4	1	6	3	8	9

Solution to Puzzle 79

8	3	2	6	4	9	5	7	1
6	1	7	8	5	3	9	2	4
9	5	4	7	2	1	3	8	6
5	7	9	1	8	4	6	3	2
3	2	6	9	7	5	1	4	8
1	4	8	3	6	2	7	5	9
2	8	1	5	9	7	4	6	3
7	6	3	4	1	8	2	9	5
4	9	5	2	3	6	8	1	7

Solution to Puzzle 80

3	2	7	1	5	6	4	8	9
4	1	9	3	8	7	5	6	2
8	5	6	9	2	4	7	3	1
1	8	3	2	4	5	9	7	6
9	7	5	8	6	1	3	2	4
2	6	4	7	9	3	8	1	5
5	9	2	6	3	8	1	4	7
7	4	8	5	1	2	6	9	3
6	3	1	4	7	9	2	5	8

Solution to Puzzle 81

8	4	2	6	7	9	3	5	1
3	9	5	8	4	1	6	7	2
1	6	7	3	5	2	8	4	9
6	5	3	2	9	4	7	1	8
7	1	8	5	6	3	9	2	4
9	2	4	1	8	7	5	3	6
5	3	9	4	2	6	1	8	7
2	7	1	9	3	8	4	6	5
4	8	6	7	1	5	2	9	3

Solution to Puzzle 82

7	8	1	3	4	5	9	2	6
2	4	6	8	9	7	3	5	1
9	5	3	6	1	2	4	8	7
6	7	9	1	8	4	5	3	2
3	1	4	5	2	6	8	7	9
8	2	5	9	7	3	1	6	4
1	3	2	7	5	9	6	4	8
5	9	7	4	6	8	2	1	3
4	6	8	2	3	1	7	9	5

Solution to Puzzle 83

5	1	4	2	6	7	3	9	8
3	6	7	9	8	1	2	4	5
2	9	8	4	3	5	6	7	1
1	7	5	3	2	4	9	8	6
9	3	6	5	1	8	7	2	4
4	8	2	6	7	9	5	1	3
8	2	1	7	5	3	4	6	9
7	4	3	8	9	6	1	5	2
6	5	9	1	4	2	8	3	7

Solution to Puzzle 84

4	8	5	9	7	2	3	1	6
1	9	2	5	6	3	7	4	8
3	7	6	4	1	8	5	9	2
7	1	9	2	5	6	4	8	3
6	2	3	8	9	4	1	7	5
5	4	8	1	3	7	2	6	9
2	3	1	7	8	9	6	5	4
8	6	7	3	4	5	9	2	1
9	5	4	6	2	1	8	3	7

Solution to Puzzle 85

2	1	8	9	4	3	6	7	5
7	9	6	8	5	1	4	3	2
4	5	3	6	7	2	1	8	9
5	8	7	1	2	6	3	9	4
9	2	1	5	3	4	8	6	7
6	3	4	7	9	8	5	2	1
8	6	2	4	1	9	7	5	3
3	4	5	2	6	7	9	1	8
1	7	9	3	8	5	2	4	6

Solution to Puzzle 86

4	8	5	9	7	2	3	1	6
1	9	2	5	6	3	7	4	8
3	7	6	4	1	8	5	9	2
7	1	9	2	5	6	4	8	3
6	2	3	8	9	4	1	7	5
5	4	8	1	3	7	2	6	9
2	3	1	7	8	9	6	5	4
8	6	7	3	4	5	9	2	1
9	5	4	6	2	1	8	3	7

Solution to Puzzle 87

4	6	8	5	1	3	2	7	9
2	3	1	7	4	9	5	6	8
5	7	9	6	2	8	4	1	3
6	1	7	9	8	2	3	5	4
8	2	3	1	5	4	7	9	6
9	5	4	3	7	6	1	8	2
7	9	2	8	3	5	6	4	1
3	8	5	4	6	1	9	2	7
1	4	6	2	9	7	8	3	5

Solution to Puzzle 88

5	6	8	9	4	1	3	7	2
4	1	9	7	3	2	5	6	8
7	2	3	6	8	5	9	1	4
1	8	5	4	6	3	2	9	7
6	9	4	2	5	7	8	3	1
3	7	2	1	9	8	4	5	6
2	5	7	8	1	9	6	4	3
8	3	6	5	7	4	1	2	9
9	4	1	3	2	6	7	8	5

Solution to Puzzle 89

8	1	9	2	6	5	3	4	7
2	7	4	9	8	3	1	6	5
5	3	6	1	4	7	9	2	8
1	9	8	6	2	4	5	7	3
4	5	7	3	1	9	6	8	2
6	2	3	7	5	8	4	9	1
3	6	2	4	7	1	8	5	9
9	4	5	8	3	2	7	1	6
7	8	1	5	9	6	2	3	4

Solution to Puzzle 90

3	4	6	5	9	8	2	7	1
5	1	8	2	3	7	9	4	6
2	9	7	6	1	4	3	8	5
8	5	1	4	6	9	7	3	2
9	7	3	8	5	2	1	6	4
4	6	2	3	7	1	5	9	8
7	3	5	1	8	6	4	2	9
6	2	9	7	4	5	8	1	3
1	8	4	9	2	3	6	5	7

Solution to Puzzle 91

3	1	7	4	8	9	2	6	5
2	5	8	3	1	6	7	4	9
9	6	4	7	2	5	3	1	8
4	2	1	9	5	7	8	3	6
5	7	3	1	6	8	9	2	4
8	9	6	2	4	3	5	7	1
1	8	9	6	7	2	4	5	3
7	4	5	8	3	1	6	9	2
6	3	2	5	9	4	1	8	7

Solution to Puzzle 92

9	8	3	6	4	2	7	5	1
2	7	4	9	5	1	6	3	8
5	6	1	8	3	7	9	2	4
4	3	2	5	7	8	1	6	9
7	9	5	3	1	6	8	4	2
8	1	6	4	2	9	5	7	3
3	5	7	1	8	4	2	9	6
6	4	8	2	9	5	3	1	7
1	2	9	7	6	3	4	8	5

Solution to Puzzle 93

9	2	4	1	8	3	5	6	7
3	7	5	9	2	6	1	8	4
8	1	6	7	4	5	2	9	3
6	4	7	8	5	1	3	2	9
5	3	1	2	9	7	6	4	8
2	8	9	6	3	4	7	5	1
7	5	3	4	6	9	8	1	2
4	6	2	3	1	8	9	7	5
1	9	8	5	7	2	4	3	6

Solution to Puzzle 94

3	8	9	7	2	4	5	1	6
1	2	5	6	8	9	7	4	3
4	6	7	1	3	5	2	8	9
7	5	4	8	9	3	1	6	2
8	9	1	5	6	2	4	3	7
6	3	2	4	7	1	8	9	5
5	7	6	9	1	8	3	2	4
2	4	8	3	5	6	9	7	1
9	1	3	2	4	7	6	5	8

Solution to Puzzle 95

2	3	1	5	9	7	6	4	8
9	4	5	8	6	1	2	7	3
7	8	6	2	3	4	1	9	5
4	5	9	3	1	2	8	6	7
8	1	7	4	5	6	3	2	9
6	2	3	9	7	8	4	5	1
5	7	4	1	2	3	9	8	6
3	6	8	7	4	9	5	1	2
1	9	2	6	8	5	7	3	4

Solution to Puzzle 96

3	4	8	6	1	5	7	2	9
9	5	1	8	2	7	4	3	6
2	7	6	9	3	4	1	5	8
6	8	2	4	5	9	3	7	1
7	1	4	3	6	8	2	9	5
5	9	3	2	7	1	6	8	4
4	3	9	1	8	2	5	6	7
8	2	5	7	4	6	9	1	3
1	6	7	5	9	3	8	4	2

Solution to Puzzle 97

5	8	3	1	7	4	6	2	9
2	1	4	5	6	9	7	8	3
9	7	6	2	8	3	4	5	1
4	5	7	8	3	1	9	6	2
3	6	9	4	2	5	8	1	7
8	2	1	6	9	7	5	3	4
7	9	8	3	1	6	2	4	5
6	3	5	7	4	2	1	9	8
1	4	2	9	5	8	3	7	6

Solution to Puzzle 98

3	1	7	4	8	9	2	6	5
2	5	8	3	1	6	7	4	9
9	6	4	7	2	5	3	1	8
4	2	1	9	5	7	8	3	6
5	7	3	1	6	8	9	2	4
8	9	6	2	4	3	5	7	1
1	8	9	6	7	2	4	5	3
7	4	5	8	3	1	6	9	2
6	3	2	5	9	4	1	8	7

Solution to Puzzle 99

4	8	5	9	7	2	3	1	6
1	9	2	5	6	3	7	4	8
3	7	6	4	1	8	5	9	2
7	1	9	2	5	6	4	8	3
6	2	3	8	9	4	1	7	5
5	4	8	1	3	7	2	6	9
2	3	1	7	8	9	6	5	4
8	6	7	3	4	5	9	2	1
9	5	4	6	2	1	8	3	7

Solution to Puzzle 100

8	5	7	2	1	6	4	9	3
3	6	2	7	9	4	8	1	5
9	1	4	3	5	8	6	2	7
2	9	5	8	3	7	1	4	6
4	3	1	5	6	2	7	8	9
7	8	6	1	4	9	3	5	2
1	2	3	4	7	5	9	6	8
5	4	9	6	8	3	2	7	1
6	7	8	9	2	1	5	3	4

Solution to Puzzle 101

2	6	5	1	9	8	3	4	7
7	8	4	2	5	3	1	6	9
3	9	1	4	7	6	2	8	5
4	5	3	7	2	9	8	1	6
9	1	6	3	8	5	7	2	4
8	7	2	6	1	4	9	5	3
1	4	8	5	3	7	6	9	2
5	3	9	8	6	2	4	7	1
6	2	7	9	4	1	5	3	8

Solution to Puzzle 102

1	8	7	6	5	3	4	9	2
6	2	9	7	4	8	1	3	5
3	5	4	9	1	2	7	6	8
9	7	3	5	8	1	2	4	6
4	1	8	2	3	6	5	7	9
5	6	2	4	9	7	8	1	3
7	4	5	3	2	9	6	8	1
2	9	1	8	6	4	3	5	7
8	3	6	1	7	5	9	2	4

Solution to Puzzle 103

6	2	5	3	8	9	4	1	7
8	7	9	6	4	1	5	2	3
4	3	1	5	2	7	8	9	6
1	8	6	2	7	4	9	3	5
5	4	7	9	3	6	2	8	1
3	9	2	8	1	5	7	6	4
7	6	4	1	9	2	3	5	8
2	5	8	4	6	3	1	7	9
9	1	3	7	5	8	6	4	2

Solution to Puzzle 104

6	7	9	8	5	2	1	3	4
3	8	1	4	6	9	7	2	5
2	4	5	1	3	7	8	6	9
7	9	3	5	2	1	4	8	6
1	5	4	6	8	3	9	7	2
8	6	2	9	7	4	5	1	3
4	2	7	3	1	5	6	9	8
9	1	6	2	4	8	3	5	7
5	3	8	7	9	6	2	4	1

Solution to Puzzle 105

5	7	9	1	6	3	4	2	8
1	2	8	5	7	4	3	6	9
4	3	6	2	9	8	1	5	7
2	9	1	8	3	6	7	4	5
7	6	5	9	4	1	2	8	3
8	4	3	7	5	2	9	1	6
6	8	7	4	2	9	5	3	1
3	5	4	6	1	7	8	9	2
9	1	2	3	8	5	6	7	4

Solution to Puzzle 106

5	4	3	7	6	9	2	8	1
7	1	6	2	5	8	3	9	4
9	8	2	4	3	1	7	6	5
3	5	8	1	4	2	6	7	9
1	9	7	6	8	5	4	2	3
6	2	4	3	9	7	5	1	8
4	3	1	8	7	6	9	5	2
8	6	5	9	2	4	1	3	7
2	7	9	5	1	3	8	4	6

Solution to Puzzle 107

6	3	1	5	7	4	8	9	2
8	2	7	1	3	9	6	5	4
9	5	4	6	8	2	7	1	3
7	6	5	9	2	3	1	4	8
1	4	3	8	5	7	9	2	6
2	9	8	4	6	1	5	3	7
3	8	6	2	1	5	4	7	9
4	1	2	7	9	8	3	6	5
5	7	9	3	4	6	2	8	1

Solution to Puzzle 108

8	5	7	4	1	9	2	6	3
2	4	9	6	3	8	7	1	5
1	6	3	7	2	5	8	9	4
3	1	2	9	8	4	6	5	7
4	9	6	5	7	3	1	2	8
7	8	5	1	6	2	4	3	9
9	3	8	2	4	1	5	7	6
6	2	4	3	5	7	9	8	1
5	7	1	8	9	6	3	4	2

Solution to Puzzle 109

9	4	2	5	3	8	6	7	1
3	7	8	1	4	6	9	5	2
6	1	5	2	7	9	3	4	8
5	6	9	8	2	4	7	1	3
2	3	1	7	6	5	4	8	9
4	8	7	9	1	3	2	6	5
1	9	4	3	5	7	8	2	6
8	5	6	4	9	2	1	3	7
7	2	3	6	8	1	5	9	4

Solution to Puzzle 110

9	8	3	6	4	2	7	5	1
2	7	4	9	5	1	6	3	8
5	6	1	8	3	7	9	2	4
4	3	2	5	7	8	1	6	9
7	9	5	3	1	6	8	4	2
8	1	6	4	2	9	5	7	3
3	5	7	1	8	4	2	9	6
6	4	8	2	9	5	3	1	7
1	2	9	7	6	3	4	8	5

Solution to Puzzle 111

8	2	5	3	4	9	7	6	1
9	1	3	8	6	7	2	4	5
6	7	4	5	1	2	8	9	3
5	3	1	6	9	8	4	7	2
7	8	2	4	3	5	9	1	6
4	6	9	2	7	1	3	5	8
1	4	6	7	2	3	5	8	9
3	5	7	9	8	6	1	2	4
2	9	8	1	5	4	6	3	7

Solution to Puzzle 112

6	4	2	5	8	1	7	3	9
9	3	5	7	2	4	1	8	6
1	8	7	3	6	9	2	4	5
5	2	9	8	7	6	4	1	3
8	1	6	4	5	3	9	7	2
3	7	4	1	9	2	6	5	8
4	9	3	2	1	8	5	6	7
7	6	1	9	3	5	8	2	4
2	5	8	6	4	7	3	9	1

Solution to Puzzle 113

3	8	4	7	1	2	9	6	5
1	9	5	6	4	8	7	2	3
2	6	7	5	3	9	8	4	1
9	3	2	4	8	5	6	1	7
8	4	6	1	9	7	3	5	2
7	5	1	3	2	6	4	9	8
6	7	9	2	5	3	1	8	4
4	2	8	9	7	1	5	3	6
5	1	3	8	6	4	2	7	9

Solution to Puzzle 114

3	8	4	7	1	2	9	6	5
1	9	5	6	4	8	7	2	3
2	6	7	5	3	9	8	4	1
9	3	2	4	8	5	6	1	7
8	4	6	1	9	7	3	5	2
7	5	1	3	2	6	4	9	8
6	7	9	2	5	3	1	8	4
4	2	8	9	7	1	5	3	6
5	1	3	8	6	4	2	7	9

Solution to Puzzle 115

3	2	1	5	8	4	6	9	7
7	5	4	6	2	9	1	3	8
6	9	8	7	1	3	4	2	5
8	7	5	9	4	2	3	1	6
9	4	3	1	6	5	7	8	2
1	6	2	8	3	7	5	4	9
2	8	7	3	5	1	9	6	4
5	1	6	4	9	8	2	7	3
4	3	9	2	7	6	8	5	1

Solution to Puzzle 116

6	5	1	8	3	4	7	2	9
3	8	7	6	2	9	5	4	1
4	9	2	5	1	7	3	8	6
1	2	4	9	8	3	6	5	7
8	6	3	7	5	1	2	9	4
9	7	5	4	6	2	8	1	3
2	3	9	1	7	5	4	6	8
7	1	8	2	4	6	9	3	5
5	4	6	3	9	8	1	7	2

Solution to Puzzle 117

3	9	4	7	8	1	5	6	2
2	5	8	3	6	4	9	7	1
7	1	6	2	9	5	8	4	3
4	3	7	8	5	6	1	2	9
9	6	5	1	2	7	3	8	4
8	2	1	4	3	9	7	5	6
6	8	2	9	7	3	4	1	5
1	7	3	5	4	2	6	9	8
5	4	9	6	1	8	2	3	7

Solution to Puzzle 118

1	7	5	8	2	6	9	3	4
8	2	3	9	4	1	5	7	6
9	4	6	5	7	3	8	2	1
4	8	1	7	6	5	2	9	3
3	6	9	1	8	2	7	4	5
7	5	2	3	9	4	6	1	8
2	3	8	6	1	7	4	5	9
5	9	4	2	3	8	1	6	7
6	1	7	4	5	9	3	8	2

Solution to Puzzle 119

5	3	2	1	6	8	4	7	9
7	1	8	4	5	9	3	6	2
6	4	9	3	7	2	1	5	8
9	5	4	7	8	3	2	1	6
2	7	3	5	1	6	8	9	4
8	6	1	2	9	4	5	3	7
3	9	6	8	4	5	7	2	1
4	2	7	6	3	1	9	8	5
1	8	5	9	2	7	6	4	3

Solution to Puzzle 120

5	4	3	7	6	9	2	8	1
7	1	6	2	5	8	3	9	4
9	8	2	4	3	1	7	6	5
3	5	8	1	4	2	6	7	9
1	9	7	6	8	5	4	2	3
6	2	4	3	9	7	5	1	8
4	3	1	8	7	6	9	5	2
8	6	5	9	2	4	1	3	7
2	7	9	5	1	3	8	4	6

Solution to Puzzle 121

5	4	2	9	6	8	1	3	7
3	9	1	4	2	7	6	8	5
6	7	8	5	3	1	4	2	9
9	8	3	6	7	4	5	1	2
2	5	7	1	8	9	3	6	4
4	1	6	3	5	2	9	7	8
1	2	5	7	9	3	8	4	6
7	6	4	8	1	5	2	9	3
8	3	9	2	4	6	7	5	1

Solution to Puzzle 122

1	3	5	9	8	7	4	2	6
2	8	9	6	5	4	3	7	1
7	6	4	1	3	2	8	9	5
5	9	6	3	2	1	7	4	8
8	4	2	5	7	9	1	6	3
3	1	7	4	6	8	9	5	2
4	5	8	2	9	3	6	1	7
9	2	3	7	1	6	5	8	4
6	7	1	8	4	5	2	3	9

Solution to Puzzle 123

2	4	5	6	8	3	7	9	1
8	7	6	4	1	9	5	3	2
1	3	9	5	7	2	8	6	4
9	2	3	1	5	8	6	4	7
5	6	1	7	9	4	2	8	3
7	8	4	2	3	6	9	1	5
4	9	8	3	2	7	1	5	6
3	5	2	8	6	1	4	7	9
6	1	7	9	4	5	3	2	8

Solution to Puzzle 124

2	6	5	1	9	8	3	4	7
7	8	4	2	5	3	1	6	9
3	9	1	4	7	6	2	8	5
4	5	3	7	2	9	8	1	6
9	1	6	3	8	5	7	2	4
8	7	2	6	1	4	9	5	3
1	4	8	5	3	7	6	9	2
5	3	9	8	6	2	4	7	1
6	2	7	9	4	1	5	3	8

Solution to Puzzle 125

6	1	2	8	7	5	4	3	9
9	3	5	1	2	4	8	6	7
4	7	8	3	9	6	1	5	2
3	8	9	4	6	7	5	2	1
2	5	7	9	8	1	6	4	3
1	6	4	2	5	3	9	7	8
8	4	3	5	1	2	7	9	6
5	9	6	7	3	8	2	1	4
7	2	1	6	4	9	3	8	5

Solution to Puzzle 126

4	3	9	7	1	5	8	2	6
8	1	6	2	3	9	5	4	7
7	5	2	4	6	8	1	3	9
5	8	4	9	7	1	3	6	2
6	7	1	3	5	2	4	9	8
9	2	3	8	4	6	7	5	1
2	6	5	1	8	4	9	7	3
3	4	8	6	9	7	2	1	5
1	9	7	5	2	3	6	8	4

Solution to Puzzle 127

9	3	8	6	7	4	1	2	5
4	5	7	2	1	9	6	3	8
1	2	6	5	8	3	4	7	9
2	4	9	1	3	6	5	8	7
3	8	1	7	5	2	9	4	6
6	7	5	9	4	8	2	1	3
5	1	3	4	9	7	8	6	2
7	9	2	8	6	1	3	5	4
8	6	4	3	2	5	7	9	1

Solution to Puzzle 128

6	4	2	5	8	1	7	3	9
9	3	5	7	2	4	1	8	6
1	8	7	3	6	9	2	4	5
5	2	9	8	7	6	4	1	3
8	1	6	4	5	3	9	7	2
3	7	4	1	9	2	6	5	8
4	9	3	2	1	8	5	6	7
7	6	1	9	3	5	8	2	4
2	5	8	6	4	7	3	9	1

Solution to Puzzle 129

1	8	7	2	9	6	4	5	3
9	3	5	7	1	4	2	8	6
6	4	2	5	3	8	7	1	9
2	6	8	4	7	9	1	3	5
4	5	3	6	8	1	9	2	7
7	1	9	3	2	5	8	6	4
8	9	6	1	4	3	5	7	2
5	2	1	9	6	7	3	4	8
3	7	4	8	5	2	6	9	1

Solution to Puzzle 130

5	4	1	8	6	7	9	3	2
2	7	8	9	3	1	6	4	5
6	9	3	4	2	5	8	1	7
7	8	9	3	4	2	5	6	1
3	5	2	6	1	8	7	9	4
1	6	4	7	5	9	2	8	3
8	2	6	1	7	3	4	5	9
4	1	5	2	9	6	3	7	8
9	3	7	5	8	4	1	2	6

Solution to Puzzle 131

2	6	3	8	9	5	1	4	7
9	8	4	1	7	3	6	2	5
1	7	5	4	6	2	9	8	3
6	4	2	9	3	1	5	7	8
5	9	8	2	4	7	3	1	6
7	3	1	5	8	6	4	9	2
8	5	9	6	2	4	7	3	1
4	1	7	3	5	8	2	6	9
3	2	6	7	1	9	8	5	4

Solution to Puzzle 132

1	5	2	4	8	9	3	7	6
7	6	8	2	5	3	4	1	9
9	3	4	6	1	7	2	8	5
4	7	1	9	2	6	5	3	8
8	9	3	7	4	5	6	2	1
6	2	5	8	3	1	9	4	7
2	8	6	5	7	4	1	9	3
5	1	7	3	9	2	8	6	4
3	4	9	1	6	8	7	5	2

Solution to Puzzle 133

4	8	5	3	1	9	2	6	7
2	9	3	7	5	6	1	8	4
1	6	7	8	2	4	3	9	5
9	4	8	2	6	7	5	1	3
3	1	2	5	9	8	7	4	6
5	7	6	1	4	3	9	2	8
7	3	4	9	8	2	6	5	1
6	5	9	4	7	1	8	3	2
8	2	1	6	3	5	4	7	9

Solution to Puzzle 134

3	6	2	8	1	7	5	9	4
1	9	8	4	6	5	7	2	3
4	7	5	9	3	2	8	1	6
2	8	4	1	5	9	3	6	7
7	5	6	2	8	3	1	4	9
9	3	1	7	4	6	2	5	8
6	4	7	3	2	1	9	8	5
8	1	3	5	9	4	6	7	2
5	2	9	6	7	8	4	3	1

Solution to Puzzle 135

2	4	9	8	6	1	7	5	3
6	5	3	2	7	9	8	4	1
8	1	7	4	3	5	6	2	9
9	3	4	1	8	2	5	6	7
7	2	1	6	5	4	9	3	8
5	6	8	7	9	3	2	1	4
1	9	5	3	2	8	4	7	6
3	8	6	5	4	7	1	9	2
4	7	2	9	1	6	3	8	5

Solution to Puzzle 136

9	2	6	1	7	4	3	5	8
7	3	5	8	2	6	1	4	9
4	8	1	9	3	5	6	2	7
3	6	9	5	8	7	2	1	4
8	1	2	4	9	3	7	6	5
5	4	7	2	6	1	9	8	3
6	9	8	3	4	2	5	7	1
2	5	3	7	1	8	4	9	6
1	7	4	6	5	9	8	3	2

Solution to Puzzle 137

9	5	7	6	8	4	2	1	3
1	8	4	3	5	2	6	7	9
6	3	2	1	9	7	4	8	5
5	4	9	2	1	6	8	3	7
8	2	3	7	4	5	9	6	1
7	6	1	9	3	8	5	2	4
3	1	8	4	6	9	7	5	2
2	9	5	8	7	1	3	4	6
4	7	6	5	2	3	1	9	8

Solution to Puzzle 138

1	6	4	9	3	2	5	8	7
3	2	8	6	5	7	1	9	4
7	5	9	4	1	8	3	6	2
5	7	2	1	6	4	8	3	9
6	9	3	8	2	5	4	7	1
8	4	1	7	9	3	2	5	6
4	3	5	2	7	6	9	1	8
2	1	7	5	8	9	6	4	3
9	8	6	3	4	1	7	2	5

Solution to Puzzle 139

8	2	1	6	3	9	5	7	4
4	6	5	8	2	7	1	3	9
9	7	3	1	5	4	2	8	6
1	9	2	3	4	8	7	6	5
3	8	6	7	9	5	4	1	2
7	5	4	2	1	6	3	9	8
2	3	9	4	8	1	6	5	7
5	4	7	9	6	3	8	2	1
6	1	8	5	7	2	9	4	3

Solution to Puzzle 140

6	7	8	3	9	5	2	4	1
1	4	2	6	8	7	9	3	5
5	3	9	1	2	4	6	7	8
4	5	7	9	1	8	3	2	6
8	9	3	2	5	6	4	1	7
2	6	1	7	4	3	8	5	9
7	8	5	4	3	9	1	6	2
9	2	4	5	6	1	7	8	3
3	1	6	8	7	2	5	9	4

Solution to Puzzle 141

6	7	8	3	9	5	2	4	1
1	4	2	6	8	7	9	3	5
5	3	9	1	2	4	6	7	8
4	5	7	9	1	8	3	2	6
8	9	3	2	5	6	4	1	7
2	6	1	7	4	3	8	5	9
7	8	5	4	3	9	1	6	2
9	2	4	5	6	1	7	8	3
3	1	6	8	7	2	5	9	4

Solution to Puzzle 142

1	9	8	5	4	3	7	6	2
5	4	7	1	2	6	8	9	3
6	2	3	8	9	7	4	5	1
2	3	6	7	1	5	9	8	4
4	7	1	6	8	9	3	2	5
8	5	9	4	3	2	1	7	6
7	8	2	3	5	4	6	1	9
9	6	4	2	7	1	5	3	8
3	1	5	9	6	8	2	4	7

Solution to Puzzle 143

1	8	2	7	3	6	4	9	5
3	4	9	5	8	2	7	1	6
7	6	5	4	1	9	8	3	2
6	5	4	3	7	1	2	8	9
8	9	7	6	2	5	3	4	1
2	3	1	8	9	4	6	5	7
5	7	6	9	4	3	1	2	8
4	2	8	1	5	7	9	6	3
9	1	3	2	6	8	5	7	4

Solution to Puzzle 144

1	2	8	7	9	5	3	6	4
4	9	3	6	1	8	2	7	5
6	5	7	3	2	4	1	9	8
5	3	1	9	8	7	4	2	6
9	8	2	5	4	6	7	3	1
7	6	4	1	3	2	8	5	9
8	1	9	2	6	3	5	4	7
3	7	6	4	5	1	9	8	2
2	4	5	8	7	9	6	1	3

Solution to Puzzle 145

7	2	5	8	6	3	1	9	4
8	6	3	4	9	1	7	5	2
1	9	4	5	2	7	6	8	3
5	8	2	6	7	4	3	1	9
6	4	9	1	3	8	2	7	5
3	1	7	9	5	2	4	6	8
2	3	6	7	8	5	9	4	1
9	5	1	2	4	6	8	3	7
4	7	8	3	1	9	5	2	6

Solution to Puzzle 146

4	8	9	1	2	6	5	3	7
2	1	3	4	7	5	9	8	6
7	5	6	3	8	9	1	4	2
8	4	2	5	9	3	7	6	1
3	6	7	8	1	2	4	5	9
5	9	1	6	4	7	8	2	3
6	3	4	7	5	1	2	9	8
1	2	5	9	3	8	6	7	4
9	7	8	2	6	4	3	1	5

Solution to Puzzle 147

9	8	2	4	7	3	5	6	1
4	1	3	6	2	5	9	7	8
7	6	5	9	8	1	4	3	2
2	7	8	5	4	9	6	1	3
1	5	9	8	3	6	2	4	7
6	3	4	2	1	7	8	5	9
3	9	6	7	5	8	1	2	4
8	4	1	3	6	2	7	9	5
5	2	7	1	9	4	3	8	6

Solution to Puzzle 148

6	1	3	5	8	9	2	4	7
5	4	2	7	1	3	9	8	6
7	8	9	2	4	6	5	1	3
4	3	8	9	2	7	6	5	1
2	7	6	4	5	1	8	3	9
9	5	1	6	3	8	4	7	2
1	6	5	8	7	2	3	9	4
8	9	7	3	6	4	1	2	5
3	2	4	1	9	5	7	6	8

Solution to Puzzle 149

5	2	7	9	3	6	1	4	8
8	9	3	7	4	1	6	2	5
1	6	4	5	8	2	7	3	9
7	3	6	2	1	8	5	9	4
2	4	1	3	5	9	8	7	6
9	8	5	4	6	7	2	1	3
4	5	8	1	2	3	9	6	7
3	1	9	6	7	5	4	8	2
6	7	2	8	9	4	3	5	1

Solution to Puzzle 150

5	3	4	1	8	2	9	6	7
9	8	6	3	7	4	2	1	5
7	2	1	6	5	9	3	4	8
4	5	2	7	1	8	6	3	9
8	6	3	9	4	5	1	7	2
1	7	9	2	3	6	8	5	4
2	9	7	4	6	1	5	8	3
3	1	5	8	9	7	4	2	6
6	4	8	5	2	3	7	9	1

Solution to Puzzle 151

5	9	6	2	4	3	8	1	7
1	3	2	8	7	9	4	6	5
8	4	7	5	1	6	9	2	3
3	5	1	4	6	7	2	9	8
2	8	4	1	9	5	3	7	6
7	6	9	3	2	8	5	4	1
9	7	8	6	5	4	1	3	2
4	2	5	7	3	1	6	8	9
6	1	3	9	8	2	7	5	4

Solution to Puzzle 152

6	1	2	5	7	9	8	3	4
3	5	4	6	2	8	1	7	9
9	8	7	1	4	3	5	6	2
4	7	1	2	6	5	3	9	8
2	3	9	8	1	7	4	5	6
5	6	8	3	9	4	2	1	7
7	2	3	4	5	6	9	8	1
8	4	6	9	3	1	7	2	5
1	9	5	7	8	2	6	4	3

Solution to Puzzle 153

6	9	1	5	4	3	2	7	8
8	2	3	9	7	1	5	6	4
7	5	4	2	8	6	9	1	3
1	7	9	3	5	8	4	2	6
5	6	8	1	2	4	3	9	7
3	4	2	6	9	7	8	5	1
2	1	7	4	3	9	6	8	5
4	8	5	7	6	2	1	3	9
9	3	6	8	1	5	7	4	2

Solution to Puzzle 154

9	4	6	8	5	2	3	1	7
1	5	3	6	9	7	4	2	8
7	2	8	4	1	3	9	6	5
8	1	4	3	7	5	2	9	6
2	3	7	9	8	6	1	5	4
5	6	9	2	4	1	8	7	3
3	9	2	7	6	4	5	8	1
4	7	5	1	2	8	6	3	9
6	8	1	5	3	9	7	4	2

Solution to Puzzle 155

7	6	8	2	4	9	1	3	5
5	4	2	8	3	1	7	9	6
3	1	9	5	6	7	8	2	4
4	9	6	7	1	2	5	8	3
8	2	7	4	5	3	9	6	1
1	3	5	6	9	8	2	4	7
6	7	4	9	2	5	3	1	8
9	5	1	3	8	4	6	7	2
2	8	3	1	7	6	4	5	9

Solution to Puzzle 156

3	6	2	7	4	1	9	8	5
9	7	4	2	8	5	6	1	3
1	8	5	9	3	6	2	4	7
7	1	3	4	6	9	5	2	8
8	4	6	5	1	2	3	7	9
5	2	9	8	7	3	1	6	4
6	5	8	3	2	4	7	9	1
2	3	7	1	9	8	4	5	6
4	9	1	6	5	7	8	3	2

Solution to Puzzle 157

2	6	3	8	9	5	1	4	7
9	8	4	1	7	3	6	2	5
1	7	5	4	6	2	9	8	3
6	4	2	9	3	1	5	7	8
5	9	8	2	4	7	3	1	6
7	3	1	5	8	6	4	9	2
8	5	9	6	2	4	7	3	1
4	1	7	3	5	8	2	6	9
3	2	6	7	1	9	8	5	4

Solution to Puzzle 158

9	3	4	8	1	7	6	5	2
2	1	7	6	9	5	8	4	3
8	5	6	4	3	2	1	7	9
6	7	2	1	5	3	9	8	4
5	4	9	7	8	6	3	2	1
3	8	1	2	4	9	7	6	5
1	6	5	3	7	4	2	9	8
7	9	8	5	2	1	4	3	6
4	2	3	9	6	8	5	1	7

Solution to Puzzle 159

6	3	5	7	9	4	2	1	8
4	8	7	6	1	2	9	3	5
9	1	2	3	5	8	6	7	4
5	2	1	8	6	9	7	4	3
7	4	9	5	2	3	1	8	6
8	6	3	4	7	1	5	2	9
1	7	8	9	3	6	4	5	2
2	9	4	1	8	5	3	6	7
3	5	6	2	4	7	8	9	1

Solution to Puzzle 160

3	6	2	7	4	1	9	8	5
9	7	4	2	8	5	6	1	3
1	8	5	9	3	6	2	4	7
7	1	3	4	6	9	5	2	8
8	4	6	5	1	2	3	7	9
5	2	9	8	7	3	1	6	4
6	5	8	3	2	4	7	9	1
2	3	7	1	9	8	4	5	6
4	9	1	6	5	7	8	3	2

Solution to Puzzle 161

3	8	1	6	2	9	5	7	4
2	9	5	7	3	4	6	8	1
4	6	7	5	8	1	2	3	9
8	4	9	3	7	6	1	5	2
1	7	3	2	4	5	8	9	6
5	2	6	1	9	8	3	4	7
7	1	8	4	6	3	9	2	5
9	5	2	8	1	7	4	6	3
6	3	4	9	5	2	7	1	8

Solution to Puzzle 162

3	1	4	2	7	6	9	8	5
9	5	6	3	8	1	7	4	2
2	7	8	5	9	4	3	1	6
6	3	7	4	2	9	8	5	1
4	8	5	6	1	3	2	9	7
1	9	2	7	5	8	6	3	4
7	2	1	8	3	5	4	6	9
5	6	3	9	4	7	1	2	8
8	4	9	1	6	2	5	7	3

Solution to Puzzle 163

9	4	1	5	2	7	3	6	8
2	6	3	1	8	9	7	5	4
5	8	7	6	3	4	9	2	1
4	3	2	8	9	6	1	7	5
1	9	6	7	4	5	8	3	2
7	5	8	3	1	2	4	9	6
8	1	5	2	7	3	6	4	9
6	7	4	9	5	8	2	1	3
3	2	9	4	6	1	5	8	7

Solution to Puzzle 164

4	5	7	3	1	6	9	8	2
1	6	2	8	9	4	7	3	5
8	9	3	7	2	5	4	6	1
3	7	5	6	4	2	8	1	9
2	1	8	9	3	7	6	5	4
6	4	9	5	8	1	3	2	7
7	8	1	4	5	3	2	9	6
5	3	4	2	6	9	1	7	8
9	2	6	1	7	8	5	4	3

Solution to Puzzle 165

5	9	6	2	7	4	8	1	3
7	2	8	1	3	9	6	4	5
4	3	1	5	8	6	2	7	9
9	4	3	6	1	2	5	8	7
8	5	2	3	9	7	1	6	4
6	1	7	4	5	8	9	3	2
3	8	4	9	6	5	7	2	1
1	7	5	8	2	3	4	9	6
2	6	9	7	4	1	3	5	8

Solution to Puzzle 166

7	9	3	8	1	4	6	2	5
8	6	4	5	2	3	7	9	1
1	2	5	7	6	9	4	3	8
4	8	6	3	9	1	5	7	2
3	5	7	2	8	6	1	4	9
2	1	9	4	7	5	3	8	6
6	3	1	9	4	8	2	5	7
9	4	2	6	5	7	8	1	3
5	7	8	1	3	2	9	6	4

Solution to Puzzle 167

8	6	2	4	5	7	9	1	3
7	4	9	1	2	3	5	6	8
3	5	1	6	9	8	4	2	7
5	1	8	9	3	2	7	4	6
4	9	7	8	1	6	2	3	5
6	2	3	7	4	5	1	8	9
1	7	4	3	8	9	6	5	2
9	8	5	2	6	1	3	7	4
2	3	6	5	7	4	8	9	1

Solution to Puzzle 168

2	6	3	8	9	5	1	4	7
9	8	4	1	7	3	6	2	5
1	7	5	4	6	2	9	8	3
6	4	2	9	3	1	5	7	8
5	9	8	2	4	7	3	1	6
7	3	1	5	8	6	4	9	2
8	5	9	6	2	4	7	3	1
4	1	7	3	5	8	2	6	9
3	2	6	7	1	9	8	5	4

Solution to Puzzle 169

6	3	5	7	9	4	2	1	8
4	8	7	6	1	2	9	3	5
9	1	2	3	5	8	6	7	4
5	2	1	8	6	9	7	4	3
7	4	9	5	2	3	1	8	6
8	6	3	4	7	1	5	2	9
1	7	8	9	3	6	4	5	2
2	9	4	1	8	5	3	6	7
3	5	6	2	4	7	8	9	1

Solution to Puzzle 170

6	1	2	8	7	5	4	3	9
9	3	5	1	2	4	8	6	7
4	7	8	3	9	6	1	5	2
3	8	9	4	6	7	5	2	1
2	5	7	9	8	1	6	4	3
1	6	4	2	5	3	9	7	8
8	4	3	5	1	2	7	9	6
5	9	6	7	3	8	2	1	4
7	2	1	6	4	9	3	8	5

Solution to Puzzle 171

8	2	3	7	6	1	4	5	9
7	4	5	2	9	3	6	8	1
6	1	9	5	4	8	2	7	3
2	5	1	9	7	6	8	3	4
4	3	6	1	8	2	5	9	7
9	8	7	4	3	5	1	2	6
1	9	2	3	5	4	7	6	8
3	6	4	8	2	7	9	1	5
5	7	8	6	1	9	3	4	2

Solution to Puzzle 172

1	8	7	6	5	3	4	9	2
6	2	9	7	4	8	1	3	5
3	5	4	9	1	2	7	6	8
9	7	3	5	8	1	2	4	6
4	1	8	2	3	6	5	7	9
5	6	2	4	9	7	8	1	3
7	4	5	3	2	9	6	8	1
2	9	1	8	6	4	3	5	7
8	3	6	1	7	5	9	2	4

Solution to Puzzle 173

9	8	2	6	4	5	1	7	3
7	6	1	9	3	8	5	2	4
3	5	4	1	7	2	6	8	9
4	1	7	2	6	3	8	9	5
2	9	5	4	8	1	7	3	6
8	3	6	5	9	7	2	4	1
1	7	8	3	5	4	9	6	2
5	4	9	7	2	6	3	1	8
6	2	3	8	1	9	4	5	7

Solution to Puzzle 174

2	3	1	8	7	6	4	9	5
8	7	9	4	2	5	1	6	3
5	6	4	1	3	9	2	7	8
4	9	2	6	5	8	3	1	7
7	1	5	3	4	2	9	8	6
6	8	3	9	1	7	5	2	4
9	2	6	5	8	3	7	4	1
1	5	7	2	6	4	8	3	9
3	4	8	7	9	1	6	5	2

Solution to Puzzle 175

1	9	7	6	4	2	5	3	8
3	2	8	1	5	7	9	6	4
6	5	4	3	8	9	2	1	7
7	4	6	9	3	5	8	2	1
5	1	9	4	2	8	6	7	3
2	8	3	7	1	6	4	5	9
8	7	2	5	9	3	1	4	6
9	3	1	2	6	4	7	8	5
4	6	5	8	7	1	3	9	2

Solution to Puzzle 176

5	4	2	9	6	8	1	3	7
3	9	1	4	2	7	6	8	5
6	7	8	5	3	1	4	2	9
9	8	3	6	7	4	5	1	2
2	5	7	1	8	9	3	6	4
4	1	6	3	5	2	9	7	8
1	2	5	7	9	3	8	4	6
7	6	4	8	1	5	2	9	3
8	3	9	2	4	6	7	5	1

Solution to Puzzle 177

1	6	4	9	3	2	5	8	7
3	2	8	6	5	7	1	9	4
7	5	9	4	1	8	3	6	2
5	7	2	1	6	4	8	3	9
6	9	3	8	2	5	4	7	1
8	4	1	7	9	3	2	5	6
4	3	5	2	7	6	9	1	8
2	1	7	5	8	9	6	4	3
9	8	6	3	4	1	7	2	5

Solution to Puzzle 178

6	3	8	9	1	2	4	5	7
1	4	2	5	7	6	9	3	8
7	9	5	3	8	4	1	6	2
5	2	6	8	4	7	3	9	1
4	8	3	1	2	9	6	7	5
9	1	7	6	5	3	8	2	4
3	5	4	2	9	8	7	1	6
8	6	1	7	3	5	2	4	9
2	7	9	4	6	1	5	8	3

Solution to Puzzle 179

8	1	3	4	5	2	9	7	6
2	5	7	1	6	9	8	3	4
4	6	9	3	8	7	2	5	1
6	7	4	5	9	3	1	2	8
3	9	1	6	2	8	7	4	5
5	2	8	7	4	1	3	6	9
1	3	6	9	7	5	4	8	2
9	8	5	2	3	4	6	1	7
7	4	2	8	1	6	5	9	3

Solution to Puzzle 180

4	5	7	3	1	6	9	8	2
1	6	2	8	9	4	7	3	5
8	9	3	7	2	5	4	6	1
3	7	5	6	4	2	8	1	9
2	1	8	9	3	7	6	5	4
6	4	9	5	8	1	3	2	7
7	8	1	4	5	3	2	9	6
5	3	4	2	6	9	1	7	8
9	2	6	1	7	8	5	4	3

Solution to Puzzle 181

2	4	9	8	6	1	7	5	3
6	5	3	2	7	9	8	4	1
8	1	7	4	3	5	6	2	9
9	3	4	1	8	2	5	6	7
7	2	1	6	5	4	9	3	8
5	6	8	7	9	3	2	1	4
1	9	5	3	2	8	4	7	6
3	8	6	5	4	7	1	9	2
4	7	2	9	1	6	3	8	5

Solution to Puzzle 182

3	1	5	6	9	8	2	4	7
6	9	2	7	3	4	5	1	8
8	4	7	5	1	2	9	3	6
2	7	1	9	8	5	4	6	3
5	3	8	4	2	6	1	7	9
9	6	4	1	7	3	8	2	5
1	5	6	8	4	7	3	9	2
4	8	3	2	6	9	7	5	1
7	2	9	3	5	1	6	8	4

Solution to Puzzle 183

1	3	2	4	5	8	7	9	6
4	8	6	7	9	1	5	2	3
7	5	9	3	2	6	1	4	8
5	1	4	8	6	3	2	7	9
6	2	7	5	4	9	8	3	1
3	9	8	1	7	2	4	6	5
9	7	5	6	1	4	3	8	2
2	4	3	9	8	5	6	1	7
8	6	1	2	3	7	9	5	4

Solution to Puzzle 184

6	3	2	8	5	9	4	1	7
5	4	9	1	2	7	8	3	6
1	7	8	4	6	3	5	2	9
2	6	4	9	7	5	3	8	1
7	8	1	6	3	4	9	5	2
3	9	5	2	8	1	7	6	4
8	1	3	7	4	6	2	9	5
4	2	6	5	9	8	1	7	3
9	5	7	3	1	2	6	4	8

Solution to Puzzle 185

5	2	7	9	3	6	1	4	8
8	9	3	7	4	1	6	2	5
1	6	4	5	8	2	7	3	9
7	3	6	2	1	8	5	9	4
2	4	1	3	5	9	8	7	6
9	8	5	4	6	7	2	1	3
4	5	8	1	2	3	9	6	7
3	1	9	6	7	5	4	8	2
6	7	2	8	9	4	3	5	1

Solution to Puzzle 186

3	8	4	7	1	2	9	6	5
1	9	5	6	4	8	7	2	3
2	6	7	5	3	9	8	4	1
9	3	2	4	8	5	6	1	7
8	4	6	1	9	7	3	5	2
7	5	1	3	2	6	4	9	8
6	7	9	2	5	3	1	8	4
4	2	8	9	7	1	5	3	6
5	1	3	8	6	4	2	7	9

Solution to Puzzle 187

6	7	4	3	8	2	9	5	1
8	2	5	1	9	7	4	3	6
3	9	1	5	6	4	7	2	8
9	4	6	8	3	5	2	1	7
2	3	8	6	7	1	5	4	9
5	1	7	2	4	9	8	6	3
1	8	9	4	2	6	3	7	5
7	5	2	9	1	3	6	8	4
4	6	3	7	5	8	1	9	2

Solution to Puzzle 188

1	6	8	5	3	2	4	7	9
7	2	3	4	9	1	6	8	5
4	9	5	6	8	7	2	3	1
8	1	2	9	4	3	7	5	6
5	3	7	8	1	6	9	2	4
9	4	6	2	7	5	3	1	8
2	5	1	3	6	4	8	9	7
3	8	4	7	5	9	1	6	2
6	7	9	1	2	8	5	4	3

Solution to Puzzle 189

3	7	5	1	6	2	4	8	9
8	6	1	4	9	3	5	2	7
2	4	9	7	8	5	1	6	3
4	9	3	8	5	7	6	1	2
7	1	6	2	4	9	8	3	5
5	2	8	3	1	6	7	9	4
6	5	7	9	2	1	3	4	8
1	8	2	5	3	4	9	7	6
9	3	4	6	7	8	2	5	1

Solution to Puzzle 190

8	2	3	7	6	1	4	5	9
7	4	5	2	9	3	6	8	1
6	1	9	5	4	8	2	7	3
2	5	1	9	7	6	8	3	4
4	3	6	1	8	2	5	9	7
9	8	7	4	3	5	1	2	6
1	9	2	3	5	4	7	6	8
3	6	4	8	2	7	9	1	5
5	7	8	6	1	9	3	4	2

Solution to Puzzle 191

3	5	8	9	6	1	2	4	7
7	6	9	4	5	2	3	1	8
2	4	1	3	8	7	5	6	9
5	2	3	6	7	4	9	8	1
1	7	4	2	9	8	6	3	5
8	9	6	1	3	5	7	2	4
9	8	2	5	4	6	1	7	3
6	3	7	8	1	9	4	5	2
4	1	5	7	2	3	8	9	6

Solution to Puzzle 192

5	2	7	9	3	6	1	4	8
8	9	3	7	4	1	6	2	5
1	6	4	5	8	2	7	3	9
7	3	6	2	1	8	5	9	4
2	4	1	3	5	9	8	7	6
9	8	5	4	6	7	2	1	3
4	5	8	1	2	3	9	6	7
3	1	9	6	7	5	4	8	2
6	7	2	8	9	4	3	5	1

Solution to Puzzle 193

5	3	4	1	8	2	9	6	7
9	8	6	3	7	4	2	1	5
7	2	1	6	5	9	3	4	8
4	5	2	7	1	8	6	3	9
8	6	3	9	4	5	1	7	2
1	7	9	2	3	6	8	5	4
2	9	7	4	6	1	5	8	3
3	1	5	8	9	7	4	2	6
6	4	8	5	2	3	7	9	1

Solution to Puzzle 194

4	1	9	3	6	5	7	2	8
8	6	7	1	2	9	3	4	5
5	2	3	8	7	4	6	9	1
9	3	1	4	8	6	5	7	2
2	4	8	5	9	7	1	3	6
6	7	5	2	1	3	4	8	9
3	5	6	9	4	8	2	1	7
7	8	2	6	3	1	9	5	4
1	9	4	7	5	2	8	6	3

Solution to Puzzle 195

2	4	8	9	7	1	5	6	3
3	6	1	8	5	4	2	7	9
9	7	5	6	3	2	1	4	8
7	1	4	2	9	5	3	8	6
5	3	9	7	8	6	4	1	2
8	2	6	4	1	3	9	5	7
6	8	3	1	4	9	7	2	5
4	9	2	5	6	7	8	3	1
1	5	7	3	2	8	6	9	4

Solution to Puzzle 196

6	3	7	4	2	8	1	9	5
9	5	2	1	3	7	4	8	6
4	1	8	5	6	9	2	3	7
7	2	1	8	4	6	3	5	9
3	6	9	2	1	5	8	7	4
8	4	5	7	9	3	6	1	2
5	8	3	6	7	4	9	2	1
2	7	6	9	8	1	5	4	3
1	9	4	3	5	2	7	6	8

Solution to Puzzle 197

4	8	5	3	1	9	2	6	7
2	9	3	7	5	6	1	8	4
1	6	7	8	2	4	3	9	5
9	4	8	2	6	7	5	1	3
3	1	2	5	9	8	7	4	6
5	7	6	1	4	3	9	2	8
7	3	4	9	8	2	6	5	1
6	5	9	4	7	1	8	3	2
8	2	1	6	3	5	4	7	9

Solution to Puzzle 198

1	7	2	3	4	8	9	6	5
6	4	9	2	5	1	7	8	3
5	3	8	7	6	9	2	1	4
4	9	7	6	8	3	1	5	2
3	8	5	9	1	2	4	7	6
2	1	6	4	7	5	3	9	8
9	5	4	8	3	7	6	2	1
7	6	1	5	2	4	8	3	9
8	2	3	1	9	6	5	4	7

Solution to Puzzle 199

7	1	5	4	9	3	8	2	6
8	2	3	5	7	6	9	4	1
6	9	4	1	8	2	3	5	7
3	4	9	2	6	5	7	1	8
2	7	8	9	4	1	5	6	3
1	5	6	8	3	7	2	9	4
9	6	7	3	5	4	1	8	2
4	8	2	7	1	9	6	3	5
5	3	1	6	2	8	4	7	9

Solution to Puzzle 200

4	5	7	3	1	6	9	8	2
1	6	2	8	9	4	7	3	5
8	9	3	7	2	5	4	6	1
3	7	5	6	4	2	8	1	9
2	1	8	9	3	7	6	5	4
6	4	9	5	8	1	3	2	7
7	8	1	4	5	3	2	9	6
5	3	4	2	6	9	1	7	8
9	2	6	1	7	8	5	4	3

Solution to Puzzle 201

4	5	3	9	8	1	6	2	7
8	7	1	2	6	4	5	9	3
9	2	6	5	7	3	1	4	8
2	3	8	6	1	5	9	7	4
1	9	7	8	4	2	3	5	6
6	4	5	3	9	7	8	1	2
3	6	2	4	5	9	7	8	1
5	1	4	7	3	8	2	6	9
7	8	9	1	2	6	4	3	5

Solution to Puzzle 202

2	7	3	8	6	9	1	4	5
4	6	1	3	2	5	8	7	9
8	5	9	4	7	1	2	3	6
7	1	6	9	4	3	5	2	8
3	4	5	2	8	6	7	9	1
9	8	2	1	5	7	3	6	4
5	2	4	6	3	8	9	1	7
6	9	8	7	1	2	4	5	3
1	3	7	5	9	4	6	8	2

Solution to Puzzle 203

6	3	1	5	7	4	8	9	2
8	2	7	1	3	9	6	5	4
9	5	4	6	8	2	7	1	3
7	6	5	9	2	3	1	4	8
1	4	3	8	5	7	9	2	6
2	9	8	4	6	1	5	3	7
3	8	6	2	1	5	4	7	9
4	1	2	7	9	8	3	6	5
5	7	9	3	4	6	2	8	1

Solution to Puzzle 204

5	4	2	9	6	8	1	3	7
3	9	1	4	2	7	6	8	5
6	7	8	5	3	1	4	2	9
9	8	3	6	7	4	5	1	2
2	5	7	1	8	9	3	6	4
4	1	6	3	5	2	9	7	8
1	2	5	7	9	3	8	4	6
7	6	4	8	1	5	2	9	3
8	3	9	2	4	6	7	5	1

Solution to Puzzle 205

3	1	4	2	7	6	9	8	5
9	5	6	3	8	1	7	4	2
2	7	8	5	9	4	3	1	6
6	3	7	4	2	9	8	5	1
4	8	5	6	1	3	2	9	7
1	9	2	7	5	8	6	3	4
7	2	1	8	3	5	4	6	9
5	6	3	9	4	7	1	2	8
8	4	9	1	6	2	5	7	3

Solution to Puzzle 206

1	2	4	7	5	3	6	8	9
3	7	8	9	6	4	2	5	1
5	9	6	8	1	2	3	4	7
6	3	9	5	2	7	8	1	4
8	1	2	3	4	9	7	6	5
7	4	5	6	8	1	9	2	3
4	8	3	1	7	6	5	9	2
2	6	7	4	9	5	1	3	8
9	5	1	2	3	8	4	7	6

Solution to Puzzle 207

6	7	9	8	1	4	5	2	3
4	5	8	9	3	2	6	1	7
3	2	1	5	6	7	4	9	8
2	1	6	7	5	9	3	8	4
8	3	7	2	4	1	9	5	6
5	9	4	6	8	3	2	7	1
7	4	3	1	2	5	8	6	9
9	6	2	3	7	8	1	4	5
1	8	5	4	9	6	7	3	2

Solution to Puzzle 208

2	5	1	6	3	7	8	4	9
8	7	6	4	9	5	2	1	3
9	4	3	1	2	8	6	7	5
4	2	8	9	5	1	3	6	7
6	1	9	3	7	4	5	8	2
5	3	7	8	6	2	4	9	1
3	8	5	7	1	6	9	2	4
7	9	4	2	8	3	1	5	6
1	6	2	5	4	9	7	3	8

Solution to Puzzle 209

3	9	4	7	8	1	5	6	2
2	5	8	3	6	4	9	7	1
7	1	6	2	9	5	8	4	3
4	3	7	8	5	6	1	2	9
9	6	5	1	2	7	3	8	4
8	2	1	4	3	9	7	5	6
6	8	2	9	7	3	4	1	5
1	7	3	5	4	2	6	9	8
5	4	9	6	1	8	2	3	7

Solution to Puzzle 210

3	2	4	8	9	1	6	5	7
6	9	7	2	3	5	4	1	8
5	1	8	4	6	7	3	9	2
1	4	6	7	2	8	5	3	9
7	3	9	6	5	4	2	8	1
8	5	2	3	1	9	7	6	4
4	8	5	9	7	6	1	2	3
9	6	3	1	4	2	8	7	5
2	7	1	5	8	3	9	4	6

Solution to Puzzle 211

5	2	4	9	3	1	7	8	6
9	6	7	4	8	5	2	3	1
8	3	1	7	6	2	9	5	4
6	5	9	1	2	8	4	7	3
1	4	8	3	7	6	5	2	9
2	7	3	5	4	9	1	6	8
4	9	6	8	5	7	3	1	2
7	1	2	6	9	3	8	4	5
3	8	5	2	1	4	6	9	7

Solution to Puzzle 212

2	6	4	1	5	7	9	8	3
8	3	5	2	6	9	4	7	1
9	7	1	3	8	4	5	2	6
5	1	6	8	7	3	2	9	4
7	2	3	9	4	1	6	5	8
4	8	9	6	2	5	1	3	7
1	5	8	7	9	6	3	4	2
6	4	2	5	3	8	7	1	9
3	9	7	4	1	2	8	6	5

Solution to Puzzle 213

2	4	3	7	6	1	5	9	8
1	9	6	3	5	8	4	7	2
5	8	7	4	2	9	1	3	6
9	3	5	2	8	4	6	1	7
8	7	4	1	9	6	2	5	3
6	2	1	5	7	3	8	4	9
4	5	2	6	3	7	9	8	1
3	6	8	9	1	5	7	2	4
7	1	9	8	4	2	3	6	5

Solution to Puzzle 214

9	8	4	7	6	2	5	3	1
3	1	6	8	5	4	2	7	9
5	7	2	1	9	3	8	6	4
1	3	8	2	7	5	4	9	6
4	6	5	9	3	8	1	2	7
2	9	7	6	4	1	3	8	5
6	2	3	4	1	9	7	5	8
7	5	1	3	8	6	9	4	2
8	4	9	5	2	7	6	1	3

Solution to Puzzle 215

3	1	5	7	8	9	2	4	6
8	6	7	3	4	2	1	5	9
9	4	2	6	1	5	8	7	3
6	3	8	5	9	1	4	2	7
1	2	4	8	7	6	3	9	5
7	5	9	4	2	3	6	1	8
4	7	1	9	3	8	5	6	2
5	9	3	2	6	4	7	8	1
2	8	6	1	5	7	9	3	4

Solution to Puzzle 216

8	6	2	3	7	1	5	9	4
3	1	5	9	4	6	2	7	8
4	9	7	2	8	5	6	3	1
6	3	9	4	2	8	7	1	5
2	5	4	6	1	7	3	8	9
1	7	8	5	3	9	4	6	2
9	2	3	1	6	4	8	5	7
5	8	6	7	9	2	1	4	3
7	4	1	8	5	3	9	2	6

Solution to Puzzle 217

3	9	1	4	8	6	2	5	7
2	6	7	1	3	5	4	8	9
4	5	8	9	7	2	1	3	6
8	3	5	7	4	9	6	1	2
1	4	6	2	5	8	9	7	3
7	2	9	3	6	1	5	4	8
5	8	2	6	1	7	3	9	4
6	7	3	5	9	4	8	2	1
9	1	4	8	2	3	7	6	5

Solution to Puzzle 218

1	2	6	7	3	4	5	8	9
8	5	3	1	2	9	4	6	7
7	4	9	6	8	5	3	1	2
5	1	2	9	4	6	8	7	3
6	9	8	3	7	1	2	5	4
4	3	7	2	5	8	1	9	6
3	8	1	4	6	7	9	2	5
9	6	4	5	1	2	7	3	8
2	7	5	8	9	3	6	4	1

Solution to Puzzle 219

9	5	8	3	7	2	4	1	6
1	2	7	6	4	8	9	3	5
3	6	4	9	5	1	8	2	7
2	4	1	5	9	6	3	7	8
7	8	9	2	3	4	6	5	1
6	3	5	8	1	7	2	4	9
4	7	6	1	2	9	5	8	3
8	1	3	4	6	5	7	9	2
5	9	2	7	8	3	1	6	4

Solution to Puzzle 220

3	9	1	4	8	6	2	5	7
2	6	7	1	3	5	4	8	9
4	5	8	9	7	2	1	3	6
8	3	5	7	4	9	6	1	2
1	4	6	2	5	8	9	7	3
7	2	9	3	6	1	5	4	8
5	8	2	6	1	7	3	9	4
6	7	3	5	9	4	8	2	1
9	1	4	8	2	3	7	6	5

Solution to Puzzle 221

4	5	7	3	1	6	9	8	2
1	6	2	8	9	4	7	3	5
8	9	3	7	2	5	4	6	1
3	7	5	6	4	2	8	1	9
2	1	8	9	3	7	6	5	4
6	4	9	5	8	1	3	2	7
7	8	1	4	5	3	2	9	6
5	3	4	2	6	9	1	7	8
9	2	6	1	7	8	5	4	3

Solution to Puzzle 222

6	4	2	5	8	1	7	3	9
9	3	5	7	2	4	1	8	6
1	8	7	3	6	9	2	4	5
5	2	9	8	7	6	4	1	3
8	1	6	4	5	3	9	7	2
3	7	4	1	9	2	6	5	8
4	9	3	2	1	8	5	6	7
7	6	1	9	3	5	8	2	4
2	5	8	6	4	7	3	9	1

Solution to Puzzle 223

6	9	1	5	4	3	2	7	8
8	2	3	9	7	1	5	6	4
7	5	4	2	8	6	9	1	3
1	7	9	3	5	8	4	2	6
5	6	8	1	2	4	3	9	7
3	4	2	6	9	7	8	5	1
2	1	7	4	3	9	6	8	5
4	8	5	7	6	2	1	3	9
9	3	6	8	1	5	7	4	2

Solution to Puzzle 224

3	4	1	7	2	5	6	9	8
6	5	9	3	1	8	2	4	7
7	8	2	9	4	6	5	1	3
2	6	5	8	7	4	9	3	1
9	3	8	2	6	1	4	7	5
1	7	4	5	9	3	8	6	2
5	2	7	4	3	9	1	8	6
8	9	6	1	5	7	3	2	4
4	1	3	6	8	2	7	5	9

Solution to Puzzle 225

2	1	7	3	8	5	4	6	9
3	8	5	4	6	9	7	1	2
4	9	6	7	2	1	8	3	5
5	2	4	8	1	6	9	7	3
6	3	9	5	4	7	2	8	1
8	7	1	2	9	3	5	4	6
7	6	2	1	5	8	3	9	4
9	5	3	6	7	4	1	2	8
1	4	8	9	3	2	6	5	7

Solution to Puzzle 226

4	5	7	3	1	6	9	8	2
1	6	2	8	9	4	7	3	5
8	9	3	7	2	5	4	6	1
3	7	5	6	4	2	8	1	9
2	1	8	9	3	7	6	5	4
6	4	9	5	8	1	3	2	7
7	8	1	4	5	3	2	9	6
5	3	4	2	6	9	1	7	8
9	2	6	1	7	8	5	4	3

Solution to Puzzle 227

1	8	2	7	3	6	4	9	5
3	4	9	5	8	2	7	1	6
7	6	5	4	1	9	8	3	2
6	5	4	3	7	1	2	8	9
8	9	7	6	2	5	3	4	1
2	3	1	8	9	4	6	5	7
5	7	6	9	4	3	1	2	8
4	2	8	1	5	7	9	6	3
9	1	3	2	6	8	5	7	4

Solution to Puzzle 228

5	2	7	9	3	6	1	4	8
8	9	3	7	4	1	6	2	5
1	6	4	5	8	2	7	3	9
7	3	6	2	1	8	5	9	4
2	4	1	3	5	9	8	7	6
9	8	5	4	6	7	2	1	3
4	5	8	1	2	3	9	6	7
3	1	9	6	7	5	4	8	2
6	7	2	8	9	4	3	5	1

Solution to Puzzle 229

1	9	7	6	4	2	5	3	8
3	2	8	1	5	7	9	6	4
6	5	4	3	8	9	2	1	7
7	4	6	9	3	5	8	2	1
5	1	9	4	2	8	6	7	3
2	8	3	7	1	6	4	5	9
8	7	2	5	9	3	1	4	6
9	3	1	2	6	4	7	8	5
4	6	5	8	7	1	3	9	2

Solution to Puzzle 230

1	2	4	7	5	3	6	8	9
3	7	8	9	6	4	2	5	1
5	9	6	8	1	2	3	4	7
6	3	9	5	2	7	8	1	4
8	1	2	3	4	9	7	6	5
7	4	5	6	8	1	9	2	3
4	8	3	1	7	6	5	9	2
2	6	7	4	9	5	1	3	8
9	5	1	2	3	8	4	7	6

Solution to Puzzle 231

8	7	2	6	4	9	3	1	5
1	3	4	2	5	8	9	6	7
6	5	9	1	3	7	4	8	2
5	9	6	8	2	4	7	3	1
3	1	7	9	6	5	2	4	8
4	2	8	7	1	3	5	9	6
2	6	3	5	9	1	8	7	4
7	4	5	3	8	6	1	2	9
9	8	1	4	7	2	6	5	3

Solution to Puzzle 232

9	8	4	7	6	2	5	3	1
3	1	6	8	5	4	2	7	9
5	7	2	1	9	3	8	6	4
1	3	8	2	7	5	4	9	6
4	6	5	9	3	8	1	2	7
2	9	7	6	4	1	3	8	5
6	2	3	4	1	9	7	5	8
7	5	1	3	8	6	9	4	2
8	4	9	5	2	7	6	1	3

Solution to Puzzle 233

2	1	8	4	3	5	9	7	6
3	7	9	1	2	6	8	5	4
6	5	4	9	8	7	2	1	3
1	8	7	3	6	2	4	9	5
5	4	3	8	1	9	6	2	7
9	6	2	7	5	4	3	8	1
8	9	6	5	4	1	7	3	2
7	2	1	6	9	3	5	4	8
4	3	5	2	7	8	1	6	9

Solution to Puzzle 234

8	7	6	5	9	1	4	3	2
5	4	9	3	2	7	8	1	6
2	1	3	4	8	6	9	5	7
1	9	2	6	7	8	5	4	3
3	5	8	2	4	9	6	7	1
4	6	7	1	3	5	2	9	8
9	3	1	8	6	4	7	2	5
7	8	5	9	1	2	3	6	4
6	2	4	7	5	3	1	8	9

Solution to Puzzle 235

8	2	1	6	4	3	9	7	5
3	6	5	9	7	2	1	4	8
9	7	4	1	5	8	3	6	2
7	5	6	4	2	1	8	9	3
1	3	2	8	9	6	7	5	4
4	8	9	5	3	7	6	2	1
6	4	7	3	8	5	2	1	9
5	1	8	2	6	9	4	3	7
2	9	3	7	1	4	5	8	6

Solution to Puzzle 236

4	8	1	9	2	6	5	7	3
2	7	6	5	3	4	8	9	1
5	9	3	1	7	8	6	4	2
8	2	7	3	6	1	9	5	4
1	4	5	2	8	9	7	3	6
6	3	9	4	5	7	1	2	8
7	5	4	6	1	2	3	8	9
9	6	8	7	4	3	2	1	5
3	1	2	8	9	5	4	6	7

Solution to Puzzle 237

3	6	2	8	1	7	5	9	4
1	9	8	4	6	5	7	2	3
4	7	5	9	3	2	8	1	6
2	8	4	1	5	9	3	6	7
7	5	6	2	8	3	1	4	9
9	3	1	7	4	6	2	5	8
6	4	7	3	2	1	9	8	5
8	1	3	5	9	4	6	7	2
5	2	9	6	7	8	4	3	1

Solution to Puzzle 238

9	5	4	6	7	1	8	2	3
7	2	3	8	5	9	4	6	1
8	6	1	2	4	3	7	9	5
6	7	2	1	8	5	9	3	4
3	8	9	4	6	7	1	5	2
1	4	5	9	3	2	6	8	7
4	9	7	5	2	8	3	1	6
2	3	8	7	1	6	5	4	9
5	1	6	3	9	4	2	7	8

Solution to Puzzle 239

6	7	9	8	5	2	1	3	4
3	8	1	4	6	9	7	2	5
2	4	5	1	3	7	8	6	9
7	9	3	5	2	1	4	8	6
1	5	4	6	8	3	9	7	2
8	6	2	9	7	4	5	1	3
4	2	7	3	1	5	6	9	8
9	1	6	2	4	8	3	5	7
5	3	8	7	9	6	2	4	1

Solution to Puzzle 240

8	7	2	4	6	1	5	3	9
9	4	3	5	7	8	6	2	1
5	6	1	3	2	9	4	8	7
2	8	7	6	1	5	9	4	3
3	5	4	7	9	2	1	6	8
6	1	9	8	4	3	7	5	2
4	9	8	2	5	7	3	1	6
1	3	6	9	8	4	2	7	5
7	2	5	1	3	6	8	9	4

Solution to Puzzle 241

6	9	1	5	4	3	2	7	8
8	2	3	9	7	1	5	6	4
7	5	4	2	8	6	9	1	3
1	7	9	3	5	8	4	2	6
5	6	8	1	2	4	3	9	7
3	4	2	6	9	7	8	5	1
2	1	7	4	3	9	6	8	5
4	8	5	7	6	2	1	3	9
9	3	6	8	1	5	7	4	2

Solution to Puzzle 242

6	4	2	9	5	7	3	8	1
8	5	1	2	3	6	7	4	9
7	9	3	8	4	1	5	6	2
9	1	5	3	6	4	2	7	8
4	7	8	5	1	2	6	9	3
3	2	6	7	9	8	4	1	5
1	3	9	6	7	5	8	2	4
2	6	4	1	8	3	9	5	7
5	8	7	4	2	9	1	3	6

Solution to Puzzle 243

9	1	2	8	6	4	7	5	3
5	8	3	7	1	2	6	9	4
4	7	6	5	3	9	8	1	2
3	2	5	9	7	1	4	6	8
1	4	7	2	8	6	9	3	5
8	6	9	3	4	5	2	7	1
6	3	4	1	2	7	5	8	9
2	9	1	6	5	8	3	4	7
7	5	8	4	9	3	1	2	6

Solution to Puzzle 244

9	3	6	1	7	2	8	4	5
4	2	1	5	9	8	3	7	6
5	7	8	4	6	3	2	9	1
8	4	9	6	5	7	1	2	3
2	5	7	8	3	1	4	6	9
1	6	3	2	4	9	5	8	7
3	8	4	7	1	6	9	5	2
7	9	5	3	2	4	6	1	8
6	1	2	9	8	5	7	3	4

Solution to Puzzle 245

8	2	1	6	7	9	3	5	4
5	4	9	2	8	3	1	7	6
3	6	7	1	4	5	2	8	9
1	7	6	5	3	4	9	2	8
9	5	3	8	2	6	4	1	7
4	8	2	7	9	1	6	3	5
6	1	8	4	5	2	7	9	3
7	3	4	9	1	8	5	6	2
2	9	5	3	6	7	8	4	1

Solution to Puzzle 246

9	2	6	1	7	4	3	5	8
7	3	5	8	2	6	1	4	9
4	8	1	9	3	5	6	2	7
3	6	9	5	8	7	2	1	4
8	1	2	4	9	3	7	6	5
5	4	7	2	6	1	9	8	3
6	9	8	3	4	2	5	7	1
2	5	3	7	1	8	4	9	6
1	7	4	6	5	9	8	3	2

Solution to Puzzle 247

1	9	8	5	4	3	7	6	2
5	4	7	1	2	6	8	9	3
6	2	3	8	9	7	4	5	1
2	3	6	7	1	5	9	8	4
4	7	1	6	8	9	3	2	5
8	5	9	4	3	2	1	7	6
7	8	2	3	5	4	6	1	9
9	6	4	2	7	1	5	3	8
3	1	5	9	6	8	2	4	7

Solution to Puzzle 248

3	8	7	6	9	4	2	1	5
5	9	4	1	8	2	6	3	7
1	2	6	3	7	5	9	4	8
6	7	5	4	3	8	1	9	2
9	4	1	5	2	7	8	6	3
8	3	2	9	6	1	7	5	4
2	5	9	8	1	3	4	7	6
7	6	3	2	4	9	5	8	1
4	1	8	7	5	6	3	2	9

Solution to Puzzle 249

4	6	8	5	1	3	2	7	9
2	3	1	7	4	9	5	6	8
5	7	9	6	2	8	4	1	3
6	1	7	9	8	2	3	5	4
8	2	3	1	5	4	7	9	6
9	5	4	3	7	6	1	8	2
7	9	2	8	3	5	6	4	1
3	8	5	4	6	1	9	2	7
1	4	6	2	9	7	8	3	5

Solution to Puzzle 250

2	4	8	9	7	1	5	6	3
3	6	1	8	5	4	2	7	9
9	7	5	6	3	2	1	4	8
7	1	4	2	9	5	3	8	6
5	3	9	7	8	6	4	1	2
8	2	6	4	1	3	9	5	7
6	8	3	1	4	9	7	2	5
4	9	2	5	6	7	8	3	1
1	5	7	3	2	8	6	9	4

Solution to Puzzle 251

5	1	4	2	6	7	3	9	8
3	6	7	9	8	1	2	4	5
2	9	8	4	3	5	6	7	1
1	7	5	3	2	4	9	8	6
9	3	6	5	1	8	7	2	4
4	8	2	6	7	9	5	1	3
8	2	1	7	5	3	4	6	9
7	4	3	8	9	6	1	5	2
6	5	9	1	4	2	8	3	7

Solution to Puzzle 252

3	1	5	6	9	8	2	4	7
6	9	2	7	3	4	5	1	8
8	4	7	5	1	2	9	3	6
2	7	1	9	8	5	4	6	3
5	3	8	4	2	6	1	7	9
9	6	4	1	7	3	8	2	5
1	5	6	8	4	7	3	9	2
4	8	3	2	6	9	7	5	1
7	2	9	3	5	1	6	8	4

Solution to Puzzle 253

6	7	9	8	1	4	5	2	3
4	5	8	9	3	2	6	1	7
3	2	1	5	6	7	4	9	8
2	1	6	7	5	9	3	8	4
8	3	7	2	4	1	9	5	6
5	9	4	6	8	3	2	7	1
7	4	3	1	2	5	8	6	9
9	6	2	3	7	8	1	4	5
1	8	5	4	9	6	7	3	2

Solution to Puzzle 254

8	2	1	6	4	3	9	7	5
3	6	5	9	7	2	1	4	8
9	7	4	1	5	8	3	6	2
7	5	6	4	2	1	8	9	3
1	3	2	8	9	6	7	5	4
4	8	9	5	3	7	6	2	1
6	4	7	3	8	5	2	1	9
5	1	8	2	6	9	4	3	7
2	9	3	7	1	4	5	8	6

Solution to Puzzle 255

9	6	3	7	1	5	4	8	2
1	8	7	4	3	2	5	9	6
5	2	4	6	9	8	3	1	7
7	9	1	8	2	4	6	5	3
2	4	6	9	5	3	8	7	1
8	3	5	1	7	6	2	4	9
4	1	2	5	6	9	7	3	8
6	7	8	3	4	1	9	2	5
3	5	9	2	8	7	1	6	4

Solution to Puzzle 256

7	8	5	6	9	3	1	2	4
9	6	4	5	2	1	3	8	7
2	1	3	8	4	7	6	5	9
3	5	6	7	8	9	2	4	1
8	4	9	2	1	6	5	7	3
1	2	7	3	5	4	8	9	6
5	7	1	9	6	8	4	3	2
4	9	8	1	3	2	7	6	5
6	3	2	4	7	5	9	1	8

Solution to Puzzle 257

1	2	4	7	5	3	6	8	9
3	7	8	9	6	4	2	5	1
5	9	6	8	1	2	3	4	7
6	3	9	5	2	7	8	1	4
8	1	2	3	4	9	7	6	5
7	4	5	6	8	1	9	2	3
4	8	3	1	7	6	5	9	2
2	6	7	4	9	5	1	3	8
9	5	1	2	3	8	4	7	6

Solution to Puzzle 258

1	2	4	7	5	3	6	8	9
3	7	8	9	6	4	2	5	1
5	9	6	8	1	2	3	4	7
6	3	9	5	2	7	8	1	4
8	1	2	3	4	9	7	6	5
7	4	5	6	8	1	9	2	3
4	8	3	1	7	6	5	9	2
2	6	7	4	9	5	1	3	8
9	5	1	2	3	8	4	7	6

Solution to Puzzle 259

6	7	3	9	1	2	4	8	5
9	1	4	3	8	5	2	6	7
8	2	5	6	7	4	9	3	1
2	4	7	8	5	9	6	1	3
3	9	1	2	6	7	8	5	4
5	8	6	4	3	1	7	9	2
7	6	9	1	4	3	5	2	8
1	5	2	7	9	8	3	4	6
4	3	8	5	2	6	1	7	9

Solution to Puzzle 260

9	7	3	4	6	1	2	5	8
1	2	8	7	5	3	4	6	9
6	4	5	8	2	9	1	7	3
4	8	6	1	9	2	7	3	5
5	1	9	3	7	6	8	2	4
2	3	7	5	4	8	6	9	1
7	6	1	9	3	4	5	8	2
8	9	2	6	1	5	3	4	7
3	5	4	2	8	7	9	1	6

Solution to Puzzle 261

7	8	4	9	5	3	2	1	6
9	6	2	8	7	1	3	4	5
3	5	1	2	4	6	7	8	9
5	4	6	1	3	7	8	9	2
2	9	7	5	6	8	1	3	4
1	3	8	4	9	2	5	6	7
8	7	5	6	1	4	9	2	3
6	1	3	7	2	9	4	5	8
4	2	9	3	8	5	6	7	1

Solution to Puzzle 262

6	1	2	8	7	5	4	3	9
9	3	5	1	2	4	8	6	7
4	7	8	3	9	6	1	5	2
3	8	9	4	6	7	5	2	1
2	5	7	9	8	1	6	4	3
1	6	4	2	5	3	9	7	8
8	4	3	5	1	2	7	9	6
5	9	6	7	3	8	2	1	4
7	2	1	6	4	9	3	8	5

Solution to Puzzle 263

9	3	4	8	1	7	6	5	2
2	1	7	6	9	5	8	4	3
8	5	6	4	3	2	1	7	9
6	7	2	1	5	3	9	8	4
5	4	9	7	8	6	3	2	1
3	8	1	2	4	9	7	6	5
1	6	5	3	7	4	2	9	8
7	9	8	5	2	1	4	3	6
4	2	3	9	6	8	5	1	7

Solution to Puzzle 264

2	1	8	4	5	9	7	3	6
4	3	7	8	2	6	1	5	9
6	9	5	1	3	7	2	8	4
1	8	2	9	7	3	6	4	5
3	6	4	5	8	1	9	2	7
7	5	9	6	4	2	8	1	3
5	4	1	7	6	8	3	9	2
9	2	6	3	1	4	5	7	8
8	7	3	2	9	5	4	6	1

Solution to Puzzle 265

5	2	4	3	1	7	8	6	9
3	1	7	6	8	9	4	5	2
8	9	6	4	2	5	1	3	7
2	8	1	9	3	6	5	7	4
4	6	5	8	7	2	3	9	1
9	7	3	5	4	1	6	2	8
7	5	8	1	9	3	2	4	6
6	4	9	2	5	8	7	1	3
1	3	2	7	6	4	9	8	5

Solution to Puzzle 266

7	1	5	4	9	3	8	2	6
8	2	3	5	7	6	9	4	1
6	9	4	1	8	2	3	5	7
3	4	9	2	6	5	7	1	8
2	7	8	9	4	1	5	6	3
1	5	6	8	3	7	2	9	4
9	6	7	3	5	4	1	8	2
4	8	2	7	1	9	6	3	5
5	3	1	6	2	8	4	7	9

Solution to Puzzle 267

8	2	9	5	1	7	3	6	4
1	5	3	6	4	2	9	8	7
7	4	6	9	8	3	1	5	2
9	7	5	2	3	1	8	4	6
2	8	1	4	9	6	7	3	5
3	6	4	7	5	8	2	1	9
4	1	2	8	6	9	5	7	3
6	9	8	3	7	5	4	2	1
5	3	7	1	2	4	6	9	8

Solution to Puzzle 268

2	6	8	1	3	5	4	7	9
5	9	4	7	6	8	2	1	3
1	3	7	4	9	2	5	8	6
3	8	6	5	2	4	1	9	7
9	4	1	6	8	7	3	2	5
7	5	2	3	1	9	6	4	8
6	1	9	2	7	3	8	5	4
4	7	3	8	5	1	9	6	2
8	2	5	9	4	6	7	3	1

Solution to Puzzle 269

5	6	2	3	7	1	9	4	8
3	8	9	4	5	6	7	1	2
4	7	1	8	2	9	6	5	3
7	2	5	1	9	3	4	8	6
1	4	3	7	6	8	2	9	5
8	9	6	2	4	5	3	7	1
6	1	8	9	3	4	5	2	7
9	5	7	6	8	2	1	3	4
2	3	4	5	1	7	8	6	9

Solution to Puzzle 270

8	1	9	2	6	5	3	4	7
2	7	4	9	8	3	1	6	5
5	3	6	1	4	7	9	2	8
1	9	8	6	2	4	5	7	3
4	5	7	3	1	9	6	8	2
6	2	3	7	5	8	4	9	1
3	6	2	4	7	1	8	5	9
9	4	5	8	3	2	7	1	6
7	8	1	5	9	6	2	3	4

Solution to Puzzle 271

8	7	6	5	9	1	4	3	2
5	4	9	3	2	7	8	1	6
2	1	3	4	8	6	9	5	7
1	9	2	6	7	8	5	4	3
3	5	8	2	4	9	6	7	1
4	6	7	1	3	5	2	9	8
9	3	1	8	6	4	7	2	5
7	8	5	9	1	2	3	6	4
6	2	4	7	5	3	1	8	9

Solution to Puzzle 272

8	4	9	2	1	6	7	5	3
3	1	2	7	8	5	9	4	6
5	7	6	4	9	3	8	2	1
7	3	4	1	2	8	6	9	5
2	5	8	3	6	9	4	1	7
9	6	1	5	7	4	3	8	2
1	9	7	8	3	2	5	6	4
6	2	5	9	4	7	1	3	8
4	8	3	6	5	1	2	7	9

Solution to Puzzle 273

9	8	2	6	4	5	1	7	3
7	6	1	9	3	8	5	2	4
3	5	4	1	7	2	6	8	9
4	1	7	2	6	3	8	9	5
2	9	5	4	8	1	7	3	6
8	3	6	5	9	7	2	4	1
1	7	8	3	5	4	9	6	2
5	4	9	7	2	6	3	1	8
6	2	3	8	1	9	4	5	7

Solution to Puzzle 274

8	3	2	6	4	9	5	7	1
6	1	7	8	5	3	9	2	4
9	5	4	7	2	1	3	8	6
5	7	9	1	8	4	6	3	2
3	2	6	9	7	5	1	4	8
1	4	8	3	6	2	7	5	9
2	8	1	5	9	7	4	6	3
7	6	3	4	1	8	2	9	5
4	9	5	2	3	6	8	1	7

Solution to Puzzle 275

6	4	1	9	2	8	7	3	5
8	5	3	4	1	7	6	2	9
2	7	9	3	5	6	1	8	4
3	1	6	5	8	4	9	7	2
9	8	7	6	3	2	4	5	1
5	2	4	1	7	9	3	6	8
7	6	5	2	4	1	8	9	3
1	9	2	8	6	3	5	4	7
4	3	8	7	9	5	2	1	6

Solution to Puzzle 276

1	2	4	7	5	3	6	8	9
3	7	8	9	6	4	2	5	1
5	9	6	8	1	2	3	4	7
6	3	9	5	2	7	8	1	4
8	1	2	3	4	9	7	6	5
7	4	5	6	8	1	9	2	3
4	8	3	1	7	6	5	9	2
2	6	7	4	9	5	1	3	8
9	5	1	2	3	8	4	7	6

Solution to Puzzle 277

1	7	5	8	2	6	9	3	4
8	2	3	9	4	1	5	7	6
9	4	6	5	7	3	8	2	1
4	8	1	7	6	5	2	9	3
3	6	9	1	8	2	7	4	5
7	5	2	3	9	4	6	1	8
2	3	8	6	1	7	4	5	9
5	9	4	2	3	8	1	6	7
6	1	7	4	5	9	3	8	2

Solution to Puzzle 278

2	5	6	4	1	3	7	9	8
3	8	7	9	2	6	5	4	1
1	9	4	5	8	7	6	2	3
5	3	1	8	6	9	2	7	4
7	6	2	3	4	1	8	5	9
9	4	8	2	7	5	3	1	6
8	7	5	6	9	4	1	3	2
4	2	3	1	5	8	9	6	7
6	1	9	7	3	2	4	8	5

Solution to Puzzle 279

2	3	7	1	9	4	6	5	8
6	8	9	2	5	7	4	1	3
1	4	5	3	6	8	9	2	7
7	6	8	5	4	2	1	3	9
4	9	2	6	1	3	8	7	5
3	5	1	8	7	9	2	6	4
5	2	4	9	3	1	7	8	6
8	7	6	4	2	5	3	9	1
9	1	3	7	8	6	5	4	2

Solution to Puzzle 280

9	4	7	5	2	8	1	3	6
3	2	6	7	1	9	8	4	5
5	8	1	6	3	4	2	9	7
7	1	9	8	6	3	4	5	2
8	6	2	9	4	5	7	1	3
4	5	3	1	7	2	6	8	9
1	9	8	2	5	7	3	6	4
2	3	5	4	8	6	9	7	1
6	7	4	3	9	1	5	2	8

Solution to Puzzle 281

1	9	6	7	5	3	8	4	2
4	3	7	8	2	1	6	5	9
8	2	5	6	4	9	1	7	3
3	7	8	9	1	2	4	6	5
9	5	4	3	6	8	7	2	1
2	6	1	4	7	5	9	3	8
6	1	3	5	9	4	2	8	7
7	8	2	1	3	6	5	9	4
5	4	9	2	8	7	3	1	6

Solution to Puzzle 282

7	5	9	2	6	1	3	4	8
4	2	8	7	5	3	1	6	9
3	6	1	4	9	8	5	7	2
2	3	6	9	7	5	8	1	4
8	1	5	3	4	2	6	9	7
9	7	4	8	1	6	2	5	3
6	4	2	5	3	9	7	8	1
5	8	7	1	2	4	9	3	6
1	9	3	6	8	7	4	2	5

Solution to Puzzle 283

7	4	2	3	9	6	1	8	5
3	1	6	8	7	5	9	4	2
5	9	8	4	1	2	3	7	6
1	8	7	2	3	9	6	5	4
4	5	3	7	6	1	2	9	8
2	6	9	5	4	8	7	3	1
9	2	5	6	8	3	4	1	7
6	7	1	9	5	4	8	2	3
8	3	4	1	2	7	5	6	9

Solution to Puzzle 284

1	6	4	9	3	2	5	8	7
3	2	8	6	5	7	1	9	4
7	5	9	4	1	8	3	6	2
5	7	2	1	6	4	8	3	9
6	9	3	8	2	5	4	7	1
8	4	1	7	9	3	2	5	6
4	3	5	2	7	6	9	1	8
2	1	7	5	8	9	6	4	3
9	8	6	3	4	1	7	2	5

Solution to Puzzle 285

9	7	5	8	6	2	4	3	1
3	8	2	4	9	1	7	5	6
6	1	4	3	5	7	9	2	8
2	9	7	5	1	6	3	8	4
1	4	6	7	3	8	5	9	2
5	3	8	9	2	4	1	6	7
4	5	1	6	8	9	2	7	3
8	2	9	1	7	3	6	4	5
7	6	3	2	4	5	8	1	9

Solution to Puzzle 286

8	5	2	7	3	9	1	6	4
7	3	1	2	6	4	8	9	5
4	9	6	5	8	1	7	3	2
6	1	7	9	5	3	4	2	8
9	8	4	6	2	7	3	5	1
5	2	3	4	1	8	9	7	6
1	6	9	8	7	2	5	4	3
3	4	5	1	9	6	2	8	7
2	7	8	3	4	5	6	1	9

Solution to Puzzle 287

1	2	4	7	5	3	6	8	9
3	7	8	9	6	4	2	5	1
5	9	6	8	1	2	3	4	7
6	3	9	5	2	7	8	1	4
8	1	2	3	4	9	7	6	5
7	4	5	6	8	1	9	2	3
4	8	3	1	7	6	5	9	2
2	6	7	4	9	5	1	3	8
9	5	1	2	3	8	4	7	6

Solution to Puzzle 288

2	4	3	7	6	1	5	9	8
1	9	6	3	5	8	4	7	2
5	8	7	4	2	9	1	3	6
9	3	5	2	8	4	6	1	7
8	7	4	1	9	6	2	5	3
6	2	1	5	7	3	8	4	9
4	5	2	6	3	7	9	8	1
3	6	8	9	1	5	7	2	4
7	1	9	8	4	2	3	6	5

Solution to Puzzle 289

9	4	1	5	2	7	3	6	8
2	6	3	1	8	9	7	5	4
5	8	7	6	3	4	9	2	1
4	3	2	8	9	6	1	7	5
1	9	6	7	4	5	8	3	2
7	5	8	3	1	2	4	9	6
8	1	5	2	7	3	6	4	9
6	7	4	9	5	8	2	1	3
3	2	9	4	6	1	5	8	7

Solution to Puzzle 290

9	5	8	3	7	2	4	1	6
1	2	7	6	4	8	9	3	5
3	6	4	9	5	1	8	2	7
2	4	1	5	9	6	3	7	8
7	8	9	2	3	4	6	5	1
6	3	5	8	1	7	2	4	9
4	7	6	1	2	9	5	8	3
8	1	3	4	6	5	7	9	2
5	9	2	7	8	3	1	6	4

Solution to Puzzle 291

6	4	2	9	5	7	3	8	1
8	5	1	2	3	6	7	4	9
7	9	3	8	4	1	5	6	2
9	1	5	3	6	4	2	7	8
4	7	8	5	1	2	6	9	3
3	2	6	7	9	8	4	1	5
1	3	9	6	7	5	8	2	4
2	6	4	1	8	3	9	5	7
5	8	7	4	2	9	1	3	6

Solution to Puzzle 292

9	1	8	6	5	3	4	2	7
2	6	7	4	1	9	8	5	3
3	5	4	2	7	8	6	9	1
5	8	9	3	4	2	7	1	6
4	7	1	5	9	6	2	3	8
6	3	2	1	8	7	5	4	9
7	4	6	9	3	5	1	8	2
8	9	5	7	2	1	3	6	4
1	2	3	8	6	4	9	7	5

Solution to Puzzle 293

8	6	5	7	3	2	9	1	4
4	3	1	9	6	8	7	5	2
2	7	9	1	4	5	6	3	8
6	8	7	5	9	1	4	2	3
5	1	4	3	2	7	8	9	6
9	2	3	6	8	4	1	7	5
1	9	6	8	5	3	2	4	7
3	4	8	2	7	9	5	6	1
7	5	2	4	1	6	3	8	9

Solution to Puzzle 294

5	6	8	9	4	1	3	7	2
4	1	9	7	3	2	5	6	8
7	2	3	6	8	5	9	1	4
1	8	5	4	6	3	2	9	7
6	9	4	2	5	7	8	3	1
3	7	2	1	9	8	4	5	6
2	5	7	8	1	9	6	4	3
8	3	6	5	7	4	1	2	9
9	4	1	3	2	6	7	8	5

Solution to Puzzle 295

5	9	6	1	4	7	3	8	2
3	2	8	5	9	6	4	1	7
4	1	7	8	3	2	5	9	6
2	7	1	3	8	9	6	5	4
6	4	5	2	7	1	9	3	8
8	3	9	6	5	4	2	7	1
9	6	2	7	1	3	8	4	5
1	8	4	9	6	5	7	2	3
7	5	3	4	2	8	1	6	9

Solution to Puzzle 296

3	1	7	4	8	9	2	6	5
2	5	8	3	1	6	7	4	9
9	6	4	7	2	5	3	1	8
4	2	1	9	5	7	8	3	6
5	7	3	1	6	8	9	2	4
8	9	6	2	4	3	5	7	1
1	8	9	6	7	2	4	5	3
7	4	5	8	3	1	6	9	2
6	3	2	5	9	4	1	8	7

Solution to Puzzle 297

2	1	6	3	4	8	9	5	7
5	4	8	7	9	6	2	1	3
3	7	9	5	2	1	6	4	8
7	9	5	2	6	4	8	3	1
6	8	1	9	3	7	5	2	4
4	2	3	8	1	5	7	9	6
1	6	2	4	8	9	3	7	5
9	5	4	6	7	3	1	8	2
8	3	7	1	5	2	4	6	9

Solution to Puzzle 298

9	1	3	6	8	2	7	5	4
5	6	7	4	9	3	2	1	8
8	4	2	1	5	7	6	9	3
3	5	8	9	7	1	4	2	6
1	2	4	5	3	6	9	8	7
7	9	6	2	4	8	1	3	5
2	7	9	3	6	5	8	4	1
4	8	5	7	1	9	3	6	2
6	3	1	8	2	4	5	7	9

Solution to Puzzle 299

2	7	3	4	6	9	5	1	8
8	5	9	7	1	3	4	2	6
1	4	6	8	2	5	3	9	7
7	6	8	1	3	4	9	5	2
9	1	2	5	8	7	6	3	4
5	3	4	6	9	2	7	8	1
3	9	7	2	4	8	1	6	5
4	8	1	9	5	6	2	7	3
6	2	5	3	7	1	8	4	9

Solution to Puzzle 300

2	9	6	4	1	7	3	8	5
5	3	7	8	6	9	2	1	4
8	1	4	3	5	2	6	7	9
3	7	2	5	8	4	9	6	1
9	4	1	7	2	6	8	5	3
6	8	5	1	9	3	4	2	7
1	2	9	6	3	5	7	4	8
4	5	3	2	7	8	1	9	6
7	6	8	9	4	1	5	3	2

Solution to Puzzle 301

9	1	8	6	5	3	4	2	7
2	6	7	4	1	9	8	5	3
3	5	4	2	7	8	6	9	1
5	8	9	3	4	2	7	1	6
4	7	1	5	9	6	2	3	8
6	3	2	1	8	7	5	4	9
7	4	6	9	3	5	1	8	2
8	9	5	7	2	1	3	6	4
1	2	3	8	6	4	9	7	5

Solution to Puzzle 302

1	2	4	7	5	3	6	8	9
3	7	8	9	6	4	2	5	1
5	9	6	8	1	2	3	4	7
6	3	9	5	2	7	8	1	4
8	1	2	3	4	9	7	6	5
7	4	5	6	8	1	9	2	3
4	8	3	1	7	6	5	9	2
2	6	7	4	9	5	1	3	8
9	5	1	2	3	8	4	7	6

Solution to Puzzle 303

7	4	8	5	3	9	1	6	2
6	9	3	1	2	7	4	5	8
5	2	1	8	4	6	9	7	3
2	3	9	6	1	4	5	8	7
1	8	7	3	9	5	2	4	6
4	5	6	7	8	2	3	9	1
8	1	5	9	7	3	6	2	4
9	7	4	2	6	1	8	3	5
3	6	2	4	5	8	7	1	9

Solution to Puzzle 304

8	4	2	6	7	9	3	5	1
3	9	5	8	4	1	6	7	2
1	6	7	3	5	2	8	4	9
6	5	3	2	9	4	7	1	8
7	1	8	5	6	3	9	2	4
9	2	4	1	8	7	5	3	6
5	3	9	4	2	6	1	8	7
2	7	1	9	3	8	4	6	5
4	8	6	7	1	5	2	9	3

Solution to Puzzle 305

3	6	1	8	5	7	4	9	2
7	4	2	3	9	6	8	1	5
8	9	5	2	1	4	3	6	7
6	5	7	1	4	3	9	2	8
9	1	3	6	2	8	7	5	4
4	2	8	5	7	9	1	3	6
1	3	6	7	8	5	2	4	9
5	7	4	9	3	2	6	8	1
2	8	9	4	6	1	5	7	3

Solution to Puzzle 306

4	6	8	5	1	3	2	7	9
2	3	1	7	4	9	5	6	8
5	7	9	6	2	8	4	1	3
6	1	7	9	8	2	3	5	4
8	2	3	1	5	4	7	9	6
9	5	4	3	7	6	1	8	2
7	9	2	8	3	5	6	4	1
3	8	5	4	6	1	9	2	7
1	4	6	2	9	7	8	3	5

Solution to Puzzle 307

9	1	8	6	5	3	4	2	7
2	6	7	4	1	9	8	5	3
3	5	4	2	7	8	6	9	1
5	8	9	3	4	2	7	1	6
4	7	1	5	9	6	2	3	8
6	3	2	1	8	7	5	4	9
7	4	6	9	3	5	1	8	2
8	9	5	7	2	1	3	6	4
1	2	3	8	6	4	9	7	5

Solution to Puzzle 308

4	3	7	5	8	6	9	2	1
8	5	2	7	1	9	4	6	3
9	1	6	3	4	2	8	7	5
5	6	9	4	7	8	3	1	2
3	7	4	2	9	1	5	8	6
2	8	1	6	5	3	7	4	9
1	4	5	9	2	7	6	3	8
7	2	3	8	6	5	1	9	4
6	9	8	1	3	4	2	5	7

Solution to Puzzle 309

5	9	6	1	4	7	3	8	2
3	2	8	5	9	6	4	1	7
4	1	7	8	3	2	5	9	6
2	7	1	3	8	9	6	5	4
6	4	5	2	7	1	9	3	8
8	3	9	6	5	4	2	7	1
9	6	2	7	1	3	8	4	5
1	8	4	9	6	5	7	2	3
7	5	3	4	2	8	1	6	9

Solution to Puzzle 310

2	1	6	3	4	8	9	5	7
5	4	8	7	9	6	2	1	3
3	7	9	5	2	1	6	4	8
7	9	5	2	6	4	8	3	1
6	8	1	9	3	7	5	2	4
4	2	3	8	1	5	7	9	6
1	6	2	4	8	9	3	7	5
9	5	4	6	7	3	1	8	2
8	3	7	1	5	2	4	6	9

Solution to Puzzle 311

1	2	4	7	5	3	6	8	9
3	7	8	9	6	4	2	5	1
5	9	6	8	1	2	3	4	7
6	3	9	5	2	7	8	1	4
8	1	2	3	4	9	7	6	5
7	4	5	6	8	1	9	2	3
4	8	3	1	7	6	5	9	2
2	6	7	4	9	5	1	3	8
9	5	1	2	3	8	4	7	6

Solution to Puzzle 312

1	2	4	7	5	3	6	8	9
3	7	8	9	6	4	2	5	1
5	9	6	8	1	2	3	4	7
6	3	9	5	2	7	8	1	4
8	1	2	3	4	9	7	6	5
7	4	5	6	8	1	9	2	3
4	8	3	1	7	6	5	9	2
2	6	7	4	9	5	1	3	8
9	5	1	2	3	8	4	7	6

Solution to Puzzle 313

4	7	3	6	2	1	5	8	9
2	9	1	8	4	5	6	7	3
5	6	8	7	3	9	4	2	1
3	4	5	9	1	2	7	6	8
7	8	9	4	6	3	2	1	5
6	1	2	5	7	8	3	9	4
9	2	4	3	8	7	1	5	6
8	3	7	1	5	6	9	4	2
1	5	6	2	9	4	8	3	7

Solution to Puzzle 314

7	6	4	8	1	2	3	9	5
8	5	3	9	6	4	1	7	2
9	2	1	3	7	5	6	8	4
1	4	6	2	9	8	5	3	7
5	8	7	1	4	3	2	6	9
2	3	9	7	5	6	8	4	1
6	7	2	5	3	9	4	1	8
3	9	5	4	8	1	7	2	6
4	1	8	6	2	7	9	5	3

Solution to Puzzle 315

6	4	1	9	2	8	7	3	5
8	5	3	4	1	7	6	2	9
2	7	9	3	5	6	1	8	4
3	1	6	5	8	4	9	7	2
9	8	7	6	3	2	4	5	1
5	2	4	1	7	9	3	6	8
7	6	5	2	4	1	8	9	3
1	9	2	8	6	3	5	4	7
4	3	8	7	9	5	2	1	6

Solution to Puzzle 316

6	7	4	3	8	2	9	5	1
8	2	5	1	9	7	4	3	6
3	9	1	5	6	4	7	2	8
9	4	6	8	3	5	2	1	7
2	3	8	6	7	1	5	4	9
5	1	7	2	4	9	8	6	3
1	8	9	4	2	6	3	7	5
7	5	2	9	1	3	6	8	4
4	6	3	7	5	8	1	9	2

Solution to Puzzle 317

6	3	7	5	4	8	9	1	2
8	5	9	2	7	1	4	3	6
2	1	4	3	9	6	7	8	5
1	7	5	4	6	9	8	2	3
3	9	8	7	5	2	1	6	4
4	2	6	8	1	3	5	7	9
5	8	1	6	3	4	2	9	7
7	6	2	9	8	5	3	4	1
9	4	3	1	2	7	6	5	8

Solution to Puzzle 318

3	8	9	7	2	4	5	1	6
1	2	5	6	8	9	7	4	3
4	6	7	1	3	5	2	8	9
7	5	4	8	9	3	1	6	2
8	9	1	5	6	2	4	3	7
6	3	2	4	7	1	8	9	5
5	7	6	9	1	8	3	2	4
2	4	8	3	5	6	9	7	1
9	1	3	2	4	7	6	5	8

Solution to Puzzle 319

2	6	8	1	3	5	4	7	9
5	9	4	7	6	8	2	1	3
1	3	7	4	9	2	5	8	6
3	8	6	5	2	4	1	9	7
9	4	1	6	8	7	3	2	5
7	5	2	3	1	9	6	4	8
6	1	9	2	7	3	8	5	4
4	7	3	8	5	1	9	6	2
8	2	5	9	4	6	7	3	1

Solution to Puzzle 320

9	3	6	1	7	2	8	4	5
4	2	1	5	9	8	3	7	6
5	7	8	4	6	3	2	9	1
8	4	9	6	5	7	1	2	3
2	5	7	8	3	1	4	6	9
1	6	3	2	4	9	5	8	7
3	8	4	7	1	6	9	5	2
7	9	5	3	2	4	6	1	8
6	1	2	9	8	5	7	3	4

Solution to Puzzle 321

4	5	7	9	6	3	1	8	2
3	2	1	7	8	4	6	5	9
8	9	6	2	1	5	7	3	4
6	8	2	4	7	1	3	9	5
1	7	5	3	2	9	8	4	6
9	4	3	6	5	8	2	1	7
7	3	9	8	4	2	5	6	1
5	6	4	1	3	7	9	2	8
2	1	8	5	9	6	4	7	3

Solution to Puzzle 322

3	4	6	5	9	8	2	7	1
5	1	8	2	3	7	9	4	6
2	9	7	6	1	4	3	8	5
8	5	1	4	6	9	7	3	2
9	7	3	8	5	2	1	6	4
4	6	2	3	7	1	5	9	8
7	3	5	1	8	6	4	2	9
6	2	9	7	4	5	8	1	3
1	8	4	9	2	3	6	5	7

Solution to Puzzle 323

9	8	2	6	4	5	1	7	3
7	6	1	9	3	8	5	2	4
3	5	4	1	7	2	6	8	9
4	1	7	2	6	3	8	9	5
2	9	5	4	8	1	7	3	6
8	3	6	5	9	7	2	4	1
1	7	8	3	5	4	9	6	2
5	4	9	7	2	6	3	1	8
6	2	3	8	1	9	4	5	7

Solution to Puzzle 324

1	5	2	4	8	9	3	7	6
7	6	8	2	5	3	4	1	9
9	3	4	6	1	7	2	8	5
4	7	1	9	2	6	5	3	8
8	9	3	7	4	5	6	2	1
6	2	5	8	3	1	9	4	7
2	8	6	5	7	4	1	9	3
5	1	7	3	9	2	8	6	4
3	4	9	1	6	8	7	5	2

Solution to Puzzle 325

9	3	5	4	6	7	8	1	2
8	4	2	9	5	1	7	6	3
6	1	7	2	3	8	9	5	4
1	5	4	7	2	9	3	8	6
3	2	9	8	1	6	4	7	5
7	6	8	3	4	5	2	9	1
4	7	1	5	8	3	6	2	9
2	8	6	1	9	4	5	3	7
5	9	3	6	7	2	1	4	8

Solution to Puzzle 326

3	4	8	6	1	5	7	2	9
9	5	1	8	2	7	4	3	6
2	7	6	9	3	4	1	5	8
6	8	2	4	5	9	3	7	1
7	1	4	3	6	8	2	9	5
5	9	3	2	7	1	6	8	4
4	3	9	1	8	2	5	6	7
8	2	5	7	4	6	9	1	3
1	6	7	5	9	3	8	4	2

Solution to Puzzle 327

9	3	4	8	1	7	6	5	2
2	1	7	6	9	5	8	4	3
8	5	6	4	3	2	1	7	9
6	7	2	1	5	3	9	8	4
5	4	9	7	8	6	3	2	1
3	8	1	2	4	9	7	6	5
1	6	5	3	7	4	2	9	8
7	9	8	5	2	1	4	3	6
4	2	3	9	6	8	5	1	7

Solution to Puzzle 328

9	2	7	3	8	1	4	5	6
8	6	5	7	9	4	1	3	2
1	3	4	2	6	5	9	8	7
6	9	8	5	7	2	3	4	1
5	4	2	1	3	9	7	6	8
3	7	1	6	4	8	5	2	9
2	1	6	9	5	3	8	7	4
4	5	9	8	2	7	6	1	3
7	8	3	4	1	6	2	9	5

Solution to Puzzle 329

1	3	2	9	5	4	7	6	8
6	9	5	2	8	7	3	1	4
7	8	4	6	3	1	9	5	2
4	5	9	7	2	8	6	3	1
3	1	8	4	6	5	2	9	7
2	7	6	3	1	9	8	4	5
8	4	7	5	9	3	1	2	6
9	6	1	8	4	2	5	7	3
5	2	3	1	7	6	4	8	9

Solution to Puzzle 330

8	3	6	7	1	9	4	5	2
1	5	4	8	6	2	9	3	7
7	2	9	3	5	4	8	1	6
2	6	1	9	4	3	7	8	5
5	9	7	1	2	8	6	4	3
3	4	8	5	7	6	2	9	1
4	7	3	6	9	5	1	2	8
6	8	2	4	3	1	5	7	9
9	1	5	2	8	7	3	6	4

Solution to Puzzle 331

4	3	6	9	5	2	8	7	1
8	5	9	7	1	6	2	4	3
2	7	1	4	8	3	9	5	6
1	6	7	3	2	8	5	9	4
9	4	5	1	6	7	3	2	8
3	2	8	5	4	9	6	1	7
7	9	2	6	3	1	4	8	5
5	8	3	2	7	4	1	6	9
6	1	4	8	9	5	7	3	2

Solution to Puzzle 332

9	4	1	5	2	7	3	6	8
2	6	3	1	8	9	7	5	4
5	8	7	6	3	4	9	2	1
4	3	2	8	9	6	1	7	5
1	9	6	7	4	5	8	3	2
7	5	8	3	1	2	4	9	6
8	1	5	2	7	3	6	4	9
6	7	4	9	5	8	2	1	3
3	2	9	4	6	1	5	8	7

Solution to Puzzle 333

1	9	8	5	4	3	7	6	2
5	4	7	1	2	6	8	9	3
6	2	3	8	9	7	4	5	1
2	3	6	7	1	5	9	8	4
4	7	1	6	8	9	3	2	5
8	5	9	4	3	2	1	7	6
7	8	2	3	5	4	6	1	9
9	6	4	2	7	1	5	3	8
3	1	5	9	6	8	2	4	7

Solution to Puzzle 334

9	6	7	4	2	8	1	5	3
8	3	4	5	1	6	9	7	2
2	1	5	3	7	9	4	6	8
7	8	9	1	5	3	2	4	6
6	2	3	7	9	4	8	1	5
5	4	1	8	6	2	3	9	7
4	7	2	9	8	5	6	3	1
3	5	6	2	4	1	7	8	9
1	9	8	6	3	7	5	2	4

Solution to Puzzle 335

1	2	4	7	5	3	6	8	9
3	7	8	9	6	4	2	5	1
5	9	6	8	1	2	3	4	7
6	3	9	5	2	7	8	1	4
8	1	2	3	4	9	7	6	5
7	4	5	6	8	1	9	2	3
4	8	3	1	7	6	5	9	2
2	6	7	4	9	5	1	3	8
9	5	1	2	3	8	4	7	6

Solution to Puzzle 336

4	5	7	3	1	6	9	8	2
1	6	2	8	9	4	7	3	5
8	9	3	7	2	5	4	6	1
3	7	5	6	4	2	8	1	9
2	1	8	9	3	7	6	5	4
6	4	9	5	8	1	3	2	7
7	8	1	4	5	3	2	9	6
5	3	4	2	6	9	1	7	8
9	2	6	1	7	8	5	4	3

Solution to Puzzle 337

6	7	3	9	1	2	4	8	5
9	1	4	3	8	5	2	6	7
8	2	5	6	7	4	9	3	1
2	4	7	8	5	9	6	1	3
3	9	1	2	6	7	8	5	4
5	8	6	4	3	1	7	9	2
7	6	9	1	4	3	5	2	8
1	5	2	7	9	8	3	4	6
4	3	8	5	2	6	1	7	9

Solution to Puzzle 338

8	3	6	7	1	9	4	5	2
1	5	4	8	6	2	9	3	7
7	2	9	3	5	4	8	1	6
2	6	1	9	4	3	7	8	5
5	9	7	1	2	8	6	4	3
3	4	8	5	7	6	2	9	1
4	7	3	6	9	5	1	2	8
6	8	2	4	3	1	5	7	9
9	1	5	2	8	7	3	6	4

Solution to Puzzle 339

4	8	5	9	7	2	3	1	6
1	9	2	5	6	3	7	4	8
3	7	6	4	1	8	5	9	2
7	1	9	2	5	6	4	8	3
6	2	3	8	9	4	1	7	5
5	4	8	1	3	7	2	6	9
2	3	1	7	8	9	6	5	4
8	6	7	3	4	5	9	2	1
9	5	4	6	2	1	8	3	7

Solution to Puzzle 340

1	5	2	4	8	9	3	7	6
7	6	8	2	5	3	4	1	9
9	3	4	6	1	7	2	8	5
4	7	1	9	2	6	5	3	8
8	9	3	7	4	5	6	2	1
6	2	5	8	3	1	9	4	7
2	8	6	5	7	4	1	9	3
5	1	7	3	9	2	8	6	4
3	4	9	1	6	8	7	5	2

Solution to Puzzle 341

2	4	8	9	7	1	5	6	3
3	6	1	8	5	4	2	7	9
9	7	5	6	3	2	1	4	8
7	1	4	2	9	5	3	8	6
5	3	9	7	8	6	4	1	2
8	2	6	4	1	3	9	5	7
6	8	3	1	4	9	7	2	5
4	9	2	5	6	7	8	3	1
1	5	7	3	2	8	6	9	4

Solution to Puzzle 342

3	4	1	7	2	5	6	9	8
6	5	9	3	1	8	2	4	7
7	8	2	9	4	6	5	1	3
2	6	5	8	7	4	9	3	1
9	3	8	2	6	1	4	7	5
1	7	4	5	9	3	8	6	2
5	2	7	4	3	9	1	8	6
8	9	6	1	5	7	3	2	4
4	1	3	6	8	2	7	5	9

Solution to Puzzle 343

1	2	8	7	9	5	3	6	4
4	9	3	6	1	8	2	7	5
6	5	7	3	2	4	1	9	8
5	3	1	9	8	7	4	2	6
9	8	2	5	4	6	7	3	1
7	6	4	1	3	2	8	5	9
8	1	9	2	6	3	5	4	7
3	7	6	4	5	1	9	8	2
2	4	5	8	7	9	6	1	3

Solution to Puzzle 344

1	7	5	8	2	6	9	3	4
8	2	3	9	4	1	5	7	6
9	4	6	5	7	3	8	2	1
4	8	1	7	6	5	2	9	3
3	6	9	1	8	2	7	4	5
7	5	2	3	9	4	6	1	8
2	3	8	6	1	7	4	5	9
5	9	4	2	3	8	1	6	7
6	1	7	4	5	9	3	8	2

Solution to Puzzle 345

7	2	8	3	5	6	4	9	1
4	3	5	7	1	9	6	8	2
6	1	9	2	8	4	5	7	3
1	8	7	6	9	2	3	5	4
3	6	4	1	7	5	9	2	8
9	5	2	4	3	8	7	1	6
8	4	6	5	2	7	1	3	9
5	9	3	8	6	1	2	4	7
2	7	1	9	4	3	8	6	5

Solution to Puzzle 346

2	8	1	9	5	4	6	7	3
3	4	6	7	8	1	2	9	5
9	5	7	3	6	2	4	8	1
4	2	3	1	9	6	8	5	7
8	7	5	4	2	3	1	6	9
1	6	9	5	7	8	3	2	4
5	3	8	2	1	9	7	4	6
7	1	2	6	4	5	9	3	8
6	9	4	8	3	7	5	1	2

Solution to Puzzle 347

7	4	8	5	3	9	1	6	2
6	9	3	1	2	7	4	5	8
5	2	1	8	4	6	9	7	3
2	3	9	6	1	4	5	8	7
1	8	7	3	9	5	2	4	6
4	5	6	7	8	2	3	9	1
8	1	5	9	7	3	6	2	4
9	7	4	2	6	1	8	3	5
3	6	2	4	5	8	7	1	9

Solution to Puzzle 348

2	7	3	8	6	9	1	4	5
4	6	1	3	2	5	8	7	9
8	5	9	4	7	1	2	3	6
7	1	6	9	4	3	5	2	8
3	4	5	2	8	6	7	9	1
9	8	2	1	5	7	3	6	4
5	2	4	6	3	8	9	1	7
6	9	8	7	1	2	4	5	3
1	3	7	5	9	4	6	8	2

Solution to Puzzle 349

6	5	7	3	8	1	2	4	9
4	1	3	9	2	6	5	7	8
2	9	8	7	5	4	6	1	3
1	8	6	2	3	9	4	5	7
5	3	4	6	7	8	1	9	2
7	2	9	1	4	5	3	8	6
8	7	1	4	6	3	9	2	5
3	4	5	8	9	2	7	6	1
9	6	2	5	1	7	8	3	4

Solution to Puzzle 350

8	6	5	7	3	2	9	1	4
4	3	1	9	6	8	7	5	2
2	7	9	1	4	5	6	3	8
6	8	7	5	9	1	4	2	3
5	1	4	3	2	7	8	9	6
9	2	3	6	8	4	1	7	5
1	9	6	8	5	3	2	4	7
3	4	8	2	7	9	5	6	1
7	5	2	4	1	6	3	8	9

Solution to Puzzle 351

2	1	3	9	7	4	6	8	5
6	9	5	8	2	1	4	7	3
7	8	4	3	5	6	1	2	9
5	7	8	2	1	3	9	4	6
3	2	6	4	9	7	5	1	8
1	4	9	5	6	8	2	3	7
9	3	2	7	4	5	8	6	1
8	5	1	6	3	2	7	9	4
4	6	7	1	8	9	3	5	2

Solution to Puzzle 352

4	8	5	9	7	2	3	1	6
1	9	2	5	6	3	7	4	8
3	7	6	4	1	8	5	9	2
7	1	9	2	5	6	4	8	3
6	2	3	8	9	4	1	7	5
5	4	8	1	3	7	2	6	9
2	3	1	7	8	9	6	5	4
8	6	7	3	4	5	9	2	1
9	5	4	6	2	1	8	3	7

Solution to Puzzle 353

5	3	4	9	6	7	2	8	1
6	2	7	8	5	1	9	3	4
1	9	8	2	4	3	7	6	5
4	6	2	7	3	9	1	5	8
9	7	1	4	8	5	3	2	6
8	5	3	1	2	6	4	7	9
7	4	6	3	1	8	5	9	2
2	8	9	5	7	4	6	1	3
3	1	5	6	9	2	8	4	7

Solution to Puzzle 354

4	7	8	5	2	6	3	1	9
5	3	1	8	7	9	4	6	2
2	6	9	3	4	1	5	8	7
8	9	3	6	5	2	1	7	4
6	1	5	7	9	4	8	2	3
7	2	4	1	8	3	6	9	5
3	8	7	2	6	5	9	4	1
1	4	6	9	3	7	2	5	8
9	5	2	4	1	8	7	3	6

Solution to Puzzle 355

4	1	5	7	9	8	2	3	6
7	3	6	1	5	2	4	8	9
8	2	9	6	4	3	5	7	1
5	4	2	9	8	6	3	1	7
6	8	7	3	2	1	9	5	4
1	9	3	5	7	4	8	6	2
2	5	4	8	6	7	1	9	3
3	7	8	2	1	9	6	4	5
9	6	1	4	3	5	7	2	8

Solution to Puzzle 356

9	8	2	4	7	3	5	6	1
4	1	3	6	2	5	9	7	8
7	6	5	9	8	1	4	3	2
2	7	8	5	4	9	6	1	3
1	5	9	8	3	6	2	4	7
6	3	4	2	1	7	8	5	9
3	9	6	7	5	8	1	2	4
8	4	1	3	6	2	7	9	5
5	2	7	1	9	4	3	8	6

Solution to Puzzle 357

3	4	1	7	2	5	6	9	8
6	5	9	3	1	8	2	4	7
7	8	2	9	4	6	5	1	3
2	6	5	8	7	4	9	3	1
9	3	8	2	6	1	4	7	5
1	7	4	5	9	3	8	6	2
5	2	7	4	3	9	1	8	6
8	9	6	1	5	7	3	2	4
4	1	3	6	8	2	7	5	9

Solution to Puzzle 358

9	7	3	4	6	1	2	5	8
1	2	8	7	5	3	4	6	9
6	4	5	8	2	9	1	7	3
4	8	6	1	9	2	7	3	5
5	1	9	3	7	6	8	2	4
2	3	7	5	4	8	6	9	1
7	6	1	9	3	4	5	8	2
8	9	2	6	1	5	3	4	7
3	5	4	2	8	7	9	1	6

Solution to Puzzle 359

9	1	2	7	6	3	5	8	4
7	5	8	4	1	9	6	3	2
3	6	4	2	5	8	7	1	9
4	2	5	3	9	7	1	6	8
1	9	3	8	4	6	2	5	7
8	7	6	5	2	1	9	4	3
6	8	1	9	7	4	3	2	5
2	4	9	1	3	5	8	7	6
5	3	7	6	8	2	4	9	1

Solution to Puzzle 360

1	2	4	7	5	3	6	8	9
3	7	8	9	6	4	2	5	1
5	9	6	8	1	2	3	4	7
6	3	9	5	2	7	8	1	4
8	1	2	3	4	9	7	6	5
7	4	5	6	8	1	9	2	3
4	8	3	1	7	6	5	9	2
2	6	7	4	9	5	1	3	8
9	5	1	2	3	8	4	7	6

Solution to Puzzle 361

1	6	8	5	3	2	4	7	9
7	2	3	4	9	1	6	8	5
4	9	5	6	8	7	2	3	1
8	1	2	9	4	3	7	5	6
5	3	7	8	1	6	9	2	4
9	4	6	2	7	5	3	1	8
2	5	1	3	6	4	8	9	7
3	8	4	7	5	9	1	6	2
6	7	9	1	2	8	5	4	3

Solution to Puzzle 362

3	6	2	8	1	7	5	9	4
1	9	8	4	6	5	7	2	3
4	7	5	9	3	2	8	1	6
2	8	4	1	5	9	3	6	7
7	5	6	2	8	3	1	4	9
9	3	1	7	4	6	2	5	8
6	4	7	3	2	1	9	8	5
8	1	3	5	9	4	6	7	2
5	2	9	6	7	8	4	3	1

Solution to Puzzle 363

3	1	4	2	7	6	9	8	5
9	5	6	3	8	1	7	4	2
2	7	8	5	9	4	3	1	6
6	3	7	4	2	9	8	5	1
4	8	5	6	1	3	2	9	7
1	9	2	7	5	8	6	3	4
7	2	1	8	3	5	4	6	9
5	6	3	9	4	7	1	2	8
8	4	9	1	6	2	5	7	3

Solution to Puzzle 364

1	2	4	7	5	3	6	8	9
3	7	8	9	6	4	2	5	1
5	9	6	8	1	2	3	4	7
6	3	9	5	2	7	8	1	4
8	1	2	3	4	9	7	6	5
7	4	5	6	8	1	9	2	3
4	8	3	1	7	6	5	9	2
2	6	7	4	9	5	1	3	8
9	5	1	2	3	8	4	7	6

Solution to Puzzle 365

9	1	5	4	7	2	8	6	3
8	7	4	6	3	9	1	2	5
2	6	3	8	5	1	9	4	7
7	8	2	5	4	6	3	9	1
3	9	6	2	1	8	7	5	4
4	5	1	3	9	7	2	8	6
6	4	9	7	2	3	5	1	8
5	2	7	1	8	4	6	3	9
1	3	8	9	6	5	4	7	2

Solution to Puzzle 366

6	1	3	5	8	9	2	4	7
5	4	2	7	1	3	9	8	6
7	8	9	2	4	6	5	1	3
4	3	8	9	2	7	6	5	1
2	7	6	4	5	1	8	3	9
9	5	1	6	3	8	4	7	2
1	6	5	8	7	2	3	9	4
8	9	7	3	6	4	1	2	5
3	2	4	1	9	5	7	6	8

Solution to Puzzle 367

5	6	8	9	4	1	3	7	2
4	1	9	7	3	2	5	6	8
7	2	3	6	8	5	9	1	4
1	8	5	4	6	3	2	9	7
6	9	4	2	5	7	8	3	1
3	7	2	1	9	8	4	5	6
2	5	7	8	1	9	6	4	3
8	3	6	5	7	4	1	2	9
9	4	1	3	2	6	7	8	5

Solution to Puzzle 368

9	5	4	6	7	1	8	2	3
7	2	3	8	5	9	4	6	1
8	6	1	2	4	3	7	9	5
6	7	2	1	8	5	9	3	4
3	8	9	4	6	7	1	5	2
1	4	5	9	3	2	6	8	7
4	9	7	5	2	8	3	1	6
2	3	8	7	1	6	5	4	9
5	1	6	3	9	4	2	7	8

Solution to Puzzle 369

4	2	5	7	3	1	6	9	8
8	7	1	9	4	6	3	2	5
3	9	6	5	2	8	4	1	7
6	3	4	1	8	5	9	7	2
2	8	7	4	6	9	5	3	1
5	1	9	2	7	3	8	6	4
1	4	8	6	9	2	7	5	3
9	5	3	8	1	7	2	4	6
7	6	2	3	5	4	1	8	9

Solution to Puzzle 370

7	4	2	3	9	6	1	8	5
3	1	6	8	7	5	9	4	2
5	9	8	4	1	2	3	7	6
1	8	7	2	3	9	6	5	4
4	5	3	7	6	1	2	9	8
2	6	9	5	4	8	7	3	1
9	2	5	6	8	3	4	1	7
6	7	1	9	5	4	8	2	3
8	3	4	1	2	7	5	6	9

Solution to Puzzle 371

4	1	3	6	7	8	2	5	9
6	8	2	9	3	5	7	4	1
7	5	9	4	2	1	6	3	8
3	9	4	5	1	6	8	2	7
1	7	5	8	9	2	4	6	3
8	2	6	3	4	7	9	1	5
9	3	7	1	6	4	5	8	2
5	6	1	2	8	9	3	7	4
2	4	8	7	5	3	1	9	6

Solution to Puzzle 372

1	5	2	4	8	9	3	7	6
7	6	8	2	5	3	4	1	9
9	3	4	6	1	7	2	8	5
4	7	1	9	2	6	5	3	8
8	9	3	7	4	5	6	2	1
6	2	5	8	3	1	9	4	7
2	8	6	5	7	4	1	9	3
5	1	7	3	9	2	8	6	4
3	4	9	1	6	8	7	5	2

Solution to Puzzle 373

1	3	2	4	5	8	7	9	6
4	8	6	7	9	1	5	2	3
7	5	9	3	2	6	1	4	8
5	1	4	8	6	3	2	7	9
6	2	7	5	4	9	8	3	1
3	9	8	1	7	2	4	6	5
9	7	5	6	1	4	3	8	2
2	4	3	9	8	5	6	1	7
8	6	1	2	3	7	9	5	4

Solution to Puzzle 374

2	3	5	1	8	9	4	7	6
7	9	6	4	3	2	5	8	1
4	8	1	7	5	6	3	9	2
6	1	9	8	7	3	2	4	5
5	4	7	6	2	1	8	3	9
8	2	3	5	9	4	6	1	7
9	6	4	2	1	8	7	5	3
3	7	8	9	6	5	1	2	4
1	5	2	3	4	7	9	6	8

Solution to Puzzle 375

5	1	2	8	7	3	6	4	9
9	4	8	1	5	6	2	7	3
7	3	6	4	2	9	8	5	1
2	6	3	5	8	4	1	9	7
4	8	5	9	1	7	3	6	2
1	9	7	3	6	2	5	8	4
3	5	9	6	4	1	7	2	8
6	2	4	7	3	8	9	1	5
8	7	1	2	9	5	4	3	6

Solution to Puzzle 376

2	6	8	7	4	1	5	3	9
4	5	1	3	9	6	8	2	7
3	7	9	8	5	2	6	1	4
6	4	7	5	2	3	1	9	8
1	3	5	6	8	9	7	4	2
9	8	2	4	1	7	3	5	6
5	1	4	2	6	8	9	7	3
8	2	3	9	7	5	4	6	1
7	9	6	1	3	4	2	8	5

Solution to Puzzle 377

9	3	2	6	1	5	7	8	4
6	4	7	8	3	2	1	9	5
8	1	5	4	9	7	2	6	3
3	2	4	7	5	9	6	1	8
7	6	9	1	4	8	3	5	2
5	8	1	3	2	6	9	4	7
2	7	6	9	8	4	5	3	1
4	9	3	5	7	1	8	2	6
1	5	8	2	6	3	4	7	9

Solution to Puzzle 378

6	7	1	2	9	5	3	8	4
2	9	4	8	3	6	5	7	1
8	3	5	4	7	1	9	6	2
3	8	9	5	2	7	1	4	6
5	2	7	1	6	4	8	9	3
4	1	6	3	8	9	2	5	7
9	6	2	7	5	3	4	1	8
7	4	3	9	1	8	6	2	5
1	5	8	6	4	2	7	3	9

Solution to Puzzle 379

5	8	3	1	7	4	6	2	9
2	1	4	5	6	9	7	8	3
9	7	6	2	8	3	4	5	1
4	5	7	8	3	1	9	6	2
3	6	9	4	2	5	8	1	7
8	2	1	6	9	7	5	3	4
7	9	8	3	1	6	2	4	5
6	3	5	7	4	2	1	9	8
1	4	2	9	5	8	3	7	6

Solution to Puzzle 380

3	1	4	2	7	6	9	8	5
9	5	6	3	8	1	7	4	2
2	7	8	5	9	4	3	1	6
6	3	7	4	2	9	8	5	1
4	8	5	6	1	3	2	9	7
1	9	2	7	5	8	6	3	4
7	2	1	8	3	5	4	6	9
5	6	3	9	4	7	1	2	8
8	4	9	1	6	2	5	7	3

Solution to Puzzle 381

8	2	1	6	4	3	9	7	5
3	6	5	9	7	2	1	4	8
9	7	4	1	5	8	3	6	2
7	5	6	4	2	1	8	9	3
1	3	2	8	9	6	7	5	4
4	8	9	5	3	7	6	2	1
6	4	7	3	8	5	2	1	9
5	1	8	2	6	9	4	3	7
2	9	3	7	1	4	5	8	6

Solution to Puzzle 382

8	2	9	5	1	7	3	6	4
1	5	3	6	4	2	9	8	7
7	4	6	9	8	3	1	5	2
9	7	5	2	3	1	8	4	6
2	8	1	4	9	6	7	3	5
3	6	4	7	5	8	2	1	9
4	1	2	8	6	9	5	7	3
6	9	8	3	7	5	4	2	1
5	3	7	1	2	4	6	9	8

Solution to Puzzle 383

6	7	8	3	9	5	2	4	1
1	4	2	6	8	7	9	3	5
5	3	9	1	2	4	6	7	8
4	5	7	9	1	8	3	2	6
8	9	3	2	5	6	4	1	7
2	6	1	7	4	3	8	5	9
7	8	5	4	3	9	1	6	2
9	2	4	5	6	1	7	8	3
3	1	6	8	7	2	5	9	4

Solution to Puzzle 384

3	4	6	5	9	8	2	7	1
5	1	8	2	3	7	9	4	6
2	9	7	6	1	4	3	8	5
8	5	1	4	6	9	7	3	2
9	7	3	8	5	2	1	6	4
4	6	2	3	7	1	5	9	8
7	3	5	1	8	6	4	2	9
6	2	9	7	4	5	8	1	3
1	8	4	9	2	3	6	5	7

Solution to Puzzle 385

8	1	9	2	6	5	3	4	7
2	7	4	9	8	3	1	6	5
5	3	6	1	4	7	9	2	8
1	9	8	6	2	4	5	7	3
4	5	7	3	1	9	6	8	2
6	2	3	7	5	8	4	9	1
3	6	2	4	7	1	8	5	9
9	4	5	8	3	2	7	1	6
7	8	1	5	9	6	2	3	4

Solution to Puzzle 386

6	7	8	3	9	5	2	4	1
1	4	2	6	8	7	9	3	5
5	3	9	1	2	4	6	7	8
4	5	7	9	1	8	3	2	6
8	9	3	2	5	6	4	1	7
2	6	1	7	4	3	8	5	9
7	8	5	4	3	9	1	6	2
9	2	4	5	6	1	7	8	3
3	1	6	8	7	2	5	9	4

Solution to Puzzle 387

6	7	9	8	5	2	1	3	4
3	8	1	4	6	9	7	2	5
2	4	5	1	3	7	8	6	9
7	9	3	5	2	1	4	8	6
1	5	4	6	8	3	9	7	2
8	6	2	9	7	4	5	1	3
4	2	7	3	1	5	6	9	8
9	1	6	2	4	8	3	5	7
5	3	8	7	9	6	2	4	1

Solution to Puzzle 388

5	4	3	7	6	9	2	8	1
7	1	6	2	5	8	3	9	4
9	8	2	4	3	1	7	6	5
3	5	8	1	4	2	6	7	9
1	9	7	6	8	5	4	2	3
6	2	4	3	9	7	5	1	8
4	3	1	8	7	6	9	5	2
8	6	5	9	2	4	1	3	7
2	7	9	5	1	3	8	4	6

Solution to Puzzle 389

9	4	2	5	3	8	6	7	1
3	7	8	1	4	6	9	5	2
6	1	5	2	7	9	3	4	8
5	6	9	8	2	4	7	1	3
2	3	1	7	6	5	4	8	9
4	8	7	9	1	3	2	6	5
1	9	4	3	5	7	8	2	6
8	5	6	4	9	2	1	3	7
7	2	3	6	8	1	5	9	4

Solution to Puzzle 390

2	7	3	8	6	9	1	4	5
4	6	1	3	2	5	8	7	9
8	5	9	4	7	1	2	3	6
7	1	6	9	4	3	5	2	8
3	4	5	2	8	6	7	9	1
9	8	2	1	5	7	3	6	4
5	2	4	6	3	8	9	1	7
6	9	8	7	1	2	4	5	3
1	3	7	5	9	4	6	8	2

Solution to Puzzle 391

3	7	5	1	6	2	4	8	9
8	6	1	4	9	3	5	2	7
2	4	9	7	8	5	1	6	3
4	9	3	8	5	7	6	1	2
7	1	6	2	4	9	8	3	5
5	2	8	3	1	6	7	9	4
6	5	7	9	2	1	3	4	8
1	8	2	5	3	4	9	7	6
9	3	4	6	7	8	2	5	1

Solution to Puzzle 392

8	5	2	7	3	9	1	6	4
7	3	1	2	6	4	8	9	5
4	9	6	5	8	1	7	3	2
6	1	7	9	5	3	4	2	8
9	8	4	6	2	7	3	5	1
5	2	3	4	1	8	9	7	6
1	6	9	8	7	2	5	4	3
3	4	5	1	9	6	2	8	7
2	7	8	3	4	5	6	1	9

Solution to Puzzle 393

8	5	6	1	2	3	7	9	4
9	3	4	6	5	7	2	1	8
7	1	2	9	8	4	3	5	6
5	9	1	2	4	6	8	7	3
6	2	3	7	1	8	5	4	9
4	7	8	5	3	9	1	6	2
3	6	9	8	7	5	4	2	1
2	8	7	4	9	1	6	3	5
1	4	5	3	6	2	9	8	7

Solution to Puzzle 394

4	2	8	5	3	7	1	6	9
7	5	3	9	1	6	2	4	8
1	6	9	4	8	2	5	3	7
9	1	4	3	6	5	8	7	2
6	7	5	8	2	9	3	1	4
3	8	2	1	7	4	6	9	5
2	3	7	6	9	8	4	5	1
5	9	1	2	4	3	7	8	6
8	4	6	7	5	1	9	2	3

Solution to Puzzle 395

9	5	4	6	7	1	8	2	3
7	2	3	8	5	9	4	6	1
8	6	1	2	4	3	7	9	5
6	7	2	1	8	5	9	3	4
3	8	9	4	6	7	1	5	2
1	4	5	9	3	2	6	8	7
4	9	7	5	2	8	3	1	6
2	3	8	7	1	6	5	4	9
5	1	6	3	9	4	2	7	8

Solution to Puzzle 396

6	7	3	9	1	2	4	5	8
1	5	4	8	3	6	7	2	9
2	8	9	4	5	7	3	1	6
9	1	6	2	7	4	5	8	3
7	3	5	1	6	8	2	9	4
8	4	2	3	9	5	1	6	7
5	2	8	7	4	9	6	3	1
3	6	7	5	8	1	9	4	2
4	9	1	6	2	3	8	7	5

Solution to Puzzle 397

9	6	4	7	3	2	1	5	8
8	3	5	1	4	6	2	9	7
2	7	1	8	9	5	4	3	6
1	2	3	6	5	7	8	4	9
6	5	8	4	2	9	7	1	3
4	9	7	3	8	1	6	2	5
5	1	6	9	7	4	3	8	2
3	4	9	2	6	8	5	7	1
7	8	2	5	1	3	9	6	4

Solution to Puzzle 398

4	3	7	5	6	9	8	1	2
8	9	5	7	1	2	3	6	4
1	6	2	3	4	8	5	9	7
3	7	4	8	9	5	6	2	1
9	5	1	4	2	6	7	3	8
6	2	8	1	3	7	4	5	9
5	8	3	2	7	1	9	4	6
7	1	6	9	5	4	2	8	3
2	4	9	6	8	3	1	7	5

Solution to Puzzle 399

9	7	4	3	2	6	1	5	8
8	2	5	7	1	9	4	6	3
1	6	3	5	4	8	7	2	9
4	5	7	6	8	2	9	3	1
6	3	1	9	7	4	5	8	2
2	9	8	1	5	3	6	4	7
3	4	6	2	9	7	8	1	5
5	8	9	4	3	1	2	7	6
7	1	2	8	6	5	3	9	4

Solution to Puzzle 400

6	3	2	8	5	9	4	1	7
5	4	9	1	2	7	8	3	6
1	7	8	4	6	3	5	2	9
2	6	4	9	7	5	3	8	1
7	8	1	6	3	4	9	5	2
3	9	5	2	8	1	7	6	4
8	1	3	7	4	6	2	9	5
4	2	6	5	9	8	1	7	3
9	5	7	3	1	2	6	4	8

Solution to Puzzle 401

3	9	1	4	8	6	2	5	7
2	6	7	1	3	5	4	8	9
4	5	8	9	7	2	1	3	6
8	3	5	7	4	9	6	1	2
1	4	6	2	5	8	9	7	3
7	2	9	3	6	1	5	4	8
5	8	2	6	1	7	3	9	4
6	7	3	5	9	4	8	2	1
9	1	4	8	2	3	7	6	5

Solution to Puzzle 402

2	4	9	8	6	1	7	5	3
6	5	3	2	7	9	8	4	1
8	1	7	4	3	5	6	2	9
9	3	4	1	8	2	5	6	7
7	2	1	6	5	4	9	3	8
5	6	8	7	9	3	2	1	4
1	9	5	3	2	8	4	7	6
3	8	6	5	4	7	1	9	2
4	7	2	9	1	6	3	8	5

Solution to Puzzle 403

1	7	6	4	8	9	3	2	5
5	8	9	7	2	3	1	4	6
4	2	3	6	5	1	8	9	7
3	9	2	8	4	7	5	6	1
8	1	4	5	3	6	2	7	9
6	5	7	9	1	2	4	8	3
9	4	5	3	6	8	7	1	2
7	3	1	2	9	4	6	5	8
2	6	8	1	7	5	9	3	4

Solution to Puzzle 404

2	3	5	1	8	9	4	7	6
7	9	6	4	3	2	5	8	1
4	8	1	7	5	6	3	9	2
6	1	9	8	7	3	2	4	5
5	4	7	6	2	1	8	3	9
8	2	3	5	9	4	6	1	7
9	6	4	2	1	8	7	5	3
3	7	8	9	6	5	1	2	4
1	5	2	3	4	7	9	6	8

Solution to Puzzle 405

5	7	9	1	6	3	4	2	8
1	2	8	5	7	4	3	6	9
4	3	6	2	9	8	1	5	7
2	9	1	8	3	6	7	4	5
7	6	5	9	4	1	2	8	3
8	4	3	7	5	2	9	1	6
6	8	7	4	2	9	5	3	1
3	5	4	6	1	7	8	9	2
9	1	2	3	8	5	6	7	4

Solution to Puzzle 406

1	2	4	7	5	3	6	8	9
3	7	8	9	6	4	2	5	1
5	9	6	8	1	2	3	4	7
6	3	9	5	2	7	8	1	4
8	1	2	3	4	9	7	6	5
7	4	5	6	8	1	9	2	3
4	8	3	1	7	6	5	9	2
2	6	7	4	9	5	1	3	8
9	5	1	2	3	8	4	7	6

Solution to Puzzle 407

1	8	4	6	3	5	7	2	9
6	2	3	7	8	9	1	5	4
9	5	7	2	1	4	8	3	6
3	4	1	8	9	2	6	7	5
7	9	2	3	5	6	4	1	8
8	6	5	1	4	7	2	9	3
4	1	6	5	7	3	9	8	2
5	7	9	4	2	8	3	6	1
2	3	8	9	6	1	5	4	7

Solution to Puzzle 408

4	6	3	2	7	5	1	8	9
9	8	5	6	1	4	7	3	2
2	7	1	9	3	8	5	6	4
8	1	4	5	9	3	6	2	7
6	3	7	1	4	2	9	5	8
5	9	2	7	8	6	3	4	1
3	5	9	8	2	7	4	1	6
1	4	8	3	6	9	2	7	5
7	2	6	4	5	1	8	9	3

Solution to Puzzle 409

5	8	3	1	7	4	6	2	9
2	1	4	5	6	9	7	8	3
9	7	6	2	8	3	4	5	1
4	5	7	8	3	1	9	6	2
3	6	9	4	2	5	8	1	7
8	2	1	6	9	7	5	3	4
7	9	8	3	1	6	2	4	5
6	3	5	7	4	2	1	9	8
1	4	2	9	5	8	3	7	6

Solution to Puzzle 410

8	4	2	6	7	9	3	5	1
3	9	5	8	4	1	6	7	2
1	6	7	3	5	2	8	4	9
6	5	3	2	9	4	7	1	8
7	1	8	5	6	3	9	2	4
9	2	4	1	8	7	5	3	6
5	3	9	4	2	6	1	8	7
2	7	1	9	3	8	4	6	5
4	8	6	7	1	5	2	9	3

Solution to Puzzle 411

4	3	7	5	6	9	8	1	2
8	9	5	7	1	2	3	6	4
1	6	2	3	4	8	5	9	7
3	7	4	8	9	5	6	2	1
9	5	1	4	2	6	7	3	8
6	2	8	1	3	7	4	5	9
5	8	3	2	7	1	9	4	6
7	1	6	9	5	4	2	8	3
2	4	9	6	8	3	1	7	5

Solution to Puzzle 412

1	7	5	8	2	6	9	3	4
8	2	3	9	4	1	5	7	6
9	4	6	5	7	3	8	2	1
4	8	1	7	6	5	2	9	3
3	6	9	1	8	2	7	4	5
7	5	2	3	9	4	6	1	8
2	3	8	6	1	7	4	5	9
5	9	4	2	3	8	1	6	7
6	1	7	4	5	9	3	8	2

Solution to Puzzle 413

4	3	6	9	5	2	8	7	1
8	5	9	7	1	6	2	4	3
2	7	1	4	8	3	9	5	6
1	6	7	3	2	8	5	9	4
9	4	5	1	6	7	3	2	8
3	2	8	5	4	9	6	1	7
7	9	2	6	3	1	4	8	5
5	8	3	2	7	4	1	6	9
6	1	4	8	9	5	7	3	2

Solution to Puzzle 414

6	5	9	4	1	8	2	3	7
8	7	3	2	6	5	1	9	4
1	4	2	9	7	3	6	5	8
5	8	4	7	2	9	3	6	1
2	9	6	3	4	1	7	8	5
3	1	7	5	8	6	9	4	2
7	2	5	6	3	4	8	1	9
9	6	1	8	5	2	4	7	3
4	3	8	1	9	7	5	2	6

Solution to Puzzle 415

3	4	1	7	2	5	6	9	8
6	5	9	3	1	8	2	4	7
7	8	2	9	4	6	5	1	3
2	6	5	8	7	4	9	3	1
9	3	8	2	6	1	4	7	5
1	7	4	5	9	3	8	6	2
5	2	7	4	3	9	1	8	6
8	9	6	1	5	7	3	2	4
4	1	3	6	8	2	7	5	9

Solution to Puzzle 416

6	1	3	5	8	9	2	4	7
5	4	2	7	1	3	9	8	6
7	8	9	2	4	6	5	1	3
4	3	8	9	2	7	6	5	1
2	7	6	4	5	1	8	3	9
9	5	1	6	3	8	4	7	2
1	6	5	8	7	2	3	9	4
8	9	7	3	6	4	1	2	5
3	2	4	1	9	5	7	6	8

Solution to Puzzle 417

1	9	6	7	5	3	8	4	2
4	3	7	8	2	1	6	5	9
8	2	5	6	4	9	1	7	3
3	7	8	9	1	2	4	6	5
9	5	4	3	6	8	7	2	1
2	6	1	4	7	5	9	3	8
6	1	3	5	9	4	2	8	7
7	8	2	1	3	6	5	9	4
5	4	9	2	8	7	3	1	6

Solution to Puzzle 418

6	3	7	4	2	8	1	9	5
9	5	2	1	3	7	4	8	6
4	1	8	5	6	9	2	3	7
7	2	1	8	4	6	3	5	9
3	6	9	2	1	5	8	7	4
8	4	5	7	9	3	6	1	2
5	8	3	6	7	4	9	2	1
2	7	6	9	8	1	5	4	3
1	9	4	3	5	2	7	6	8

Solution to Puzzle 419

9	1	8	3	5	4	7	2	6
3	4	5	6	7	2	1	8	9
2	6	7	1	8	9	3	4	5
1	8	4	7	3	5	9	6	2
5	3	2	9	6	8	4	7	1
7	9	6	2	4	1	5	3	8
6	5	3	8	9	7	2	1	4
8	2	9	4	1	3	6	5	7
4	7	1	5	2	6	8	9	3

Solution to Puzzle 420

1	7	4	2	6	8	5	3	9
5	6	3	4	9	7	2	8	1
2	8	9	5	1	3	4	7	6
3	5	1	7	4	9	6	2	8
8	2	7	6	3	1	9	4	5
4	9	6	8	5	2	3	1	7
7	3	5	1	2	6	8	9	4
9	4	8	3	7	5	1	6	2
6	1	2	9	8	4	7	5	3

Solution to Puzzle 421

8	4	9	2	5	7	6	3	1
3	2	5	1	6	8	7	4	9
7	1	6	3	4	9	5	8	2
5	9	1	7	8	4	3	2	6
4	3	7	9	2	6	8	1	5
2	6	8	5	3	1	4	9	7
6	7	2	4	9	3	1	5	8
1	5	3	8	7	2	9	6	4
9	8	4	6	1	5	2	7	3

Solution to Puzzle 422

1	4	8	9	5	7	2	3	6
9	7	2	1	6	3	5	4	8
5	3	6	2	8	4	1	7	9
4	6	1	7	9	5	8	2	3
2	9	3	8	4	1	7	6	5
7	8	5	3	2	6	9	1	4
6	5	7	4	1	9	3	8	2
8	1	9	6	3	2	4	5	7
3	2	4	5	7	8	6	9	1

Solution to Puzzle 423

8	2	1	6	3	9	5	7	4
4	6	5	8	2	7	1	3	9
9	7	3	1	5	4	2	8	6
1	9	2	3	4	8	7	6	5
3	8	6	7	9	5	4	1	2
7	5	4	2	1	6	3	9	8
2	3	9	4	8	1	6	5	7
5	4	7	9	6	3	8	2	1
6	1	8	5	7	2	9	4	3

Solution to Puzzle 424

1	4	6	7	5	3	9	2	8
2	5	3	4	8	9	7	1	6
9	8	7	1	2	6	5	4	3
6	3	5	2	7	8	1	9	4
7	9	1	3	6	4	2	8	5
4	2	8	9	1	5	6	3	7
5	6	4	8	9	2	3	7	1
3	1	2	5	4	7	8	6	9
8	7	9	6	3	1	4	5	2

Solution to Puzzle 425

9	8	2	6	4	5	1	7	3
7	6	1	9	3	8	5	2	4
3	5	4	1	7	2	6	8	9
4	1	7	2	6	3	8	9	5
2	9	5	4	8	1	7	3	6
8	3	6	5	9	7	2	4	1
1	7	8	3	5	4	9	6	2
5	4	9	7	2	6	3	1	8
6	2	3	8	1	9	4	5	7

Solution to Puzzle 426

7	9	3	8	1	4	6	2	5
8	6	4	5	2	3	7	9	1
1	2	5	7	6	9	4	3	8
4	8	6	3	9	1	5	7	2
3	5	7	2	8	6	1	4	9
2	1	9	4	7	5	3	8	6
6	3	1	9	4	8	2	5	7
9	4	2	6	5	7	8	1	3
5	7	8	1	3	2	9	6	4

Solution to Puzzle 427

1	8	7	2	9	6	4	5	3
9	3	5	7	1	4	2	8	6
6	4	2	5	3	8	7	1	9
2	6	8	4	7	9	1	3	5
4	5	3	6	8	1	9	2	7
7	1	9	3	2	5	8	6	4
8	9	6	1	4	3	5	7	2
5	2	1	9	6	7	3	4	8
3	7	4	8	5	2	6	9	1

Solution to Puzzle 428

8	1	7	2	5	9	4	3	6
3	6	9	8	7	4	5	1	2
4	5	2	6	3	1	9	8	7
2	7	5	9	1	8	3	6	4
9	4	8	3	6	7	2	5	1
1	3	6	5	4	2	8	7	9
6	8	4	1	2	5	7	9	3
7	9	1	4	8	3	6	2	5
5	2	3	7	9	6	1	4	8

Solution to Puzzle 429

2	3	8	5	7	9	1	4	6
1	7	5	3	4	6	8	2	9
6	9	4	8	1	2	3	5	7
9	8	7	1	2	5	4	6	3
5	6	1	4	3	7	2	9	8
4	2	3	6	9	8	5	7	1
7	1	9	2	5	3	6	8	4
3	5	6	7	8	4	9	1	2
8	4	2	9	6	1	7	3	5

Solution to Puzzle 430

8	5	1	6	2	4	7	3	9
9	2	7	1	3	8	5	4	6
4	3	6	9	5	7	8	1	2
5	1	4	3	8	2	6	9	7
6	7	3	4	9	5	2	8	1
2	8	9	7	6	1	3	5	4
1	9	8	5	7	6	4	2	3
7	4	5	2	1	3	9	6	8
3	6	2	8	4	9	1	7	5

Solution to Puzzle 431

5	1	4	2	6	7	3	9	8
3	6	7	9	8	1	2	4	5
2	9	8	4	3	5	6	7	1
1	7	5	3	2	4	9	8	6
9	3	6	5	1	8	7	2	4
4	8	2	6	7	9	5	1	3
8	2	1	7	5	3	4	6	9
7	4	3	8	9	6	1	5	2
6	5	9	1	4	2	8	3	7

Solution to Puzzle 432

1	3	2	4	5	8	7	9	6
4	8	6	7	9	1	5	2	3
7	5	9	3	2	6	1	4	8
5	1	4	8	6	3	2	7	9
6	2	7	5	4	9	8	3	1
3	9	8	1	7	2	4	6	5
9	7	5	6	1	4	3	8	2
2	4	3	9	8	5	6	1	7
8	6	1	2	3	7	9	5	4

Solution to Puzzle 433

9	7	5	8	6	2	4	3	1
3	8	2	4	9	1	7	5	6
6	1	4	3	5	7	9	2	8
2	9	7	5	1	6	3	8	4
1	4	6	7	3	8	5	9	2
5	3	8	9	2	4	1	6	7
4	5	1	6	8	9	2	7	3
8	2	9	1	7	3	6	4	5
7	6	3	2	4	5	8	1	9

Solution to Puzzle 434

9	4	7	2	6	8	1	5	3
8	1	5	4	3	7	6	2	9
2	6	3	9	5	1	4	8	7
1	3	2	7	8	4	5	9	6
6	5	4	3	9	2	8	7	1
7	8	9	6	1	5	2	3	4
3	9	1	5	2	6	7	4	8
5	7	8	1	4	3	9	6	2
4	2	6	8	7	9	3	1	5

Solution to Puzzle 435

6	3	8	9	1	2	4	5	7
1	4	2	5	7	6	9	3	8
7	9	5	3	8	4	1	6	2
5	2	6	8	4	7	3	9	1
4	8	3	1	2	9	6	7	5
9	1	7	6	5	3	8	2	4
3	5	4	2	9	8	7	1	6
8	6	1	7	3	5	2	4	9
2	7	9	4	6	1	5	8	3

Solution to Puzzle 436

2	6	8	7	4	1	5	3	9
4	5	1	3	9	6	8	2	7
3	7	9	8	5	2	6	1	4
6	4	7	5	2	3	1	9	8
1	3	5	6	8	9	7	4	2
9	8	2	4	1	7	3	5	6
5	1	4	2	6	8	9	7	3
8	2	3	9	7	5	4	6	1
7	9	6	1	3	4	2	8	5

Solution to Puzzle 437

1	2	4	7	5	3	6	8	9
3	7	8	9	6	4	2	5	1
5	9	6	8	1	2	3	4	7
6	3	9	5	2	7	8	1	4
8	1	2	3	4	9	7	6	5
7	4	5	6	8	1	9	2	3
4	8	3	1	7	6	5	9	2
2	6	7	4	9	5	1	3	8
9	5	1	2	3	8	4	7	6

Solution to Puzzle 438

8	7	2	4	6	1	5	3	9
9	4	3	5	7	8	6	2	1
5	6	1	3	2	9	4	8	7
2	8	7	6	1	5	9	4	3
3	5	4	7	9	2	1	6	8
6	1	9	8	4	3	7	5	2
4	9	8	2	5	7	3	1	6
1	3	6	9	8	4	2	7	5
7	2	5	1	3	6	8	9	4

Solution to Puzzle 439

1	7	5	8	2	6	9	3	4
8	2	3	9	4	1	5	7	6
9	4	6	5	7	3	8	2	1
4	8	1	7	6	5	2	9	3
3	6	9	1	8	2	7	4	5
7	5	2	3	9	4	6	1	8
2	3	8	6	1	7	4	5	9
5	9	4	2	3	8	1	6	7
6	1	7	4	5	9	3	8	2

Solution to Puzzle 440

6	9	1	5	4	3	2	7	8
8	2	3	9	7	1	5	6	4
7	5	4	2	8	6	9	1	3
1	7	9	3	5	8	4	2	6
5	6	8	1	2	4	3	9	7
3	4	2	6	9	7	8	5	1
2	1	7	4	3	9	6	8	5
4	8	5	7	6	2	1	3	9
9	3	6	8	1	5	7	4	2

Solution to Puzzle 441

5	9	2	3	7	6	4	8	1
3	7	8	1	5	4	2	9	6
1	4	6	2	8	9	3	5	7
2	8	5	4	9	7	1	6	3
9	6	4	5	3	1	7	2	8
7	1	3	8	6	2	9	4	5
8	2	7	6	4	3	5	1	9
4	5	9	7	1	8	6	3	2
6	3	1	9	2	5	8	7	4

Solution to Puzzle 442

3	4	6	5	9	8	2	7	1
5	1	8	2	3	7	9	4	6
2	9	7	6	1	4	3	8	5
8	5	1	4	6	9	7	3	2
9	7	3	8	5	2	1	6	4
4	6	2	3	7	1	5	9	8
7	3	5	1	8	6	4	2	9
6	2	9	7	4	5	8	1	3
1	8	4	9	2	3	6	5	7

Solution to Puzzle 443

2	7	3	8	6	9	1	4	5
4	6	1	3	2	5	8	7	9
8	5	9	4	7	1	2	3	6
7	1	6	9	4	3	5	2	8
3	4	5	2	8	6	7	9	1
9	8	2	1	5	7	3	6	4
5	2	4	6	3	8	9	1	7
6	9	8	7	1	2	4	5	3
1	3	7	5	9	4	6	8	2

Solution to Puzzle 444

8	3	2	6	4	9	5	7	1
6	1	7	8	5	3	9	2	4
9	5	4	7	2	1	3	8	6
5	7	9	1	8	4	6	3	2
3	2	6	9	7	5	1	4	8
1	4	8	3	6	2	7	5	9
2	8	1	5	9	7	4	6	3
7	6	3	4	1	8	2	9	5
4	9	5	2	3	6	8	1	7

Solution to Puzzle 445

8	7	2	6	4	9	3	1	5
1	3	4	2	5	8	9	6	7
6	5	9	1	3	7	4	8	2
5	9	6	8	2	4	7	3	1
3	1	7	9	6	5	2	4	8
4	2	8	7	1	3	5	9	6
2	6	3	5	9	1	8	7	4
7	4	5	3	8	6	1	2	9
9	8	1	4	7	2	6	5	3

Solution to Puzzle 446

1	2	4	7	5	3	6	8	9
3	7	8	9	6	4	2	5	1
5	9	6	8	1	2	3	4	7
6	3	9	5	2	7	8	1	4
8	1	2	3	4	9	7	6	5
7	4	5	6	8	1	9	2	3
4	8	3	1	7	6	5	9	2
2	6	7	4	9	5	1	3	8
9	5	1	2	3	8	4	7	6

Solution to Puzzle 447

4	8	5	3	1	9	2	6	7
2	9	3	7	5	6	1	8	4
1	6	7	8	2	4	3	9	5
9	4	8	2	6	7	5	1	3
3	1	2	5	9	8	7	4	6
5	7	6	1	4	3	9	2	8
7	3	4	9	8	2	6	5	1
6	5	9	4	7	1	8	3	2
8	2	1	6	3	5	4	7	9

Solution to Puzzle 448

5	3	2	7	8	6	9	1	4
1	7	9	3	4	5	8	6	2
4	8	6	9	2	1	3	5	7
2	1	7	6	9	3	5	4	8
8	9	5	4	1	2	7	3	6
3	6	4	5	7	8	1	2	9
9	5	1	2	6	7	4	8	3
6	4	3	8	5	9	2	7	1
7	2	8	1	3	4	6	9	5

Solution to Puzzle 449

3	1	7	4	8	9	2	6	5
2	5	8	3	1	6	7	4	9
9	6	4	7	2	5	3	1	8
4	2	1	9	5	7	8	3	6
5	7	3	1	6	8	9	2	4
8	9	6	2	4	3	5	7	1
1	8	9	6	7	2	4	5	3
7	4	5	8	3	1	6	9	2
6	3	2	5	9	4	1	8	7

Solution to Puzzle 450

1	2	4	7	5	3	6	8	9
3	7	8	9	6	4	2	5	1
5	9	6	8	1	2	3	4	7
6	3	9	5	2	7	8	1	4
8	1	2	3	4	9	7	6	5
7	4	5	6	8	1	9	2	3
4	8	3	1	7	6	5	9	2
2	6	7	4	9	5	1	3	8
9	5	1	2	3	8	4	7	6

Solution to Puzzle 451

9	4	7	2	6	8	1	5	3
8	1	5	4	3	7	6	2	9
2	6	3	9	5	1	4	8	7
1	3	2	7	8	4	5	9	6
6	5	4	3	9	2	8	7	1
7	8	9	6	1	5	2	3	4
3	9	1	5	2	6	7	4	8
5	7	8	1	4	3	9	6	2
4	2	6	8	7	9	3	1	5

Solution to Puzzle 452

4	3	7	5	8	6	9	2	1
8	5	2	7	1	9	4	6	3
9	1	6	3	4	2	8	7	5
5	6	9	4	7	8	3	1	2
3	7	4	2	9	1	5	8	6
2	8	1	6	5	3	7	4	9
1	4	5	9	2	7	6	3	8
7	2	3	8	6	5	1	9	4
6	9	8	1	3	4	2	5	7

Solution to Puzzle 453

2	3	8	5	7	9	1	4	6
1	7	5	3	4	6	8	2	9
6	9	4	8	1	2	3	5	7
9	8	7	1	2	5	4	6	3
5	6	1	4	3	7	2	9	8
4	2	3	6	9	8	5	7	1
7	1	9	2	5	3	6	8	4
3	5	6	7	8	4	9	1	2
8	4	2	9	6	1	7	3	5

Solution to Puzzle 454

4	2	5	7	3	1	6	9	8
8	7	1	9	4	6	3	2	5
3	9	6	5	2	8	4	1	7
6	3	4	1	8	5	9	7	2
2	8	7	4	6	9	5	3	1
5	1	9	2	7	3	8	6	4
1	4	8	6	9	2	7	5	3
9	5	3	8	1	7	2	4	6
7	6	2	3	5	4	1	8	9

Solution to Puzzle 455

6	5	1	8	3	4	7	2	9
3	8	7	6	2	9	5	4	1
4	9	2	5	1	7	3	8	6
1	2	4	9	8	3	6	5	7
8	6	3	7	5	1	2	9	4
9	7	5	4	6	2	8	1	3
2	3	9	1	7	5	4	6	8
7	1	8	2	4	6	9	3	5
5	4	6	3	9	8	1	7	2

Solution to Puzzle 456

4	6	8	1	2	9	5	7	3
5	1	2	7	6	3	4	8	9
3	7	9	8	4	5	6	1	2
1	3	4	2	5	7	8	9	6
6	8	7	4	9	1	3	2	5
2	9	5	6	3	8	7	4	1
8	4	3	5	1	2	9	6	7
9	2	6	3	7	4	1	5	8
7	5	1	9	8	6	2	3	4

Solution to Puzzle 457

4	1	3	6	7	8	2	5	9
6	8	2	9	3	5	7	4	1
7	5	9	4	2	1	6	3	8
3	9	4	5	1	6	8	2	7
1	7	5	8	9	2	4	6	3
8	2	6	3	4	7	9	1	5
9	3	7	1	6	4	5	8	2
5	6	1	2	8	9	3	7	4
2	4	8	7	5	3	1	9	6

Solution to Puzzle 458

9	5	4	6	7	1	8	2	3
7	2	3	8	5	9	4	6	1
8	6	1	2	4	3	7	9	5
6	7	2	1	8	5	9	3	4
3	8	9	4	6	7	1	5	2
1	4	5	9	3	2	6	8	7
4	9	7	5	2	8	3	1	6
2	3	8	7	1	6	5	4	9
5	1	6	3	9	4	2	7	8

Solution to Puzzle 459

1	2	4	7	5	3	6	8	9
3	7	8	9	6	4	2	5	1
5	9	6	8	1	2	3	4	7
6	3	9	5	2	7	8	1	4
8	1	2	3	4	9	7	6	5
7	4	5	6	8	1	9	2	3
4	8	3	1	7	6	5	9	2
2	6	7	4	9	5	1	3	8
9	5	1	2	3	8	4	7	6

Solution to Puzzle 460

5	4	1	8	6	7	9	3	2
2	7	8	9	3	1	6	4	5
6	9	3	4	2	5	8	1	7
7	8	9	3	4	2	5	6	1
3	5	2	6	1	8	7	9	4
1	6	4	7	5	9	2	8	3
8	2	6	1	7	3	4	5	9
4	1	5	2	9	6	3	7	8
9	3	7	5	8	4	1	2	6

Solution to Puzzle 461

2	1	8	4	5	9	7	3	6
4	3	7	8	2	6	1	5	9
6	9	5	1	3	7	2	8	4
1	8	2	9	7	3	6	4	5
3	6	4	5	8	1	9	2	7
7	5	9	6	4	2	8	1	3
5	4	1	7	6	8	3	9	2
9	2	6	3	1	4	5	7	8
8	7	3	2	9	5	4	6	1

Solution to Puzzle 462

1	2	4	7	5	3	6	8	9
3	7	8	9	6	4	2	5	1
5	9	6	8	1	2	3	4	7
6	3	9	5	2	7	8	1	4
8	1	2	3	4	9	7	6	5
7	4	5	6	8	1	9	2	3
4	8	3	1	7	6	5	9	2
2	6	7	4	9	5	1	3	8
9	5	1	2	3	8	4	7	6

Solution to Puzzle 463

2	5	1	6	3	7	8	4	9
8	7	6	4	9	5	2	1	3
9	4	3	1	2	8	6	7	5
4	2	8	9	5	1	3	6	7
6	1	9	3	7	4	5	8	2
5	3	7	8	6	2	4	9	1
3	8	5	7	1	6	9	2	4
7	9	4	2	8	3	1	5	6
1	6	2	5	4	9	7	3	8

Solution to Puzzle 464

1	6	8	5	3	2	4	7	9
7	2	3	4	9	1	6	8	5
4	9	5	6	8	7	2	3	1
8	1	2	9	4	3	7	5	6
5	3	7	8	1	6	9	2	4
9	4	6	2	7	5	3	1	8
2	5	1	3	6	4	8	9	7
3	8	4	7	5	9	1	6	2
6	7	9	1	2	8	5	4	3

Solution to Puzzle 465

6	9	8	3	4	5	1	7	2
3	5	7	9	1	2	6	8	4
2	4	1	7	8	6	3	9	5
8	1	2	5	9	7	4	3	6
5	7	4	6	3	1	9	2	8
9	3	6	8	2	4	5	1	7
1	6	5	2	7	3	8	4	9
4	2	9	1	6	8	7	5	3
7	8	3	4	5	9	2	6	1

Solution to Puzzle 466

3	6	8	1	9	2	4	7	5
2	7	1	3	5	4	8	6	9
9	4	5	8	6	7	3	1	2
5	8	2	9	7	6	1	3	4
4	3	6	2	1	8	9	5	7
1	9	7	4	3	5	6	2	8
6	2	9	5	8	1	7	4	3
7	5	3	6	4	9	2	8	1
8	1	4	7	2	3	5	9	6

Solution to Puzzle 467

3	9	1	4	8	6	2	5	7
2	6	7	1	3	5	4	8	9
4	5	8	9	7	2	1	3	6
8	3	5	7	4	9	6	1	2
1	4	6	2	5	8	9	7	3
7	2	9	3	6	1	5	4	8
5	8	2	6	1	7	3	9	4
6	7	3	5	9	4	8	2	1
9	1	4	8	2	3	7	6	5

Solution to Puzzle 468

8	7	2	6	4	9	3	1	5
1	3	4	2	5	8	9	6	7
6	5	9	1	3	7	4	8	2
5	9	6	8	2	4	7	3	1
3	1	7	9	6	5	2	4	8
4	2	8	7	1	3	5	9	6
2	6	3	5	9	1	8	7	4
7	4	5	3	8	6	1	2	9
9	8	1	4	7	2	6	5	3

Solution to Puzzle 469

4	8	1	9	2	6	5	7	3
2	7	6	5	3	4	8	9	1
5	9	3	1	7	8	6	4	2
8	2	7	3	6	1	9	5	4
1	4	5	2	8	9	7	3	6
6	3	9	4	5	7	1	2	8
7	5	4	6	1	2	3	8	9
9	6	8	7	4	3	2	1	5
3	1	2	8	9	5	4	6	7

Solution to Puzzle 470

9	7	4	3	2	6	1	5	8
8	2	5	7	1	9	4	6	3
1	6	3	5	4	8	7	2	9
4	5	7	6	8	2	9	3	1
6	3	1	9	7	4	5	8	2
2	9	8	1	5	3	6	4	7
3	4	6	2	9	7	8	1	5
5	8	9	4	3	1	2	7	6
7	1	2	8	6	5	3	9	4

Solution to Puzzle 471

6	5	7	3	8	1	2	4	9
4	1	3	9	2	6	5	7	8
2	9	8	7	5	4	6	1	3
1	8	6	2	3	9	4	5	7
5	3	4	6	7	8	1	9	2
7	2	9	1	4	5	3	8	6
8	7	1	4	6	3	9	2	5
3	4	5	8	9	2	7	6	1
9	6	2	5	1	7	8	3	4

Solution to Puzzle 472

6	7	9	8	5	2	1	3	4
3	8	1	4	6	9	7	2	5
2	4	5	1	3	7	8	6	9
7	9	3	5	2	1	4	8	6
1	5	4	6	8	3	9	7	2
8	6	2	9	7	4	5	1	3
4	2	7	3	1	5	6	9	8
9	1	6	2	4	8	3	5	7
5	3	8	7	9	6	2	4	1

Solution to Puzzle 473

3	2	4	8	9	1	6	5	7
6	9	7	2	3	5	4	1	8
5	1	8	4	6	7	3	9	2
1	4	6	7	2	8	5	3	9
7	3	9	6	5	4	2	8	1
8	5	2	3	1	9	7	6	4
4	8	5	9	7	6	1	2	3
9	6	3	1	4	2	8	7	5
2	7	1	5	8	3	9	4	6

Solution to Puzzle 474

6	7	1	2	9	5	3	8	4
2	9	4	8	3	6	5	7	1
8	3	5	4	7	1	9	6	2
3	8	9	5	2	7	1	4	6
5	2	7	1	6	4	8	9	3
4	1	6	3	8	9	2	5	7
9	6	2	7	5	3	4	1	8
7	4	3	9	1	8	6	2	5
1	5	8	6	4	2	7	3	9

Solution to Puzzle 475

3	4	1	7	2	5	6	9	8
6	5	9	3	1	8	2	4	7
7	8	2	9	4	6	5	1	3
2	6	5	8	7	4	9	3	1
9	3	8	2	6	1	4	7	5
1	7	4	5	9	3	8	6	2
5	2	7	4	3	9	1	8	6
8	9	6	1	5	7	3	2	4
4	1	3	6	8	2	7	5	9

Solution to Puzzle 476

1	5	2	4	8	9	3	7	6
7	6	8	2	5	3	4	1	9
9	3	4	6	1	7	2	8	5
4	7	1	9	2	6	5	3	8
8	9	3	7	4	5	6	2	1
6	2	5	8	3	1	9	4	7
2	8	6	5	7	4	1	9	3
5	1	7	3	9	2	8	6	4
3	4	9	1	6	8	7	5	2

Solution to Puzzle 477

3	9	4	7	8	1	5	6	2
2	5	8	3	6	4	9	7	1
7	1	6	2	9	5	8	4	3
4	3	7	8	5	6	1	2	9
9	6	5	1	2	7	3	8	4
8	2	1	4	3	9	7	5	6
6	8	2	9	7	3	4	1	5
1	7	3	5	4	2	6	9	8
5	4	9	6	1	8	2	3	7

Solution to Puzzle 478

8	2	5	3	4	9	7	6	1
9	1	3	8	6	7	2	4	5
6	7	4	5	1	2	8	9	3
5	3	1	6	9	8	4	7	2
7	8	2	4	3	5	9	1	6
4	6	9	2	7	1	3	5	8
1	4	6	7	2	3	5	8	9
3	5	7	9	8	6	1	2	4
2	9	8	1	5	4	6	3	7

Solution to Puzzle 479

1	3	2	4	5	8	7	9	6
4	8	6	7	9	1	5	2	3
7	5	9	3	2	6	1	4	8
5	1	4	8	6	3	2	7	9
6	2	7	5	4	9	8	3	1
3	9	8	1	7	2	4	6	5
9	7	5	6	1	4	3	8	2
2	4	3	9	8	5	6	1	7
8	6	1	2	3	7	9	5	4

Solution to Puzzle 480

8	5	1	4	7	6	2	3	9
9	7	2	8	1	3	5	4	6
3	6	4	2	9	5	7	1	8
5	2	3	9	6	1	4	8	7
1	8	6	7	4	2	3	9	5
7	4	9	5	3	8	1	6	2
4	9	5	1	8	7	6	2	3
6	1	7	3	2	9	8	5	4
2	3	8	6	5	4	9	7	1

Solution to Puzzle 481

3	4	8	6	1	5	7	2	9
9	5	1	8	2	7	4	3	6
2	7	6	9	3	4	1	5	8
6	8	2	4	5	9	3	7	1
7	1	4	3	6	8	2	9	5
5	9	3	2	7	1	6	8	4
4	3	9	1	8	2	5	6	7
8	2	5	7	4	6	9	1	3
1	6	7	5	9	3	8	4	2

Solution to Puzzle 482

1	9	7	6	4	2	5	3	8
3	2	8	1	5	7	9	6	4
6	5	4	3	8	9	2	1	7
7	4	6	9	3	5	8	2	1
5	1	9	4	2	8	6	7	3
2	8	3	7	1	6	4	5	9
8	7	2	5	9	3	1	4	6
9	3	1	2	6	4	7	8	5
4	6	5	8	7	1	3	9	2

Solution to Puzzle 483

9	5	2	8	7	4	1	3	6
4	6	3	2	5	1	8	9	7
1	7	8	9	3	6	5	4	2
5	2	7	4	1	9	6	8	3
3	8	4	7	6	5	2	1	9
6	9	1	3	2	8	7	5	4
2	3	9	1	8	7	4	6	5
8	4	6	5	9	2	3	7	1
7	1	5	6	4	3	9	2	8

Solution to Puzzle 484

3	6	2	7	4	1	9	8	5
9	7	4	2	8	5	6	1	3
1	8	5	9	3	6	2	4	7
7	1	3	4	6	9	5	2	8
8	4	6	5	1	2	3	7	9
5	2	9	8	7	3	1	6	4
6	5	8	3	2	4	7	9	1
2	3	7	1	9	8	4	5	6
4	9	1	6	5	7	8	3	2

Solution to Puzzle 485

1	2	4	7	5	3	6	8	9
3	7	8	9	6	4	2	5	1
5	9	6	8	1	2	3	4	7
6	3	9	5	2	7	8	1	4
8	1	2	3	4	9	7	6	5
7	4	5	6	8	1	9	2	3
4	8	3	1	7	6	5	9	2
2	6	7	4	9	5	1	3	8
9	5	1	2	3	8	4	7	6

Solution to Puzzle 486

1	2	4	7	5	3	6	8	9
3	7	8	9	6	4	2	5	1
5	9	6	8	1	2	3	4	7
6	3	9	5	2	7	8	1	4
8	1	2	3	4	9	7	6	5
7	4	5	6	8	1	9	2	3
4	8	3	1	7	6	5	9	2
2	6	7	4	9	5	1	3	8
9	5	1	2	3	8	4	7	6

Solution to Puzzle 487

6	7	4	3	8	2	9	5	1
8	2	5	1	9	7	4	3	6
3	9	1	5	6	4	7	2	8
9	4	6	8	3	5	2	1	7
2	3	8	6	7	1	5	4	9
5	1	7	2	4	9	8	6	3
1	8	9	4	2	6	3	7	5
7	5	2	9	1	3	6	8	4
4	6	3	7	5	8	1	9	2

Solution to Puzzle 488

9	6	3	7	1	5	4	8	2
1	8	7	4	3	2	5	9	6
5	2	4	6	9	8	3	1	7
7	9	1	8	2	4	6	5	3
2	4	6	9	5	3	8	7	1
8	3	5	1	7	6	2	4	9
4	1	2	5	6	9	7	3	8
6	7	8	3	4	1	9	2	5
3	5	9	2	8	7	1	6	4

Solution to Puzzle 489

1	3	2	9	5	4	7	6	8
6	9	5	2	8	7	3	1	4
7	8	4	6	3	1	9	5	2
4	5	9	7	2	8	6	3	1
3	1	8	4	6	5	2	9	7
2	7	6	3	1	9	8	4	5
8	4	7	5	9	3	1	2	6
9	6	1	8	4	2	5	7	3
5	2	3	1	7	6	4	8	9

Solution to Puzzle 490

1	2	4	7	5	3	6	8	9
3	7	8	9	6	4	2	5	1
5	9	6	8	1	2	3	4	7
6	3	9	5	2	7	8	1	4
8	1	2	3	4	9	7	6	5
7	4	5	6	8	1	9	2	3
4	8	3	1	7	6	5	9	2
2	6	7	4	9	5	1	3	8
9	5	1	2	3	8	4	7	6

Solution to Puzzle 491

8	4	2	6	7	9	3	5	1
3	9	5	8	4	1	6	7	2
1	6	7	3	5	2	8	4	9
6	5	3	2	9	4	7	1	8
7	1	8	5	6	3	9	2	4
9	2	4	1	8	7	5	3	6
5	3	9	4	2	6	1	8	7
2	7	1	9	3	8	4	6	5
4	8	6	7	1	5	2	9	3

Solution to Puzzle 492

5	2	4	9	3	1	7	8	6
9	6	7	4	8	5	2	3	1
8	3	1	7	6	2	9	5	4
6	5	9	1	2	8	4	7	3
1	4	8	3	7	6	5	2	9
2	7	3	5	4	9	1	6	8
4	9	6	8	5	7	3	1	2
7	1	2	6	9	3	8	4	5
3	8	5	2	1	4	6	9	7

Solution to Puzzle 493

9	1	4	2	6	8	3	5	7
5	6	8	7	3	1	4	2	9
7	2	3	4	9	5	6	8	1
3	7	1	9	5	6	8	4	2
8	5	2	3	4	7	9	1	6
4	9	6	1	8	2	7	3	5
6	4	9	5	1	3	2	7	8
1	8	7	6	2	4	5	9	3
2	3	5	8	7	9	1	6	4

Solution to Puzzle 494

8	2	3	7	6	1	4	5	9
7	4	5	2	9	3	6	8	1
6	1	9	5	4	8	2	7	3
2	5	1	9	7	6	8	3	4
4	3	6	1	8	2	5	9	7
9	8	7	4	3	5	1	2	6
1	9	2	3	5	4	7	6	8
3	6	4	8	2	7	9	1	5
5	7	8	6	1	9	3	4	2

Solution to Puzzle 495

5	3	9	8	2	7	1	6	4
2	7	1	4	3	6	8	9	5
6	4	8	1	9	5	2	3	7
4	6	7	5	1	3	9	8	2
1	8	2	9	7	4	3	5	6
3	9	5	2	6	8	7	4	1
7	5	4	3	8	2	6	1	9
9	2	3	6	5	1	4	7	8
8	1	6	7	4	9	5	2	3

Solution to Puzzle 496

1	2	4	7	5	3	6	8	9
3	7	8	9	6	4	2	5	1
5	9	6	8	1	2	3	4	7
6	3	9	5	2	7	8	1	4
8	1	2	3	4	9	7	6	5
7	4	5	6	8	1	9	2	3
4	8	3	1	7	6	5	9	2
2	6	7	4	9	5	1	3	8
9	5	1	2	3	8	4	7	6

Solution to Puzzle 497

7	8	3	2	1	6	5	9	4
2	1	4	9	5	8	3	7	6
6	9	5	7	4	3	2	8	1
9	2	7	6	8	1	4	3	5
1	3	6	5	7	4	9	2	8
5	4	8	3	2	9	1	6	7
4	5	2	8	3	7	6	1	9
3	7	9	1	6	5	8	4	2
8	6	1	4	9	2	7	5	3

Solution to Puzzle 498

6	7	4	8	5	3	9	2	1
2	9	3	7	4	1	8	6	5
8	5	1	6	2	9	3	4	7
4	3	6	9	1	8	5	7	2
9	8	2	5	6	7	4	1	3
5	1	7	2	3	4	6	8	9
3	2	9	4	7	6	1	5	8
7	4	8	1	9	5	2	3	6
1	6	5	3	8	2	7	9	4

Solution to Puzzle 499

9	5	4	6	7	1	8	2	3
7	2	3	8	5	9	4	6	1
8	6	1	2	4	3	7	9	5
6	7	2	1	8	5	9	3	4
3	8	9	4	6	7	1	5	2
1	4	5	9	3	2	6	8	7
4	9	7	5	2	8	3	1	6
2	3	8	7	1	6	5	4	9
5	1	6	3	9	4	2	7	8

Solution to Puzzle 500

9	8	4	7	6	2	5	3	1
3	1	6	8	5	4	2	7	9
5	7	2	1	9	3	8	6	4
1	3	8	2	7	5	4	9	6
4	6	5	9	3	8	1	2	7
2	9	7	6	4	1	3	8	5
6	2	3	4	1	9	7	5	8
7	5	1	3	8	6	9	4	2
8	4	9	5	2	7	6	1	3

Solution to Puzzle 501

3	9	4	7	8	1	5	6	2
2	5	8	3	6	4	9	7	1
7	1	6	2	9	5	8	4	3
4	3	7	8	5	6	1	2	9
9	6	5	1	2	7	3	8	4
8	2	1	4	3	9	7	5	6
6	8	2	9	7	3	4	1	5
1	7	3	5	4	2	6	9	8
5	4	9	6	1	8	2	3	7

Solution to Puzzle 502

4	2	1	8	3	9	6	7	5
6	3	7	1	5	2	9	8	4
5	8	9	6	7	4	3	1	2
7	9	8	3	1	5	2	4	6
3	4	2	9	6	7	8	5	1
1	5	6	2	4	8	7	3	9
8	1	3	4	2	6	5	9	7
2	7	4	5	9	3	1	6	8
9	6	5	7	8	1	4	2	3

Solution to Puzzle 503

4	8	2	5	7	3	6	9	1
1	5	3	2	6	9	4	7	8
9	7	6	8	1	4	3	5	2
6	1	4	3	9	7	8	2	5
7	3	5	1	8	2	9	6	4
8	2	9	4	5	6	7	1	3
5	6	1	9	3	8	2	4	7
3	4	7	6	2	5	1	8	9
2	9	8	7	4	1	5	3	6

Solution to Puzzle 504

2	7	8	6	9	3	5	4	1
4	3	9	5	7	1	8	2	6
1	5	6	4	2	8	3	9	7
9	2	3	1	5	7	6	8	4
8	4	7	3	6	2	1	5	9
6	1	5	8	4	9	2	7	3
7	6	1	2	8	4	9	3	5
5	9	2	7	3	6	4	1	8
3	8	4	9	1	5	7	6	2

Solution to Puzzle 505

3	2	4	8	9	1	6	5	7
6	9	7	2	3	5	4	1	8
5	1	8	4	6	7	3	9	2
1	4	6	7	2	8	5	3	9
7	3	9	6	5	4	2	8	1
8	5	2	3	1	9	7	6	4
4	8	5	9	7	6	1	2	3
9	6	3	1	4	2	8	7	5
2	7	1	5	8	3	9	4	6

Solution to Puzzle 506

2	7	8	6	9	3	5	4	1
4	3	9	5	7	1	8	2	6
1	5	6	4	2	8	3	9	7
9	2	3	1	5	7	6	8	4
8	4	7	3	6	2	1	5	9
6	1	5	8	4	9	2	7	3
7	6	1	2	8	4	9	3	5
5	9	2	7	3	6	4	1	8
3	8	4	9	1	5	7	6	2

Solution to Puzzle 507

9	4	1	5	2	7	3	6	8
2	6	3	1	8	9	7	5	4
5	8	7	6	3	4	9	2	1
4	3	2	8	9	6	1	7	5
1	9	6	7	4	5	8	3	2
7	5	8	3	1	2	4	9	6
8	1	5	2	7	3	6	4	9
6	7	4	9	5	8	2	1	3
3	2	9	4	6	1	5	8	7

Solution to Puzzle 508

9	1	2	7	6	3	5	8	4
7	5	8	4	1	9	6	3	2
3	6	4	2	5	8	7	1	9
4	2	5	3	9	7	1	6	8
1	9	3	8	4	6	2	5	7
8	7	6	5	2	1	9	4	3
6	8	1	9	7	4	3	2	5
2	4	9	1	3	5	8	7	6
5	3	7	6	8	2	4	9	1

Solution to Puzzle 509

7	1	6	4	3	8	2	5	9
4	2	8	6	9	5	7	3	1
3	5	9	2	7	1	8	6	4
8	7	3	9	4	2	5	1	6
6	4	1	8	5	3	9	7	2
2	9	5	1	6	7	4	8	3
9	8	7	3	2	6	1	4	5
1	3	2	5	8	4	6	9	7
5	6	4	7	1	9	3	2	8

Solution to Puzzle 510

8	2	9	5	1	7	3	6	4
1	5	3	6	4	2	9	8	7
7	4	6	9	8	3	1	5	2
9	7	5	2	3	1	8	4	6
2	8	1	4	9	6	7	3	5
3	6	4	7	5	8	2	1	9
4	1	2	8	6	9	5	7	3
6	9	8	3	7	5	4	2	1
5	3	7	1	2	4	6	9	8

Solution to Puzzle 511

2	3	5	1	8	9	4	7	6
7	9	6	4	3	2	5	8	1
4	8	1	7	5	6	3	9	2
6	1	9	8	7	3	2	4	5
5	4	7	6	2	1	8	3	9
8	2	3	5	9	4	6	1	7
9	6	4	2	1	8	7	5	3
3	7	8	9	6	5	1	2	4
1	5	2	3	4	7	9	6	8

Solution to Puzzle 512

1	8	7	6	5	3	4	9	2
6	2	9	7	4	8	1	3	5
3	5	4	9	1	2	7	6	8
9	7	3	5	8	1	2	4	6
4	1	8	2	3	6	5	7	9
5	6	2	4	9	7	8	1	3
7	4	5	3	2	9	6	8	1
2	9	1	8	6	4	3	5	7
8	3	6	1	7	5	9	2	4

Solution to Puzzle 513

6	9	8	3	4	5	1	7	2
3	5	7	9	1	2	6	8	4
2	4	1	7	8	6	3	9	5
8	1	2	5	9	7	4	3	6
5	7	4	6	3	1	9	2	8
9	3	6	8	2	4	5	1	7
1	6	5	2	7	3	8	4	9
4	2	9	1	6	8	7	5	3
7	8	3	4	5	9	2	6	1

Solution to Puzzle 514

9	7	5	3	8	1	2	4	6
4	2	8	6	9	5	1	3	7
6	1	3	4	7	2	9	5	8
2	5	4	7	6	8	3	1	9
7	3	6	5	1	9	8	2	4
8	9	1	2	4	3	6	7	5
3	6	9	1	5	4	7	8	2
1	4	7	8	2	6	5	9	3
5	8	2	9	3	7	4	6	1

Solution to Puzzle 515

1	5	2	4	8	9	3	7	6
7	6	8	2	5	3	4	1	9
9	3	4	6	1	7	2	8	5
4	7	1	9	2	6	5	3	8
8	9	3	7	4	5	6	2	1
6	2	5	8	3	1	9	4	7
2	8	6	5	7	4	1	9	3
5	1	7	3	9	2	8	6	4
3	4	9	1	6	8	7	5	2

Solution to Puzzle 516

2	8	1	9	5	4	6	7	3
3	4	6	7	8	1	2	9	5
9	5	7	3	6	2	4	8	1
4	2	3	1	9	6	8	5	7
8	7	5	4	2	3	1	6	9
1	6	9	5	7	8	3	2	4
5	3	8	2	1	9	7	4	6
7	1	2	6	4	5	9	3	8
6	9	4	8	3	7	5	1	2

Solution to Puzzle 517

6	7	3	9	1	2	4	8	5
9	1	4	3	8	5	2	6	7
8	2	5	6	7	4	9	3	1
2	4	7	8	5	9	6	1	3
3	9	1	2	6	7	8	5	4
5	8	6	4	3	1	7	9	2
7	6	9	1	4	3	5	2	8
1	5	2	7	9	8	3	4	6
4	3	8	5	2	6	1	7	9

Solution to Puzzle 518

1	4	8	9	5	7	2	3	6
9	7	2	1	6	3	5	4	8
5	3	6	2	8	4	1	7	9
4	6	1	7	9	5	8	2	3
2	9	3	8	4	1	7	6	5
7	8	5	3	2	6	9	1	4
6	5	7	4	1	9	3	8	2
8	1	9	6	3	2	4	5	7
3	2	4	5	7	8	6	9	1

Solution to Puzzle 519

9	6	3	7	1	5	4	8	2
1	8	7	4	3	2	5	9	6
5	2	4	6	9	8	3	1	7
7	9	1	8	2	4	6	5	3
2	4	6	9	5	3	8	7	1
8	3	5	1	7	6	2	4	9
4	1	2	5	6	9	7	3	8
6	7	8	3	4	1	9	2	5
3	5	9	2	8	7	1	6	4

Solution to Puzzle 520

5	8	3	1	7	4	6	2	9
2	1	4	5	6	9	7	8	3
9	7	6	2	8	3	4	5	1
4	5	7	8	3	1	9	6	2
3	6	9	4	2	5	8	1	7
8	2	1	6	9	7	5	3	4
7	9	8	3	1	6	2	4	5
6	3	5	7	4	2	1	9	8
1	4	2	9	5	8	3	7	6

Solution to Puzzle 521

1	5	2	4	8	9	3	7	6
7	6	8	2	5	3	4	1	9
9	3	4	6	1	7	2	8	5
4	7	1	9	2	6	5	3	8
8	9	3	7	4	5	6	2	1
6	2	5	8	3	1	9	4	7
2	8	6	5	7	4	1	9	3
5	1	7	3	9	2	8	6	4
3	4	9	1	6	8	7	5	2

Solution to Puzzle 522

2	8	3	5	7	4	1	6	9
6	4	7	9	8	1	3	2	5
5	1	9	2	6	3	8	4	7
8	2	5	7	3	9	4	1	6
9	6	4	1	2	5	7	3	8
7	3	1	8	4	6	5	9	2
3	9	6	4	5	8	2	7	1
1	5	2	3	9	7	6	8	4
4	7	8	6	1	2	9	5	3

Solution to Puzzle 523

7	5	9	2	6	1	3	4	8
4	2	8	7	5	3	1	6	9
3	6	1	4	9	8	5	7	2
2	3	6	9	7	5	8	1	4
8	1	5	3	4	2	6	9	7
9	7	4	8	1	6	2	5	3
6	4	2	5	3	9	7	8	1
5	8	7	1	2	4	9	3	6
1	9	3	6	8	7	4	2	5

Solution to Puzzle 524

5	3	9	8	2	7	1	6	4
2	7	1	4	3	6	8	9	5
6	4	8	1	9	5	2	3	7
4	6	7	5	1	3	9	8	2
1	8	2	9	7	4	3	5	6
3	9	5	2	6	8	7	4	1
7	5	4	3	8	2	6	1	9
9	2	3	6	5	1	4	7	8
8	1	6	7	4	9	5	2	3

Solution to Puzzle 525

4	5	7	3	1	6	9	8	2
1	6	2	8	9	4	7	3	5
8	9	3	7	2	5	4	6	1
3	7	5	6	4	2	8	1	9
2	1	8	9	3	7	6	5	4
6	4	9	5	8	1	3	2	7
7	8	1	4	5	3	2	9	6
5	3	4	2	6	9	1	7	8
9	2	6	1	7	8	5	4	3

Solution to Puzzle 526

7	6	1	3	5	8	9	4	2
2	3	9	4	1	7	5	6	8
8	5	4	2	6	9	3	7	1
6	2	8	9	4	3	7	1	5
3	1	5	7	8	6	4	2	9
9	4	7	5	2	1	6	8	3
1	7	2	6	9	5	8	3	4
4	9	3	8	7	2	1	5	6
5	8	6	1	3	4	2	9	7

Solution to Puzzle 527

2	9	6	8	7	5	3	4	1
3	1	7	9	2	4	8	6	5
5	4	8	3	1	6	9	7	2
6	3	1	4	5	9	2	8	7
9	8	2	7	6	1	5	3	4
7	5	4	2	8	3	6	1	9
1	2	3	6	9	7	4	5	8
4	7	9	5	3	8	1	2	6
8	6	5	1	4	2	7	9	3

Solution to Puzzle 528

3	4	1	7	2	5	6	9	8
6	5	9	3	1	8	2	4	7
7	8	2	9	4	6	5	1	3
2	6	5	8	7	4	9	3	1
9	3	8	2	6	1	4	7	5
1	7	4	5	9	3	8	6	2
5	2	7	4	3	9	1	8	6
8	9	6	1	5	7	3	2	4
4	1	3	6	8	2	7	5	9

Solution to Puzzle 529

4	2	5	7	3	1	6	9	8
8	7	1	9	4	6	3	2	5
3	9	6	5	2	8	4	1	7
6	3	4	1	8	5	9	7	2
2	8	7	4	6	9	5	3	1
5	1	9	2	7	3	8	6	4
1	4	8	6	9	2	7	5	3
9	5	3	8	1	7	2	4	6
7	6	2	3	5	4	1	8	9

Solution to Puzzle 530

6	7	3	9	1	2	4	5	8
1	5	4	8	3	6	7	2	9
2	8	9	4	5	7	3	1	6
9	1	6	2	7	4	5	8	3
7	3	5	1	6	8	2	9	4
8	4	2	3	9	5	1	6	7
5	2	8	7	4	9	6	3	1
3	6	7	5	8	1	9	4	2
4	9	1	6	2	3	8	7	5

Solution to Puzzle 531

6	7	9	8	5	2	1	3	4
3	8	1	4	6	9	7	2	5
2	4	5	1	3	7	8	6	9
7	9	3	5	2	1	4	8	6
1	5	4	6	8	3	9	7	2
8	6	2	9	7	4	5	1	3
4	2	7	3	1	5	6	9	8
9	1	6	2	4	8	3	5	7
5	3	8	7	9	6	2	4	1

Solution to Puzzle 532

7	3	6	5	9	8	2	4	1
9	1	8	2	4	3	6	7	5
5	2	4	7	6	1	3	9	8
8	7	1	9	2	5	4	6	3
2	5	9	4	3	6	8	1	7
6	4	3	1	8	7	9	5	2
4	8	7	6	5	2	1	3	9
3	6	5	8	1	9	7	2	4
1	9	2	3	7	4	5	8	6

Solution to Puzzle 533

1	2	4	7	5	3	6	8	9
3	7	8	9	6	4	2	5	1
5	9	6	8	1	2	3	4	7
6	3	9	5	2	7	8	1	4
8	1	2	3	4	9	7	6	5
7	4	5	6	8	1	9	2	3
4	8	3	1	7	6	5	9	2
2	6	7	4	9	5	1	3	8
9	5	1	2	3	8	4	7	6

Solution to Puzzle 534

6	3	7	4	2	8	1	9	5
9	5	2	1	3	7	4	8	6
4	1	8	5	6	9	2	3	7
7	2	1	8	4	6	3	5	9
3	6	9	2	1	5	8	7	4
8	4	5	7	9	3	6	1	2
5	8	3	6	7	4	9	2	1
2	7	6	9	8	1	5	4	3
1	9	4	3	5	2	7	6	8

Solution to Puzzle 535

1	7	4	2	6	8	5	3	9
5	6	3	4	9	7	2	8	1
2	8	9	5	1	3	4	7	6
3	5	1	7	4	9	6	2	8
8	2	7	6	3	1	9	4	5
4	9	6	8	5	2	3	1	7
7	3	5	1	2	6	8	9	4
9	4	8	3	7	5	1	6	2
6	1	2	9	8	4	7	5	3

Solution to Puzzle 536

9	2	4	6	1	8	5	3	7
5	7	3	4	2	9	1	8	6
6	8	1	3	5	7	2	4	9
2	4	5	8	9	1	7	6	3
3	6	7	2	4	5	8	9	1
1	9	8	7	6	3	4	2	5
4	5	9	1	3	2	6	7	8
8	1	6	9	7	4	3	5	2
7	3	2	5	8	6	9	1	4

Solution to Puzzle 537

3	4	8	6	1	5	7	2	9
9	5	1	8	2	7	4	3	6
2	7	6	9	3	4	1	5	8
6	8	2	4	5	9	3	7	1
7	1	4	3	6	8	2	9	5
5	9	3	2	7	1	6	8	4
4	3	9	1	8	2	5	6	7
8	2	5	7	4	6	9	1	3
1	6	7	5	9	3	8	4	2

Solution to Puzzle 538

2	6	4	5	1	8	7	3	9
9	3	1	6	7	4	8	2	5
8	5	7	9	2	3	1	6	4
4	8	6	2	3	5	9	7	1
5	7	2	4	9	1	3	8	6
1	9	3	7	8	6	4	5	2
7	2	5	3	4	9	6	1	8
3	4	8	1	6	2	5	9	7
6	1	9	8	5	7	2	4	3

Solution to Puzzle 539

9	7	3	4	6	1	2	5	8
1	2	8	7	5	3	4	6	9
6	4	5	8	2	9	1	7	3
4	8	6	1	9	2	7	3	5
5	1	9	3	7	6	8	2	4
2	3	7	5	4	8	6	9	1
7	6	1	9	3	4	5	8	2
8	9	2	6	1	5	3	4	7
3	5	4	2	8	7	9	1	6

Solution to Puzzle 540

2	6	8	7	4	1	5	3	9
4	5	1	3	9	6	8	2	7
3	7	9	8	5	2	6	1	4
6	4	7	5	2	3	1	9	8
1	3	5	6	8	9	7	4	2
9	8	2	4	1	7	3	5	6
5	1	4	2	6	8	9	7	3
8	2	3	9	7	5	4	6	1
7	9	6	1	3	4	2	8	5

Solution to Puzzle 541

5	2	4	3	1	7	8	6	9
3	1	7	6	8	9	4	5	2
8	9	6	4	2	5	1	3	7
2	8	1	9	3	6	5	7	4
4	6	5	8	7	2	3	9	1
9	7	3	5	4	1	6	2	8
7	5	8	1	9	3	2	4	6
6	4	9	2	5	8	7	1	3
1	3	2	7	6	4	9	8	5

Solution to Puzzle 542

2	7	3	4	6	9	5	1	8
8	5	9	7	1	3	4	2	6
1	4	6	8	2	5	3	9	7
7	6	8	1	3	4	9	5	2
9	1	2	5	8	7	6	3	4
5	3	4	6	9	2	7	8	1
3	9	7	2	4	8	1	6	5
4	8	1	9	5	6	2	7	3
6	2	5	3	7	1	8	4	9

Solution to Puzzle 543

4	6	8	1	2	9	5	7	3
5	1	2	7	6	3	4	8	9
3	7	9	8	4	5	6	1	2
1	3	4	2	5	7	8	9	6
6	8	7	4	9	1	3	2	5
2	9	5	6	3	8	7	4	1
8	4	3	5	1	2	9	6	7
9	2	6	3	7	4	1	5	8
7	5	1	9	8	6	2	3	4

Solution to Puzzle 544

9	2	4	6	1	8	5	3	7
5	7	3	4	2	9	1	8	6
6	8	1	3	5	7	2	4	9
2	4	5	8	9	1	7	6	3
3	6	7	2	4	5	8	9	1
1	9	8	7	6	3	4	2	5
4	5	9	1	3	2	6	7	8
8	1	6	9	7	4	3	5	2
7	3	2	5	8	6	9	1	4

Solution to Puzzle 545

2	6	3	8	9	5	1	4	7
9	8	4	1	7	3	6	2	5
1	7	5	4	6	2	9	8	3
6	4	2	9	3	1	5	7	8
5	9	8	2	4	7	3	1	6
7	3	1	5	8	6	4	9	2
8	5	9	6	2	4	7	3	1
4	1	7	3	5	8	2	6	9
3	2	6	7	1	9	8	5	4

Solution to Puzzle 546

5	4	1	8	6	7	9	3	2
2	7	8	9	3	1	6	4	5
6	9	3	4	2	5	8	1	7
7	8	9	3	4	2	5	6	1
3	5	2	6	1	8	7	9	4
1	6	4	7	5	9	2	8	3
8	2	6	1	7	3	4	5	9
4	1	5	2	9	6	3	7	8
9	3	7	5	8	4	1	2	6

Solution to Puzzle 547

1	6	4	9	3	2	5	8	7
3	2	8	6	5	7	1	9	4
7	5	9	4	1	8	3	6	2
5	7	2	1	6	4	8	3	9
6	9	3	8	2	5	4	7	1
8	4	1	7	9	3	2	5	6
4	3	5	2	7	6	9	1	8
2	1	7	5	8	9	6	4	3
9	8	6	3	4	1	7	2	5

Solution to Puzzle 548

8	7	2	4	6	1	5	3	9
9	4	3	5	7	8	6	2	1
5	6	1	3	2	9	4	8	7
2	8	7	6	1	5	9	4	3
3	5	4	7	9	2	1	6	8
6	1	9	8	4	3	7	5	2
4	9	8	2	5	7	3	1	6
1	3	6	9	8	4	2	7	5
7	2	5	1	3	6	8	9	4

Solution to Puzzle 549

3	2	4	8	9	1	6	5	7
6	9	7	2	3	5	4	1	8
5	1	8	4	6	7	3	9	2
1	4	6	7	2	8	5	3	9
7	3	9	6	5	4	2	8	1
8	5	2	3	1	9	7	6	4
4	8	5	9	7	6	1	2	3
9	6	3	1	4	2	8	7	5
2	7	1	5	8	3	9	4	6

Solution to Puzzle 550

5	9	6	1	4	7	3	8	2
3	2	8	5	9	6	4	1	7
4	1	7	8	3	2	5	9	6
2	7	1	3	8	9	6	5	4
6	4	5	2	7	1	9	3	8
8	3	9	6	5	4	2	7	1
9	6	2	7	1	3	8	4	5
1	8	4	9	6	5	7	2	3
7	5	3	4	2	8	1	6	9

Solution to Puzzle 551

1	2	4	7	5	3	6	8	9
3	7	8	9	6	4	2	5	1
5	9	6	8	1	2	3	4	7
6	3	9	5	2	7	8	1	4
8	1	2	3	4	9	7	6	5
7	4	5	6	8	1	9	2	3
4	8	3	1	7	6	5	9	2
2	6	7	4	9	5	1	3	8
9	5	1	2	3	8	4	7	6

Solution to Puzzle 552

4	2	5	7	3	1	6	9	8
8	7	1	9	4	6	3	2	5
3	9	6	5	2	8	4	1	7
6	3	4	1	8	5	9	7	2
2	8	7	4	6	9	5	3	1
5	1	9	2	7	3	8	6	4
1	4	8	6	9	2	7	5	3
9	5	3	8	1	7	2	4	6
7	6	2	3	5	4	1	8	9

Solution to Puzzle 553

8	4	9	2	5	7	6	3	1
3	2	5	1	6	8	7	4	9
7	1	6	3	4	9	5	8	2
5	9	1	7	8	4	3	2	6
4	3	7	9	2	6	8	1	5
2	6	8	5	3	1	4	9	7
6	7	2	4	9	3	1	5	8
1	5	3	8	7	2	9	6	4
9	8	4	6	1	5	2	7	3

Solution to Puzzle 554

5	3	9	8	2	7	1	6	4
2	7	1	4	3	6	8	9	5
6	4	8	1	9	5	2	3	7
4	6	7	5	1	3	9	8	2
1	8	2	9	7	4	3	5	6
3	9	5	2	6	8	7	4	1
7	5	4	3	8	2	6	1	9
9	2	3	6	5	1	4	7	8
8	1	6	7	4	9	5	2	3

Solution to Puzzle 555

7	2	6	3	1	8	5	9	4
4	3	1	2	9	5	8	7	6
8	9	5	6	7	4	2	1	3
5	4	9	1	8	6	7	3	2
3	1	8	4	2	7	9	6	5
2	6	7	9	5	3	4	8	1
1	8	4	5	3	9	6	2	7
6	7	2	8	4	1	3	5	9
9	5	3	7	6	2	1	4	8

Solution to Puzzle 556

8	5	1	6	2	4	7	3	9
9	2	7	1	3	8	5	4	6
4	3	6	9	5	7	8	1	2
5	1	4	3	8	2	6	9	7
6	7	3	4	9	5	2	8	1
2	8	9	7	6	1	3	5	4
1	9	8	5	7	6	4	2	3
7	4	5	2	1	3	9	6	8
3	6	2	8	4	9	1	7	5

Solution to Puzzle 557

1	2	4	7	5	3	6	8	9
3	7	8	9	6	4	2	5	1
5	9	6	8	1	2	3	4	7
6	3	9	5	2	7	8	1	4
8	1	2	3	4	9	7	6	5
7	4	5	6	8	1	9	2	3
4	8	3	1	7	6	5	9	2
2	6	7	4	9	5	1	3	8
9	5	1	2	3	8	4	7	6

Solution to Puzzle 558

5	2	4	9	3	1	7	8	6
9	6	7	4	8	5	2	3	1
8	3	1	7	6	2	9	5	4
6	5	9	1	2	8	4	7	3
1	4	8	3	7	6	5	2	9
2	7	3	5	4	9	1	6	8
4	9	6	8	5	7	3	1	2
7	1	2	6	9	3	8	4	5
3	8	5	2	1	4	6	9	7

Solution to Puzzle 559

4	3	9	7	1	5	8	2	6
8	1	6	2	3	9	5	4	7
7	5	2	4	6	8	1	3	9
5	8	4	9	7	1	3	6	2
6	7	1	3	5	2	4	9	8
9	2	3	8	4	6	7	5	1
2	6	5	1	8	4	9	7	3
3	4	8	6	9	7	2	1	5
1	9	7	5	2	3	6	8	4

Solution to Puzzle 560

1	5	2	4	8	9	3	7	6
7	6	8	2	5	3	4	1	9
9	3	4	6	1	7	2	8	5
4	7	1	9	2	6	5	3	8
8	9	3	7	4	5	6	2	1
6	2	5	8	3	1	9	4	7
2	8	6	5	7	4	1	9	3
5	1	7	3	9	2	8	6	4
3	4	9	1	6	8	7	5	2

Solution to Puzzle 561

7	6	4	8	1	2	3	9	5
8	5	3	9	6	4	1	7	2
9	2	1	3	7	5	6	8	4
1	4	6	2	9	8	5	3	7
5	8	7	1	4	3	2	6	9
2	3	9	7	5	6	8	4	1
6	7	2	5	3	9	4	1	8
3	9	5	4	8	1	7	2	6
4	1	8	6	2	7	9	5	3

Solution to Puzzle 562

2	1	6	3	4	8	9	5	7
5	4	8	7	9	6	2	1	3
3	7	9	5	2	1	6	4	8
7	9	5	2	6	4	8	3	1
6	8	1	9	3	7	5	2	4
4	2	3	8	1	5	7	9	6
1	6	2	4	8	9	3	7	5
9	5	4	6	7	3	1	8	2
8	3	7	1	5	2	4	6	9

Solution to Puzzle 563

1	8	7	2	9	6	4	5	3
9	3	5	7	1	4	2	8	6
6	4	2	5	3	8	7	1	9
2	6	8	4	7	9	1	3	5
4	5	3	6	8	1	9	2	7
7	1	9	3	2	5	8	6	4
8	9	6	1	4	3	5	7	2
5	2	1	9	6	7	3	4	8
3	7	4	8	5	2	6	9	1

Solution to Puzzle 564

7	8	4	2	6	5	3	1	9
2	1	3	9	8	4	5	6	7
6	9	5	3	7	1	2	4	8
4	6	2	7	9	3	8	5	1
1	7	9	8	5	6	4	2	3
5	3	8	4	1	2	7	9	6
8	2	1	5	3	9	6	7	4
3	4	6	1	2	7	9	8	5
9	5	7	6	4	8	1	3	2

Solution to Puzzle 565

2	4	5	6	8	3	7	9	1
8	7	6	4	1	9	5	3	2
1	3	9	5	7	2	8	6	4
9	2	3	1	5	8	6	4	7
5	6	1	7	9	4	2	8	3
7	8	4	2	3	6	9	1	5
4	9	8	3	2	7	1	5	6
3	5	2	8	6	1	4	7	9
6	1	7	9	4	5	3	2	8

Solution to Puzzle 566

1	2	4	7	5	3	6	8	9
3	7	8	9	6	4	2	5	1
5	9	6	8	1	2	3	4	7
6	3	9	5	2	7	8	1	4
8	1	2	3	4	9	7	6	5
7	4	5	6	8	1	9	2	3
4	8	3	1	7	6	5	9	2
2	6	7	4	9	5	1	3	8
9	5	1	2	3	8	4	7	6

Solution to Puzzle 567

6	3	7	5	4	8	9	1	2
8	5	9	2	7	1	4	3	6
2	1	4	3	9	6	7	8	5
1	7	5	4	6	9	8	2	3
3	9	8	7	5	2	1	6	4
4	2	6	8	1	3	5	7	9
5	8	1	6	3	4	2	9	7
7	6	2	9	8	5	3	4	1
9	4	3	1	2	7	6	5	8

Solution to Puzzle 568

5	9	6	1	4	7	3	8	2
3	2	8	5	9	6	4	1	7
4	1	7	8	3	2	5	9	6
2	7	1	3	8	9	6	5	4
6	4	5	2	7	1	9	3	8
8	3	9	6	5	4	2	7	1
9	6	2	7	1	3	8	4	5
1	8	4	9	6	5	7	2	3
7	5	3	4	2	8	1	6	9

Solution to Puzzle 569

6	4	2	9	5	7	3	8	1
8	5	1	2	3	6	7	4	9
7	9	3	8	4	1	5	6	2
9	1	5	3	6	4	2	7	8
4	7	8	5	1	2	6	9	3
3	2	6	7	9	8	4	1	5
1	3	9	6	7	5	8	2	4
2	6	4	1	8	3	9	5	7
5	8	7	4	2	9	1	3	6

Solution to Puzzle 570

9	8	3	6	4	2	7	5	1
2	7	4	9	5	1	6	3	8
5	6	1	8	3	7	9	2	4
4	3	2	5	7	8	1	6	9
7	9	5	3	1	6	8	4	2
8	1	6	4	2	9	5	7	3
3	5	7	1	8	4	2	9	6
6	4	8	2	9	5	3	1	7
1	2	9	7	6	3	4	8	5

Solution to Puzzle 571

2	6	5	1	9	8	3	4	7
7	8	4	2	5	3	1	6	9
3	9	1	4	7	6	2	8	5
4	5	3	7	2	9	8	1	6
9	1	6	3	8	5	7	2	4
8	7	2	6	1	4	9	5	3
1	4	8	5	3	7	6	9	2
5	3	9	8	6	2	4	7	1
6	2	7	9	4	1	5	3	8

Solution to Puzzle 572

4	1	5	7	9	8	2	3	6
7	3	6	1	5	2	4	8	9
8	2	9	6	4	3	5	7	1
5	4	2	9	8	6	3	1	7
6	8	7	3	2	1	9	5	4
1	9	3	5	7	4	8	6	2
2	5	4	8	6	7	1	9	3
3	7	8	2	1	9	6	4	5
9	6	1	4	3	5	7	2	8

Solution to Puzzle 573

5	7	9	1	6	3	4	2	8
1	2	8	5	7	4	3	6	9
4	3	6	2	9	8	1	5	7
2	9	1	8	3	6	7	4	5
7	6	5	9	4	1	2	8	3
8	4	3	7	5	2	9	1	6
6	8	7	4	2	9	5	3	1
3	5	4	6	1	7	8	9	2
9	1	2	3	8	5	6	7	4

Solution to Puzzle 574

2	3	5	8	1	7	9	4	6
9	4	8	6	5	2	1	7	3
1	6	7	3	9	4	5	2	8
3	7	9	4	8	5	2	6	1
8	2	1	9	6	3	4	5	7
6	5	4	7	2	1	8	3	9
7	1	2	5	3	8	6	9	4
5	9	3	1	4	6	7	8	2
4	8	6	2	7	9	3	1	5

Solution to Puzzle 575

9	6	7	3	8	4	2	5	1
2	5	8	7	1	6	9	3	4
1	4	3	9	2	5	7	8	6
4	8	9	1	3	7	5	6	2
7	3	6	5	4	2	1	9	8
5	2	1	8	6	9	3	4	7
3	7	4	6	5	1	8	2	9
8	9	2	4	7	3	6	1	5
6	1	5	2	9	8	4	7	3

Solution to Puzzle 576

2	1	6	3	4	8	9	5	7
5	4	8	7	9	6	2	1	3
3	7	9	5	2	1	6	4	8
7	9	5	2	6	4	8	3	1
6	8	1	9	3	7	5	2	4
4	2	3	8	1	5	7	9	6
1	6	2	4	8	9	3	7	5
9	5	4	6	7	3	1	8	2
8	3	7	1	5	2	4	6	9

Solution to Puzzle 577

8	6	2	4	5	7	9	1	3
7	4	9	1	2	3	5	6	8
3	5	1	6	9	8	4	2	7
5	1	8	9	3	2	7	4	6
4	9	7	8	1	6	2	3	5
6	2	3	7	4	5	1	8	9
1	7	4	3	8	9	6	5	2
9	8	5	2	6	1	3	7	4
2	3	6	5	7	4	8	9	1

Solution to Puzzle 578

6	7	1	2	9	5	3	8	4
2	9	4	8	3	6	5	7	1
8	3	5	4	7	1	9	6	2
3	8	9	5	2	7	1	4	6
5	2	7	1	6	4	8	9	3
4	1	6	3	8	9	2	5	7
9	6	2	7	5	3	4	1	8
7	4	3	9	1	8	6	2	5
1	5	8	6	4	2	7	3	9

Solution to Puzzle 579

9	4	6	8	5	2	3	1	7
1	5	3	6	9	7	4	2	8
7	2	8	4	1	3	9	6	5
8	1	4	3	7	5	2	9	6
2	3	7	9	8	6	1	5	4
5	6	9	2	4	1	8	7	3
3	9	2	7	6	4	5	8	1
4	7	5	1	2	8	6	3	9
6	8	1	5	3	9	7	4	2

Solution to Puzzle 580

7	2	5	8	6	3	1	9	4
8	6	3	4	9	1	7	5	2
1	9	4	5	2	7	6	8	3
5	8	2	6	7	4	3	1	9
6	4	9	1	3	8	2	7	5
3	1	7	9	5	2	4	6	8
2	3	6	7	8	5	9	4	1
9	5	1	2	4	6	8	3	7
4	7	8	3	1	9	5	2	6

Solution to Puzzle 581

3	1	4	2	7	6	9	8	5
9	5	6	3	8	1	7	4	2
2	7	8	5	9	4	3	1	6
6	3	7	4	2	9	8	5	1
4	8	5	6	1	3	2	9	7
1	9	2	7	5	8	6	3	4
7	2	1	8	3	5	4	6	9
5	6	3	9	4	7	1	2	8
8	4	9	1	6	2	5	7	3

Solution to Puzzle 582

8	5	1	4	7	6	2	3	9
9	7	2	8	1	3	5	4	6
3	6	4	2	9	5	7	1	8
5	2	3	9	6	1	4	8	7
1	8	6	7	4	2	3	9	5
7	4	9	5	3	8	1	6	2
4	9	5	1	8	7	6	2	3
6	1	7	3	2	9	8	5	4
2	3	8	6	5	4	9	7	1

Solution to Puzzle 583

5	3	2	1	6	8	4	7	9
7	1	8	4	5	9	3	6	2
6	4	9	3	7	2	1	5	8
9	5	4	7	8	3	2	1	6
2	7	3	5	1	6	8	9	4
8	6	1	2	9	4	5	3	7
3	9	6	8	4	5	7	2	1
4	2	7	6	3	1	9	8	5
1	8	5	9	2	7	6	4	3

Solution to Puzzle 584

7	5	1	8	6	3	9	2	4
8	3	2	4	1	9	6	5	7
9	4	6	7	5	2	3	8	1
5	2	8	1	9	7	4	3	6
3	6	7	2	8	4	1	9	5
1	9	4	6	3	5	2	7	8
4	8	5	9	2	1	7	6	3
2	1	3	5	7	6	8	4	9
6	7	9	3	4	8	5	1	2

Solution to Puzzle 585

9	2	4	6	1	8	5	3	7
5	7	3	4	2	9	1	8	6
6	8	1	3	5	7	2	4	9
2	4	5	8	9	1	7	6	3
3	6	7	2	4	5	8	9	1
1	9	8	7	6	3	4	2	5
4	5	9	1	3	2	6	7	8
8	1	6	9	7	4	3	5	2
7	3	2	5	8	6	9	1	4

Solution to Puzzle 586

2	1	6	3	4	8	9	5	7
5	4	8	7	9	6	2	1	3
3	7	9	5	2	1	6	4	8
7	9	5	2	6	4	8	3	1
6	8	1	9	3	7	5	2	4
4	2	3	8	1	5	7	9	6
1	6	2	4	8	9	3	7	5
9	5	4	6	7	3	1	8	2
8	3	7	1	5	2	4	6	9

Solution to Puzzle 587

3	9	4	7	8	1	5	6	2
2	5	8	3	6	4	9	7	1
7	1	6	2	9	5	8	4	3
4	3	7	8	5	6	1	2	9
9	6	5	1	2	7	3	8	4
8	2	1	4	3	9	7	5	6
6	8	2	9	7	3	4	1	5
1	7	3	5	4	2	6	9	8
5	4	9	6	1	8	2	3	7

Solution to Puzzle 588

6	7	3	9	1	2	4	8	5
9	1	4	3	8	5	2	6	7
8	2	5	6	7	4	9	3	1
2	4	7	8	5	9	6	1	3
3	9	1	2	6	7	8	5	4
5	8	6	4	3	1	7	9	2
7	6	9	1	4	3	5	2	8
1	5	2	7	9	8	3	4	6
4	3	8	5	2	6	1	7	9